Praise for *Fragile Freedom*

'*Fragile Freedom* is an unforgettable story told with raw authenticity and startling honesty. I read it in two sittings – couldn't put it down – it blew me away. Highly recommended.'

Catherine Simpson, author of *One Body*

'I couldn't put this book down. Gulara's brave and incisive story telling – of her true and riveting life story – captures an important cultural moment in her Eastern European country of birth while highlighting some of the dangers and traumas that so many women of so many different cultures have faced and continue to face in many places around the world. This is an important book. Gulara and her work have the potential to support healing for an untold number of women around the world today.'

Edward Mannix, author of *Reinventing Truth* and *Impossible Compassion*, and founder of The Compassion Key®

GULARA VINCENT

# FRAGILE
# FREEDOM

*A young woman's unlikely
emancipation in post-Soviet Azerbaijan*

*To Alex*
*Thank you for loving all of me, even when I didn't*

# CONTENTS

1.

# PROSECUTOR'S OFFICE

## *1st September 1992*

'What if they ask me something about the law, Mama? I know nothing about it,' I gasped, as she half pulled me along the increasingly busy streets of our hometown, Ganja, towards the Prosecutor's Office. I ached for her to stop, give me a hug and say that it was all a mistake and that we would go home now.

'Stop moaning and keep walking. No one is going to ask you anything important!' Face fixed forwards, she kept up a fast pace despite her black leather stilettos, the uneven ground and the beads of sweat glistening on her brow in the already warm sunshine. An old lady with a pristine head-covering, who had just stalked out of a nearby pharmacy, stared sternly at us. She reminded me so much of my grandmother, I tried to speed up while whispering urgently in Mama's ear.

'But it's the Prosecutor's Office! I should know something.'

'If you don't keep walking, and stop your chatter, we will be late!'

I didn't like it when Mama was short with me and bit

1

my tongue. As we passed a tall block of concrete flats on Khatai Avenue, which even post-independence locals still called Lenin Avenue, my mind flashed through the chain of events that had got me a job in the Prosecutor's Office, without ever setting foot in it.

I was just seventeen, newly enrolled at Baku State University and my law course was to be taught mostly by correspondence. I needed a day job, to do my studies independently, attend regular, short study sessions in Baku and pass exams twice each academic year in order to progress to the next. The first set of introductory lectures was only three weeks away. The Prosecutor, who had agreed for me to work as a filing assistant in the office, was a brother of the Minister of Internal Affairs, which was probably how he got his job, I thought. The Minister of Internal Affairs was head of the political party called the 'Grey Wolves', of which Mama was a keen member. Her connections were why I was trotting along beside her today, the first day of my new, currently mysterious, job.

As we approached the huge, high-arched portico of the Prosecutor's Office, a tall man with greying, curly hair greeted Mama like a long-lost relative. Another of her political party buddies, I assumed. I brooded quietly while they exchanged pleasantries and launched into a predictable lament about the future of our 'noble' country, Azerbaijan. I mentally rolled my eyes, because I had heard it all before. Besides, I thought my troubles were more important, especially on that day.

So, what if it had been a year since the Soviet Union collapsed and 'the country's transition to independence should have stabilised by now'? Yes, 'political chaos and economic devastation weakened the country', 'recession was unprecedented' and 'who knows how long it will take to transform its economic system into a market economy?' The answer, from me, would have been, no one! No one knew what to do! Everything had been planned for us by the Soviet Union for the past seventy years. What was the point of worrying that unemployment had soared as our own government was forced to close factories? How was anyone going to 'stop young men from leaving Azerbaijan to sell fruit and herbs in Russian bazaars'? If that's what they wanted to do, why shouldn't they use their 'new freedoms' to do just that?

I had listened to Mama discussing these concerns with so many people. I was tired of the narrative. Her political activism had skyrocketed with her aspirations to serve the 'new' country and now she had decided to move to Baku with her second family. The thought made me so sad. Yet again, I was left behind with Nana. I had always dreamt of living permanently with Mama. She was so much more permissive than Nana. She would let me wear trousers, meet up with friends and have fun. Although Nana had mellowed since her husband's death three years ago, she was still keen on 'observing the correct traditions' and worried terribly about what neighbours might say about pretty much everything.

Mama and the man had moved on to the dreaded topic of the war with Armenia over the Nagorno-Karabakh region, which was still shackling our country. It had been raging since 1988, when ethnic Armenians living in Nagorno-Karabakh demanded the transfer of this autonomous region of Azerbaijan to Armenia. We had already lost Lachin, a region adjacent to Armenia, the occupation of which, on the 18th of May 1992 had created a direct land connection between Armenia and Nagorno-Karabakh. Mama and the man were locked into their conversation, oblivious of others, oblivious of me. Her hand gripped tighter on my arm.

'It's all Russia's doing,' the man said, red-faced with passion. 'They always divided and ruled us. It's ridiculous that they are saying they are engaged in conflict resolution! They themselves are supplying guns and military to Armenia.'

*How can talk change anything?* I thought but didn't say. In my mind, I could see what I imagined to be a huge office clock, counting down time inside the office. What if I really was late? I tried to pull my arm away, but Mama stayed solid, ignoring me, so, trying to calm myself, I turned my attention to the Soviet-era buildings surrounding the Prosecutor's Office. These concrete five-storey blocks of flats had small, flimsy balconies adorned with lines of clothing drying in the sun. I noticed a bearded man in his undershirt smoking on one of the balconies, watching people walk by. The smell of chopped onions fried in butter wafted from somewhere. I looked up to find its source. A gentle breeze stirred laced, lime-coloured net curtains at a first-floor, open window. Behind them was the silhouette, probably of a woman, who was no doubt eavesdropping on Mama's conversation. I could not blame her; if you were a housewife these days, what else was there to do but cook, watch TV, gossip or pry on other people? Nana always said, 'Remember, Gulush, even the walls have ears in this country.'

That memory cast me, for a moment, back to two years ago, when as Nana and I listened to the gunfire of Armenian troops advancing on our hometown, she had told me she would kill me rather than let them 'have their way' with me. I shuddered, despite the warming air. Mama was talking about the floods of refugees now. Of course, I felt sympathy for people who had to abandon their homes and flee into poverty and despair – it could have been our family – but we couldn't really help them. We had our own lives to struggle with.

Getting any job was a major milestone these days, especially somewhere as prestigious as the Prosecutor's Office. Irrespective of your job title, the name of the organisation alone instilled respect, as well as fear, in most people, me included.

Just at the point where I was about to explode outwards and say something, Mama finally bid farewell to her comrade. She whisked me up the steps of the imposing, municipal building set in its own square courtyard. It was so different from the flats around it. Its huge, sturdy door creaked open into a large hall with a tall ceiling. There was a glass police booth opposite the entrance door and a staircase leading upstairs on the right-hand side. To the left, I saw five men sitting motionless on a long wooden bench. They were handcuffed. They didn't look up, as men normally did when they heard the click of Mama's stilettos. They remained staring down at the patterned tiled floor. I tensed a little. Was I going to have to work with real criminals?

The young policeman straightened up at his desk as Mama approached him. He had definitely noticed her.

'I'm here to see Zakir *bay*,' Mama announced, unconsciously running a slim, manicured hand through her thick dark hair. 'He's expecting us.'

The young man was momentarily fascinated before his professionalism kicked back in. He nodded. 'Just a minute.' And picked up his phone.

While he spoke to someone on the phone and Mama rearranged her hair, I sneaked a peek at the prisoners. They looked like a row of bedraggled and dirty crows, with stubbly faces, rough cropped hair and soiled clothes. One felt my gaze and glanced up. His dark eyes were filled with a hopeless resignation I could not understand. I shivered and looked away. The entrance hall was dimly lit and felt cold, despite the heat of the early September sun outside. Summer's unbearable thirty-five to forty degrees Celsius had eased off a few days ago but the balmy twenty-five-degree warmth outside was not enough to penetrate the air of this space.

The policeman pointed and I followed Mama up the marble staircase, the sound of her high heels echoed by my smaller ones against the cold stone walls. On the next floor, we walked down a long corridor. The doors of the offices were open. I peered in as we passed by. Every office was occupied by a man.

Was I going to work with all these men? I was not even allowed to be seen on the rare occasions when my uncles' friends visited the house. Since childhood, I had been taught that men were dangerous and to be feared. I was not meant to be friendly with them, but on the other hand, I had to avoid antagonising them in any way. The thought of working alongside so many men felt overwhelming. I felt

6

my face reddening, so turned to look out of the windows on the right side of the corridor to escape my feelings. A wall of pink, pale yellow and maroon roses greeted me. It was a surprise to find that such a forbidding and functional building had such a well-tended garden nestled behind it. The sight of it calmed me instantly.

As we neared the Prosecutor's room, two bodyguards intercepted us. The tallest had a dark complexion, short, ebony curls and stern features, while the other had cropped, gingery blond hair and a mischievous sparkle in his grey eyes. While the taller man questioned Mama, the other seemed to be trying to suppress the smile that lingered at the edges of his pale lips. Now it was me who was focusing on the floor, forcing myself not to look at their bulging arm muscles, the revolvers under their smart, black suits and the Kalashnikovs slung casually over their shoulders. My knees shook and I felt a little breathless as we were finally ushered into the reception room. I wondered if the Prosecutor had bodyguards because of his brother's position as the Minister of Internal Affairs, because of the war with Armenia, or because of the prisoners I had seen downstairs.

The reception was spacious, but the chestnut cupboards made the room look smaller and darker. A big *chinar* tree stirred its magnificent green branches outside the large windows, framed with cream, stripy curtains and covered with iron mesh, presumably for security purposes. The thought of criminals breaking in unsettled me, so I watched the receptionist, pushing back her dark-brown hair with blonde highlights as she busied herself with the kettle, after asking us to take a seat on the soft velvet-covered, formal chairs. She wore a starched white shirt and a brown, midi-length, pleated leather skirt. I wondered if my blue floral dress was too casual for this place. Was this woman kind and friendly? Would she like me? She seemed reserved and distant for now. Perhaps she would like Mama and so like me, I reasoned.

Everyone liked Mama. I glanced at her and smiled. Her black dress was fashionable, and covered her knees, while emphasising her slim waistline and well-proportioned curves. Her mouth was painted a classy red and her eyes well defined by mascara and black eyeliner. Nana had fought with her about make-up when she lived with us but now that she was married again, Nana's level of criticism had waned.

At first sight, Mama and I looked like we weren't even related. I did not have her black wavy tresses. Much to my uncles' annoyance, I kept my light chestnut hair cut just below my earlobes, which today were adorned with blue seashell-shaped earrings that matched my dress and my grey-blue eyes. My skin was fairer than Mama's, lightly tanned on my arms and neck. The rest of my body had not seen the sunshine since our last beach holiday five years ago. I was, of course, not wearing any make-up. I thought my eyebrows were huge but knew I would have to wait until I got married before I could pluck and shape them. Nana would not even let me shave my armpits. The only time I attempted it, she was so furious I thought she might kill me. Consequently, I tried to keep the tops of my arms covered because I thought it would conceal the smell of my sweat, but that was hard to do on scorching summer days. Mama always told me I worried too much about little things.

As the receptionist brewed black tea on an electric hot plate, I imagined how the Prosecutor might look. He would have an expensive suit hugging a tall, lean body, with sleek hair and cold, steely eyes. His shirt would be starched, with a fancy grey silk tie and a gold ring on his finger. My heart jumped as I started to worry again. Would I have to shake hands with him? He would notice my sweaty palms. But, before I could dry them on my dress, we were summoned.

Another spacious room, but this one was full of light streaming in from three large windows, decorated with milky-coffee-coloured linen curtains. A giant map of Azerbaijan dominated one wall. There was a long, dark wooden table, which could easily have seated ten people, surrounded by elegant chairs. The Prosecutor sat silhouetted by the light, at its far end, in a cloud of smoke. The smell of stale tobacco smoke did not surprise me because, without exception, all the men I knew were smokers, as if smoking were an essential requirement of manliness. What did surprise me, though, once my eyes had adjusted to the light, was the Prosecutor's appearance. He was nothing like I had imagined. He could have been a farmer, with his loose, brown jumper pulled over a stripy shirt, which, Nana would have said, looked like it had been 'chewed by a dog'. She despised men whose wives 'didn't take the time to have their clothes starched and ironed'. What was more, he had no tie and his unkempt, curly hair spilled over his brows, almost covering his pebble-brown eyes, which seemed warm and wise, and I found myself relaxing a little bit.

'Take a seat,' he said. He motioned towards the two chairs nearest to him. After he had shaken Mama's hand, he picked up a phone next to him. 'Arzu, please bring in some tea and call Masha here.'

I moved the chair carefully so as not to scrape it on the polished floor and perched on the edge of my seat. A few moments later, as Mama and the Prosecutor talked, Arzu, the receptionist we had already seen, walked in with a tray, then placed pear-shaped crystal glasses full of hot, black tea in front of the Prosecutor, Mama and finally me. I picked up my steaming glass immediately, to give myself something to do, but my hand was shaking so badly, hot liquid burnt my fingers and I had to slip it quickly back onto the saucer. Mama and the Prosecutor didn't notice because, at that moment, the door behind us opened and a short woman with a cloud of fuzzy hair and eyeliner as thick as Cleopatra's walked in. She wore a long, satin, black skirt with a matching loose top.

'Masha, I've got you a new assistant,' the Prosecutor said, gesturing grandly towards me, 'I hope you will teach her well.'

'Of course,' Masha replied. Her voice was calm, clipped and professional. 'Follow me,' she said, briefly beckoning me, before turning to leave.

I hesitated because Mama remained seated, but the Prosecutor nodded his head, so I shot out of my seat after Masha. She was walking briskly and had already passed Arzu. We continued past the two bodyguards, then back down the long corridor with its open doors.

Masha's office was the last one, facing the staircase and right next door to a toilet. It was womb-like inside, being compact and self-contained with little furniture. Every inch of wall space in this dimly lit windowless room was lined with shelves crammed with folders. There was a set of tall doors at the back of the office, through which Masha led me into a smaller back room, which might have been a balcony in the past. The walls to the left and right of us were also covered with shelves from floor to ceiling, and at the end of the room there was a set of tall windows overlooking residential buildings. As Masha started to talk me through my new duties, I could hear Mama's steps approaching the open door. For a precious moment, she beamed at me, her face full of pride, but then she drew Masha back into the outer room to speak to her. I couldn't make out the words but there was some urgency in her voice.

For some reason, this triggered a unique memory from when I was ten. Mama had been about to leave our country, with her then new husband, to live in Latvia. The day before her departure, she had come to my school and had fervently asked my class teacher to look out for me in her absence. Now I felt like a schoolgirl again, assigned to the care of others while Mama left me. This time it was to go to Baku to pursue her political aspirations. She had already sold her three-bedroom flat in Ganja to buy a smaller place in Baku. Her money could only get her a studio flat in the outskirts of the capital. There simply was no space for me in the new home, even if I had been able to leave Nana.

I looked away, out of the windows, to hide my tear-filled eyes. It was, after all, partly my choice to stay this time. Nana had brought me up as her own since I was almost three weeks old. Now it was my duty to stay to support her, or she would be completely alone. Her sons, my two uncles, had moved away and her husband, Baba, had died three years ago, after a painful illness. Nana had stopped making dresses to earn her living a few months ago, when her eyesight deteriorated. Stern and as harsh as she could be, I knew she loved me as fiercely as I loved her. Despite this, my heart ached when Mama, her talk with Masha complete, said her goodbyes and left. Now it was me who was peering from behind the net curtains, just like the woman in the flats, watching her leave. As I lingered by the window, trying to compose myself, a flashy, white GAZ-31, a Russian-manufactured Volga car, pulled up in front of the entrance door. A large man climbed out of the driver's seat and greeted another smoking outside.

'That's the Prosecutor's chauffeur, Mahir,' Masha said, appearing next to me. 'Come along now, and I'll show you what you need to do.'

We sat at my tiny desk and she gave me a grey A4 form containing typed-up information. 'This is the paperwork that comes from the police stations. We oversee their activities, so it's important to keep track of relevant investigators and their caseload. This case belongs to—' she paused to consult her register— 'Alekberov. This is where you write their surname.'

I took a pen and, as instructed, wrote 'Alekberov' in the relevant section, trying to make each letter legible, despite my shaking hand.

'Hmm,' Masha purred next to me, 'I see you have studied in Russian. That's not how we spell it in Azerbaijani. You'll have to write Ələkbərov.'

She underlined the three letters that I had got wrong in just one word while enunciating each letter clearly. I flushed violently. So much for worrying about my non-existent knowledge of law, I thought, it seemed I didn't even know

12

the basics. It was so unfair. During Soviet rule, Russian was deemed to be the 'progressive language' as opposed to Azerbaijani. While I had read hundreds of Russian classics during my school years, I had only read two books in Azerbaijani. *Extraordinary Adventures of Mulla Nasruddin* and a book of Azerbaijani fairy tales. Not surprisingly, my command of Russian was now excellent, but my mother tongue was mostly conversational.

With Azerbaijan's independence a year ago, things were changing fast. The government had introduced a Latin alphabet, which replaced the Cyrillic alphabet imposed by Stalin during the cyrillisation campaign in the late 1930s. My grandmother, who was a school-aged girl at the time, had just learnt the Latin spelling of the Azerbaijani language when she was forced to switch to the Cyrillic alphabet along with the majority of the Soviet Union. Now that the process was being reversed, Nana, who was an avid reader, was deprived of the simple pleasure of reading a newspaper as she found it difficult to read the Latin script.

Now I had a steep learning curve ahead of me too. I had to master both legal terminology and my mother tongue to do this job. Though temporarily daunted by the challenge, I was determined to succeed, so I dutifully corrected my mistakes with Masha's instruction.

★★★

Within two weeks of starting the new job, I felt like an adult, leaving home every day with a sense of purpose and having grown-up friends. Most of my schoolmates were married off or engaged within weeks of graduating from school, but my life was different. I had a job and a legitimate excuse to be out every working day. I still felt frightened when the Prosecutor's entourage marched up and down the corridor and I fled to the back room, pretending to put the kettle on or check on a file.

Masha's room was the beating heart of the Prosecutor's Office. Every day, the investigators brought her grey pages of A4 paper with case details, typed by a receptionist or the investigators themselves, to be filed away. The Prosecutor's Office had jurisdiction over murder and rape cases. I mostly filed paperwork pertaining to murder cases, while Masha looked after the rape caseload.

The office also oversaw the activities of police officers' theft and burglary caseloads. Sometimes they had to bring in detained suspects for the Prosecutor to question before issuing an arrest warrant. The detainees normally sat downstairs on the wooden bench until the Prosecutor called them in and signed off the paperwork. From what Masha said, I gathered it was a mere formality.

The personalities of the many investigators I met at this time blurred into one. They were all the same to me, grim and officious. The handsome, blue-eyed policeman Tolik was the exception. He seemed so much kinder and warmer than the others.

'Hi Masha,' he said, the first time I saw him. 'I didn't know you had a new beauty in your office. Hello stranger, I'm Tavakkul, but you can call me Tolik. Everyone who knows me does.' He extended his hand. I shook it gingerly and felt myself blushing. His skin was so pale and surprisingly soft.

I was speechless. I looked at Masha. She understood

and spoke for me, while I filed the pieces of paper Tolik had just deposited on her table. 'Gulush is a law student. She currently works with me.'

'Congratulations to you, Gulush.' Tolik beamed at me. 'You're in such capable hands.' He rummaged in his brown leather briefcase, producing two Snickers and two Mars bars. Masha did not bat an eye at the sight of these treats. She winked at me and pointed to our kettle.

'Tea, Tolik?'

'Thanks for being so prompt and efficient with the paperwork, Masha. Sorry, I can't. Got to deal with the detainee downstairs. Burglary,' he sighed.

'Well, you've got a confession…' Masha peered at the file he was holding in his hands.

'Yeah, but…'

Mahir, the chauffeur, walked into the office, instantly filling up the space and making it feel crammed. He eyed Tolik, then the rest of the room, before saying a curt hello and taking his usual seat.

'Gulush, put the kettle on.'

The kettle hissed and I wondered whether Mahir might feel as protective of me as my uncles did. He probably did not approve of this policeman befriending me. I dutifully retreated into the back room to pour three glasses of tea, while Tolik took his leave. As soon as he was gone, Masha peeled the wrappers off two of the bars and chopped them into six chunks to share with me and Mahir.

'Good timing as ever, Mahir,' she said.

Mahir chewed his chunks slowly with obvious enjoyment. He had a shock of black curly hair, which he tried to tame into neat waves. His top lip was covered with a thick black moustache. He looked a bit like Winnie-the-Pooh, with his big hands and round belly, but he was never as relaxed as that character. His brown eyes were constantly restless and searching. I supposed he always had to be alert in his job. These were still dangerous times. I knew Mahir smoked a lot, there were always butts next to the car. He even smoked in Masha's room sometimes when she wasn't about. She had told me that Mahir was married and had two young boys. He seemed a very caring son, too, as he regularly checked on his mother. Sometimes, when Masha went to the toilet, Mahir hijacked her swivelling armchair to call his household. Mahir and Masha often bickered over seats and chocolates like brother and sister. I loved their banter; it felt familiar, like it used to be at home when my mum, uncles and grandparents all lived together.

I still missed Mama, though it wasn't as bad as when I was ten, because I felt as if she had never wholly returned after that time. Her attention had continued to be split between her new family, politics, other life demands and me. I think I tried to fill up the void inside me with my connection with Masha, who turned out to be my mum's age. Just days after I started work, we had marked Masha's thirty-seventh birthday with lunch. Mahir, Masha, Arzu and I brought some fancy food from home and laid it out on Masha's T-shaped table. I had helped Nana to make chicken cooked with fried onions and fluffy potatoes; I also brought a jar of pickled hot green peppers that Nana and I conserved every summer. Masha brought a layered salad of pickled herring, boiled potatoes, eggs, carrots and beetroots, mixed with soured cream and decorated with dill. Arzu contributed an Edam cheese, which her cousin had got from Moscow, and fresh cornichons. Last, but not least, Mahir produced tandoor-baked bread, still warm to touch, a bunch of fresh tarragon and a roll of pâté that his wife had made. Since the Prosecutor was out all day, Mahir also helped himself to a glass of vodka from one of the crates in the meeting room.

'Does the office buy all this cognac and vodka, Mahir?' I asked, as he poured himself another generous glass full. It might look as if he was having a glass of water, but the smell was unmistakable.

'This?' Mahir laughed. 'Of course not.' He squeezed half a lemon into a separate glass of water. My mouth was watering. 'These are gifts from local factories. You want some?'

I recoiled in shock. I hadn't drunk alcohol since my fifth birthday when I mistook champagne for lemonade and greatly entertained my uncles with my facial expressions. Mahir leant back on his chair and explained patiently. 'The Prosecutor's Office curates the Kapaz region of the city. There are different factories in the area.' He took a big bite of chicken and continued talking with his mouth full. 'Including wine factories, for example. Directors of the factories send gifts from time to time, to pay the dues. You understand? If something goes wrong for the director, like there's a disgruntled employee or there's an imminent inspection, they get backed up by the Prosecutor's Office.' He downed his vodka and wiped his pursed lips with the back of his hand, before sipping on the lemon water.

Masha nodded in agreement, as she scooped up a piece of meat with her bread. She ate delicately, avoiding smearing her lipstick as I tried to take this new information in – that the crates in the meeting room were all bribes.

'Oh, by the way, there's something I need to drop off at yours after work, Gulush,' Mahir said unexpectedly. 'So don't leave without me.'

The thought of appearing with a man in my household startled me. Nana would be sure to fret about my reputation in the neighbourhood. Young women of marriageable age could not be seen with men who were not their immediate family.

'You can't,' I replied, trying to sound firm.

'Really?' Mahir raised his eyebrows at Masha. 'Gulush, give me your address.' He wiped his oily hands on a large handkerchief he had teased out of his trouser pocket with his fingertips, then grabbed a piece of scrap paper from Masha's desk and looked at me expectantly. 'I have a sack of rice and flour to drop off at yours,' he said, waving his left hand in the air to hurry me up.

I tried hard to make sense of what he was saying. He sighed. 'So young, so… Remember what I told you about the wine? Well, the same applies to other things. It's just a little gift, Gulush, not a proposal of marriage. Now just tell me your address, otherwise I'll have to follow you.' He laughed, showing his teeth.

Masha gave me a reassuring pat on the arm, so I dictated the address, wondering all the while what reaction to expect from Nana when I returned home. Even before I could understand what she meant, she had drummed it into me that my virtue was my only asset and any stain on my reputation would ruin my life for good.

When Nana met me by the blue iron gates of our home that evening, she was actually smiling. The *khalat* she wore, a floral cotton dress buttoned from top to bottom, which she had made years ago, looked tired like she usually did, but the sky was still bright, even though it was dinner time and she had sat out to catch the last rays of the sun. I had timed my journey perfectly. I had left work at 6pm and, as I had got lucky catching the first trolley-bus, it only took forty minutes. Perhaps Mahir hadn't been yet.

'Nana! How are you?' I kissed her round wrinkled cheek and looked into her hooded brown eyes fearfully. Sometimes Nana would smile just before she shouted.

'I am fine, and so's that Mahir. What a good colleague you have there, Gulush. So respectful and protective towards you. He said he's always looking out for you like you were his own sister. What a man, such a man.'

I sighed with relief, as she bustled me towards the house. As soon as I opened our tall wooden door, I felt overwhelmed by the smell of freshly baked bread. 'Have you already…?' I asked.

'Yes, of course.' She smiled, revealing her fake teeth. 'My hands were itching to cook something delicious. You can't buy such good stuff in the shops. Not that you can find much in the shops anyway,' she added.

Since the collapse of the Soviet Union, shop shelves had looked forlorn and were even emptier than during Soviet rule when we had to produce coupons to get rations of stinky margarine, scraps of beef clinging to hefty bones and sugar lumps. Some private individuals were able to bring supplies from Iran and Turkey these days, but since Nana's state pension was our main income, we had not been able to afford to buy that type of produce. That too was about to change.

19

★★★

At the start of my third week at work, Masha distributed people's salaries. Throughout the day, staff members trickled into Masha's office to sign a register, as she counted their earnings and handed it over to them. I did not expect to be paid yet, as I had only worked for two full weeks so far, but to my surprise, she slipped me four 250-manat notes. The government had introduced the new Azerbaijani manat a month earlier. With denominations of one, ten and 250, it was currently being used alongside the Russian ruble. I stared at the four notes in silent stupor. 1000 manats was the equivalent of 10,000 Russian rubles!

'What is this, Masha?'

'A gift,' she said, smiling, while busying herself with mugs in the corner. She turned around eventually and threw her hands in the air. 'Such a child! Take the money and put it away. This is how things work here. The Prosecutor gets gifts and then passes some around. You have to pay for your bus fare to get to work, right? And buy some food, too. When given, take it, when beaten, run away!' she concluded with a Russian saying, before packing up her bag to leave for home.

When I handed the money to Nana that evening, she was so excited that she did not seem to know what to do with herself. She stood and beamed at me for a moment. Then turned and locked it carefully away in her chest of drawers. Nana had worked from the age of eleven, when WWII began. Orphaned a year earlier, she had been forced to quit school and get a job at a match factory to support her aunt and two cousins with whom she lived in Ganja.

As far as I knew, no one had supported her financially before. Even when my Baba was alive, she had taken pride in being financially independent, working from home as a seamstress.

Having made tea, she went to rummage in her understairs store for some preserved apricots she had saved for special occasions. Each whole apricot looked so succulent, with golden syrup streaming out of it. Slicing my first one open, I discovered that before cooking, each apricot stone had been replaced with a tasty nut kernel. After filling up on tea and these exquisitely sweet desserts, it took us both a long time to wind down and fall asleep that night.

## 2.

# BAKU STATE UNIVERSITY

My first three weeks at work flew by. Soon it was time for me to head to Baku for my orientation week at Baku State University. The day before I went, I had another gift from the Prosecutor. This time it was a crisp 100 US dollar note. I had never seen one before. Masha pressed it into my palm and ordered me to put it in my bag straightaway. She did not need to ask me twice, because I could immediately picture Nana's relief. A study session in Baku was an expensive activity.

The next day, Nana accompanied me on the eight-hour bus journey along bumpy roads. It included a long break in Kurdamir, the halfway point between Ganja and Baku. I hated Kurdamir since it felt barren and rough. When the bus stopped at a cheap-looking eatery on an otherwise deserted road, Nana and I loitered outside, dusty wind ruffling our hair, waiting for the other passengers to have a meal inside, sitting at rusting metal tables, on hard chairs.

'They probably use some old, rangy meat in there. Dogs wouldn't eat that food. I don't know why people stuff their faces with it. I wouldn't even buy tea here. I bet they add baking soda to make you thirsty and drink more,' Nana rumbled on disapprovingly, while I looked longingly at the steaming enamel teapots and listened to the clatter of cutlery on plates and the chatter of our fellow travellers. I knew it was pointless to argue with Nana when she looked so resolute, but at least I was allowed to visit the nearby toilet block. As I expected, there was no running water, just three cubicles with squatting toilets in them and no doors. I checked each cubicle in turn, but they rivalled each other in the amount of poo left not only where intended, but also all over the floor. The ground by the useless, rusting sinks, was also dotted with poo, and there was not a scrap of newspaper used in lieu of toilet paper in sight. After a few seconds of examining the scene, assaulted by the sights and smells, I gave up on the idea. Long after I left the block to go back to Nana, the stench, she remarked, clung to me. It seemed ages before the driver shouted for the passengers and we resumed our journey. I felt every bump. By the time we reached Azad's, my uncle's brother-in-law, in Baku, my bladder was threatening to explode. His wife, Yasmin, politely accepted the bags of gifts I thrust into her hands as I made a beeline for the toilet.

As tradition required, we had arrived with presents for the household. In the bags was packed fresh, clotted cream, which Nana claimed was so thick you had to cut it with a knife. There were two shoulders of freshly slaughtered lamb, succulent fruits, walnuts still milky and soft in their shells, as well as aromatic herbs and other odds and ends.

Azad and Yasmin's two-bedroom flat seemed spacious, light and so modern. It had central heating to defeat the cold of winter, as well as an indoor toilet and separate bathroom. The latter was my ultimate dream, as a teenager. I hated even the thought of going to our outdoor toilet in the spidery night, while using our bathhouse, so far down the garden, had always felt like a major operation to coordinate.

I liked Azad a lot. He was a military officer. He and his siblings had grown up in East Germany, before the Soviet Block collapsed, where his dad had served in the Soviet Red Army. It was perhaps because of that upbringing that Azad was so different from other men I knew. Unlike the men in my family, Azad was affectionate with his two daughters, who often gave him big hugs. On our first evening together, I watched Azad and his family gathered round the TV, laughing at the stand-up Russian comedian Zadornov's jokes. They really enjoyed each other's company. His wife, Yasmin, was inquisitive but kind. She spent most of her time keeping the house spotless and looking after their two daughters. As soon as the girls were sent to their bedroom, the conversation turned to the dreadful topic of war in Nagorno-Karabakh.

'What do they say about the war, Azad? Is there any hope?' Nana asked. She took a sip from her black tea with lemon. I spooned some rich, cherry jam onto a small saucer, for now interested in the subject. As a senior member of the army, Azad currently had a cushy job in the barracks, but as the war with Armenia kept escalating, it was highly likely that he could be sent to the front-line.

Disappointingly, Azad was non-committal about how the war might affect him. He skilfully directed the discussion to Nana's health. I sighed and focused on licking my spoon clean. We all knew that topic was another fertile ground for conversation with Nana. She had always had some sort of ailment, from failing kidneys and high blood pressure to heart palpitations. I vividly remembered, though I was only five, the time when the local hospital sent her to die at home because her kidneys seemed to be failing. Nearly twelve years later, Nana was still going strong. The family thought this was largely due to herbal medicine that had saved her life. Despite this, Nana was always able to rattle off a long list of aches and pains. Yasmin, after listening patiently for a few minutes, seized this opportunity as a reason to make Nana's bed on the sofa.

'You should really rest now, Rosa *khala*,' she said kindly. Nana, paused mid-sentence, frowned, but grunted her assent.

I was sent to share a double bed with my two young cousins. Although the girls were six and eight years younger than me respectively, I didn't mind. I had played with them a lot when they lived in Ganja. Staying in their room felt like a sleepover, something that I had seldom done due to Nana's overprotectiveness. She would not even let me stay with Mama when I came to Baku, because she thought the distance from Mama's flat to the university was too great and she deemed that Mama's new partner was a stranger to me and therefore not safe to be around.

Next morning, after Nana's inevitable, prolonged speech on how I should be careful in Baku and not mix with anyone, I got ready to go. I pulled on my favourite long-sleeved, light-pink shirt. It reminded me of apricot blossom in the garden. Nana had made it a year ago when we went to one of Baba's relative's wedding. I tucked the soft shirt neatly into my midi black skirt and, after some debate with Nana over a farewell breakfast of eggy bread, I agreed to carry an old-fashioned hand-knitted cardigan over my arm. I did not intend to wear it. The weather was still sunny outside, thankfully, but since I knew Baku's winds could suddenly become piercing, I decided she was right this time.

'I have promised to give *nazir* to the poor and elderly when you return home safely,' she said, kissing my forehead, as if I was going on a dangerous sea voyage rather than around a modern city. I left the flat slightly tearful, however, because although I revelled in my newfound freedom, I was sad to be parted from Nana. Despite Yasmin and Azad's welcoming attitude, I felt I could not fully relax. I had never been away from my immediate family before.

Azad's flat was only a ten-minute walk away from Baku State University. I felt quite nervous as I stepped out into the sunshine, but I had Yasmin's clear instructions, which I intended to follow absolutely. There were so many sets of steps to go down. When I reached the bottom of the hill, I looked back at Azad's nine-storey block of flats looming above me. Climbing back up after a long day was not going to be easy.

★★★

From day one, Yasmin spent every evening with me in the kitchen, quizzing me about university life. Her large eyes seemed full of wonder, perhaps because she had left school young. Her curiosity, although welcome, was a bit overwhelming some nights. I was not used to being the centre of attention. After listening to my description of the university and its formalities, she asked: 'Have you made any friends yet?'

'Well, there's this girl, Lala, she's quite friendly,' I replied. 'She's taller than me. She's got brown, curly hair, green eyes and she's a bit spotty. She doesn't look like a typical Azerbaijani, but then neither do I. I told her she resembled Fatma Girik, the Turkish actress. She just laughed because 'girik' means broken in Azerbaijani, though I'm not sure it means the same in Turkish. I liked her. She obviously has a sense of humour. Of course, she's a Russian-speaker too, her Azerbaijani is so heavily accented.'

A frown brushed across Yasmin's face when I said that. Was I being insensitive? Yasmin had attended the Azerbaijani-language stream at school where all subjects were taught in our mother tongue, and, despite being fluent in Russian, I knew she felt rather insecure about her language skills when compared to Azad and her daughters, who mostly spoke in Russian.

'I think she's a Lezgi, ' I added hastily to explain Lala's preference for the Russian language. 'I am in the Russian-language stream at law school. Everyone has to be fluent in Russian.' Yasmin had turned to cast onions in a pan. 'It's caused me so much trouble at the office,' I added dramatically. 'My written Azerbaijani is terrible.'

'What about boys?' Yasmin changed the subject, sitting back at the table to prepare more vegetables. She wouldn't let me help to start with, partly because I had assignments to do and partly because she doubted my capabilities.

What about them? Was Yasmin gathering intelligence to report back to Nana?

'It's a very mixed group,' I replied. 'I suppose that's because we were admitted based on written test results. Some have been trying to get in for years and have finally managed to at last. Most of my class are grown-up men with families and other responsibilities. I expected there to be more young people. Maybe it's because it's a part correspondence course designed to fit round a paid job. A lot of younger students don't have to work like I do. It's mostly like being back at the Prosecutor's Office, only with lectures and seminars.'

'Sounds like it will be the best place to learn in,' Yasmin replied thoughtfully.

I tried hard to mask my disappointment. Deep down, I had been counting on meeting a good-looking, wealthy young man, who lived in Baku, had a secure job in law enforcement and a nice house. Someone who would offer to marry me, as soon as possible. If I didn't meet anyone in Baku, chances were that Nana would arrange a marriage for me. She often said that Romeos and Juliets of this world didn't survive the day-to-day demands of life, whereas an arranged marriage was fortified by the support of both families and was likely to last. The thought of marrying someone I didn't even know properly felt depressing. Mistaking my sudden silence for tiredness, Yasmin poured us some more tea and then went to see to the girls, leaving me to put my feet up and daydream in front of the TV.

★★★

Since there were no obvious candidates for marriage in my class, I decided to concentrate on getting to know Lala. We quickly discovered that we shared a love for good food, which was plentiful in the nearby cafés, and sentimental Indian movies, which made us laugh until our cheeks ached.

Lala was a ray of light in a dreary university environment.

Baku State University, though it looked imposing from the outside, was shabby and in need of repair on the inside. The collapse of the Soviet Union meant that many institutions did not have sufficient funds to invest in their infrastructure. The induction for my law course involved sitting in a succession of large classrooms with broken windows, listening to the howling wind and waiting for lecturers to show up. A lot of what we had to listen to seemed boring and monotonous. Many of the lecturers had other law-related jobs besides teaching. Delivering introductory lectures to correspondence course students was obviously low on their priority list. Those lecturers who bothered to turn up were dull and uninspiring. They droned on, reading their handwritten notes, which we were expected to transcribe word for word. They also did not expect anyone to ask questions.

I found it difficult to concentrate on note-taking, especially with cold feet and hands, so, at first, I sat there in a stupor, thinking I could simply read up on the subjects in relevant textbooks later on. I soon discovered the major flaw in that plan. The university library did not have enough textbooks for everyone. The students who were in full-time education were prioritised over my cohort.

'Try Akhundov,' said a rigid-faced librarian, closing her hatch in my face.

'Who's Akhundov?' I asked Lala.

'It's the central library, silly. It was named after Akhundov. You know, the writer, Mirza Fatali Akhundov? I think he was most famous for his elegy, "Eastern Poem to Lament the Death of Pushkin". Was it 1837 when Pushkin was killed? I don't know, but I know where the library is. I'll take you there after the class.'

The Akhundov library reminded me of a local museum in Ganja, where Mama had worked when I was young, but much grander. The library could not have been more central. It was only a five-minute walk away from Torgovaya, the large pedestrian shopping street, and just around the corner from the Opera and Ballet Theatre. The latter building had stunning architecture, built back in 1911, according to its wall plaque. The Akhundov library was not as old as that, but it had full-size statues adorning its façade. I recognised some as famous Azerbaijani poets.

'That's Nizami Ganjavi, isn't it?' I pointed out the twelfth-century Azerbaijani poet to Lala. 'Look, Mahsati is there too!' She was a poet from the same era as Ganjavi. It was unusual for women to be celebrated, I thought. She must have been really special. I recognised them because they came from my hometown, but other figures were less familiar. 'Is that man Uzeyir Hajibayov? Wasn't he a composer?'

'I think he was also a playwright... Maybe that's why he's there,' Lala said, squinting upwards in the sunlight.

'Who's that one?'

'Rustaveli,' Lala replied.

I wondered why they had a medieval Georgian poet's statue in the line-up. Pushkin was there as well. Cars whizzed by on Khagani Street behind us and Rashid Behbudov Avenue on our right, as we stood admiring the frontage. The end of September air was balmy and bright. It felt too nice outside to want to go into the library, but eventually necessity forced us inside.

We trooped up the grand marble staircase and, after browsing the catalogues, found the relevant weighty tomes. Lala and I grinned as we pulled the books off the shelf and sat down at a table in a vast reading room, which could easily have accommodated hundreds of readers but was mostly empty. However, when we turned to the appropriate chapters, we were in for a shock. Half of the pages were missing. Someone had just torn out pages instead of taking notes. Lala swore out loud. I looked around to see if anyone had heard. Luckily, the smattering of people there were sitting at the other end of the room. It might explain why the library was so empty, if the students stole pages instead of staying in the library.

From then on, I made an extra effort to absorb every word the lecturers said, however boring, since they were the only teaching materials I was likely to get to help me prepare for my exams. Buying textbooks was not an option because the older editions were no longer reprinted and the new ones were not available yet. The teachers were using old Soviet texts and simply omitting any references to the Soviet authorities. The laws of Azerbaijan had hardly changed yet, apart from the deletion of references to the Soviet Socialist Republic from the title and texts of the legislation.

Despite our first experience, we returned to the library later in the week in the hope of finding alternative sources for our study of an important module, the theory of state and law. This was taught by a somewhat fierce older woman. She had published the first edition of her book on the subject in 1955, when my mother was a newborn. This time we were successful. We were particularly anxious to get everything right for this assignment. The rumours were that she disliked beautiful young women but had a soft spot for good-looking young men. Anyone who failed the exam she set had only two options: to drop out or to pay a bribe of 1000 USD to pass a resit. Neither of these was an option for me. During her lectures you could feel the whole class perspiring with concentration, the air empty of any sound but her frighteningly calm, creaky voice.

Despite all the stresses, my friendship with Lala blossomed. We found a Presto café in the city centre, not far from the fountain square, which we both loved. We escaped there every day to wind down and to moan about the plight of students. The café was on two floors. Downstairs was always overrun with people ordering food, but there was always a quiet spot upstairs, by the large windows where we could watch passers-by in the street below.

Our order was always the same: a Presto bun filled with Russian salad, chopped up gherkins and sausage, along with a glass of Coca-Cola. Lala's parents, who used to be engineers at a factory that went bust after the Soviet Union collapsed, were even poorer than my family, so I was glad to have the money from the Prosecutor's Office so I could treat us both. It couldn't compare to the homemade food that Nana used to make before the economy disintegrated. My favourites had always been minced lamb with crushed mint and basil wrapped in vine leaves, or *pilav* rice with caramelised onions, creamy chestnuts, sweet raisins, dried apricots and more lamb. However, although the Presto fare was somewhat unimpressive taste-wise, I loved the novelty of fast food and the freedom to go to cafés. This was something I could never do in my more conservative hometown, Ganja.

One afternoon, when the café was almost empty upstairs, Lala surprised me by pulling out a packet of cigarettes and casually lighting up. She offered one to me, but I pushed it away. I was amazed I hadn't noticed that her clothes smelt of them, under the notes of floral perfume. This was probably because, unusually for Azerbaijan, I had grown up in a family where all the women smoked. Baba had had a sister whose dying wish was to be buried with her strong filter-less cigarettes. Even Nana smoked, although secretly. She said it helped to numb the pain she still felt over the loss of her twenty-three-year-old son, who was killed in a tragic accident before I was born. For years, I had to buy her cigarettes from a local corner shop under the pretext of having male visitors at home. I didn't feel I could do something so reckless as Lala, smoking in a public place. I thought to be seen doing that could sabotage my chances of a good marriage.

***

At the end of my first week at university, Lala and I were heading to the Presto café chatting happily when someone called out my name, and the voice was a man's.

'Hey, Gulush!'

I looked around but couldn't see anyone, so quickly dismissed the thought that there was someone who knew me in this busy city. Azad was at work every day, and our class had all beetled home to their wives and families. Besides, Gulush had always been my nickname at home. Unfortunately, my colleagues had chosen to call me that at work, after Mama had said it on the first day. At school, and now at university, I was called Gulya, my Russianised nickname, which I much preferred.

'Gulush, over here,' the voice insisted. I stopped and turned again to see Mahir standing by the white GAZ-31.

'Mahir? What are you doing here?' It felt almost like seeing a family member, to see that familiar face. Sudden excitement surged through me. 'This is Lala, she's my university friend,' I gabbled. 'Lala, this is Mahir, my work colleague.' They exchanged polite smiles.

'I'm here with Zakir *bay,* on official business, you know,' Mahir said importantly. 'I thought I'd stop by to say hello.' He was leaning on the car now. The armpits of his white shirt were slightly sweaty and his ample belly was hanging over his thick trouser belt.

'How long have you been waiting?' I was more than curious.

'What does it matter, Gulush? Hop into the car and let's take a ride.'

My usual anxiety of being seen with a man who was not an immediate family member kicked in. I looked at Lala for an excuse to get away, but she simply shrugged. She didn't seem to be concerned by the invitation, why should I be? People were obviously more relaxed about taking a ride in other people's cars in Baku. It was a big, modern city and everyone minded their own business.

'I'll just drop you off wherever you were going,' Mahir added. Perhaps he had noticed my hesitation. He opened the car's back door for us. As Lala stepped towards the car, I noticed that she was the same height as Mahir, but he was twice as wide as her. At least I was not going to be alone with him. I sat next to Lala on the back seat and, as soon as I shut the door, he took off, driving confidently towards the city centre.

'Have you eaten today?' he asked, while we were waiting for the traffic lights.

I hoped he wasn't going to ask us out. I was not allowed to go to a café with a man, I was sure of that. I tried to fudge it. 'Yes, I have.'

'What, breakfast?' He chortled.

Lala shrugged again, so I relaxed a little.

'Yes, breakfast.'

'Come on, Gulush, I won't bite. Let's have a quick meal and then you two go back to your studies. I haven't eaten anything today, not even breakfast. I could use some intelligent company.'

I looked out at the trees and the unknown streets whizzing by. No one had to know about our meal out. He was a work colleague. This was not going to ruin my reputation.

'OK,' I said. Then I added, with determination in my voice, 'One meal.'

Mahir did a sharp U-turn and drove into a district I did not recognise. He parked by an empty courtyard, filled with the seductive smells of lamb kebabs. A young man rushed up to Mahir to welcome him. We were ushered into a room built of concrete blocks and decorated with cheap, yellow, floral wallpaper. There was a square table and four wooden chairs. Before we had even sat down, a waiter burst in carrying a tray heavy with starters. Mahir, obviously familiar with the menu, ordered the waiter to leave the warm flat bread, feta cheese, fresh tomatoes, cucumbers and pickles and waved away other less appealing starters. I suddenly felt ravenous and eagerly helped myself to bread and cheese. My face flushed with delight, but catching Mahir's knowing smile, I reddened further. Lala followed my example.

'Easy, Gulush,' Mahir said, 'don't fill up on the starters.'

He was right to warn me. Shortly the waiter reappeared with plates of succulent lamb kebabs sizzling on their skewers. We were still tearing pieces of lamb off the ribs when the *Tabaka*, a whole pan-fried chicken, arrived. I didn't wait to be asked. I broke off a chicken leg and started chewing on it.

A part of me sometimes felt embarrassed by my enthusiasm for food, especially eating with other people. I had been taught that "real ladies" should be reserved around food. The tradition was to refuse anything offered to you at least three times. Today I couldn't resist. The last time I had such delectable dishes was at Baba's funeral. Even though I had started bringing money in, Nana insisted on remaining 'frugal', so she could save enough money to buy me a decent dowry. Remembering this, I willed myself to slow down.

'What have I missed at the office?' I said, in a rather grown-up voice. Lala did not have the experience of a paid job, despite her family's circumstances.

'Change is coming, big change…' Mahir paused and lit another cigarette. Was he going to elaborate on that statement? In the silence, Lala broke off a larger piece of the succulent chicken, licking her fingers in delight. She hardly ever had any nice food at home. Mahir blew a smoke ring. 'You haven't heard this from me,' he said, 'but our Zakir *bay* is transferring to Baku. By the time you return, we will have a new boss.'

This news stunned me into silence. As Lala started to chat on about university, I was worrying about the security of my job and who the new Prosecutor would be. The waiter collected the plates and brought in a pot of black tea together with the bill. Since offering to pay was considered an affront to a gentleman's masculinity, Lala and I sat back and let Mahir settle the bill. He included a generous tip for the young waiter. I wasn't sure either of us could have afforded to pay for even our part of the meal anyway.

'Student life is tough, I know.' Mahir sipped his tea. 'I am glad I could come and treat you hard-working people.' I was a bit curious how a driver could afford such a kind gesture.

Once in the car, we raced back then halted in front of the library. As there was no parking, Lala and I slid quickly out, voicing our thanks, but turning to wave him off, to our surprise, he came out.

'Enjoy the rest of your study session, Lala,' he said as a way of bidding farewell to her. 'And Gulush, come back to work quickly. It's not the same in Masha's room without you. She doesn't make tea when I come round nowadays.' He pouted, then reached out to shake my hand and pressed something into my palm. I noticed Lala step towards the library when he leant in closer. 'Don't make a fuss, Gulush. It's a present.'

I stared at the 100 USD note in my hand.

'This is from work? But I've had one already.'

'Yes, of course, it's from work,' he said. A broad smile lit up his round face. 'Buy yourself something nice.'

With a backwards wave, he revved the GAZ-31's powerful engine, causing some pedestrians to look round, and sped off.

I stood dumbfounded on the pavement as his car disappeared around the corner, until Lala's arm curled around mine. 'He seems nice,' she said. 'Lucky you to have such a generous friend. Thank you for letting me come along. That meal was delicious, but look at my belly now!' She laughed and I joined in. Then, linked by our arms and our shared, secret experience, we sauntered into the library feeling content.

★★★

I had prearranged to meet Mama at the main university building on the penultimate day of my current study session. She didn't have a landline at home, and I had no easy means of contacting her during my stay. The plan had been that I visit her family, but as I anticipated my first study period would be all-consuming, I decided, before we met up, that spending several hours getting across Baku to Mama's flat would be too much to fit in. At some level, I think I didn't want to see her new life, a life I could not share with her. This was something I would never admit to her. Instead, I made lots of excuses and amped up my angst about the first-year exams. I was genuinely sad to not see my siblings, though. I treated her at the Presto café. She didn't rate it as much as Lala and I did. As we chatted, I realised she was wearing an old navy dress she had worn in Ganja, had little make-up on and flat shoes. She seemed less glamorous than I remembered, even though she still looked beautiful. Before I said my reluctant goodbyes, I pressed the 100 USD Mahir had given me into her palm. I asked her to buy something nice for my brother and sister.

Her eyes lit up. Living in Baku could not be easy without a regular income and support from her extended family.

The next day, I caught the bus back home. I spent hours narrating the highlights of my first study session to Nana who had been eagerly awaiting my return. She cooked my favourite vine leaf dolma with minced lamb she had bought from a local butcher and a special soup made with Greek-style yoghurt and fresh, fragrant, finely chopped dill, parsley, coriander and mint. A bunch of autumnal roses from the garden decorated the table. It was the first time I had been away from home by myself, and homecoming felt sweet.

Returning to the Prosecutor's Office, however, felt remarkably difficult. I had just begun to get to know my colleagues when I left for Baku. While I was away, life had moved on. Ali *muellim*, the new Prosecutor, was old news to them, and it seemed like they were all at ease with the change. Unlike his predecessor, he preferred to be addressed *muellim*, a 'teacher', a respectful address of a man since the Soviet times, whereas *bay* became popular post-independence.

Every time I heard his measured footsteps down the corridor, I would bury myself in some sort of paperwork. I started reading the murder cases out of sheer desperation. I wanted to look busy. I would try, at first, to work out some simple elements, such as a criminal act and criminal intent. Then gradually, as my curiosity took over, I tried to detect some objective components of the crimes, in the way one of our lecturers had explained. Discerning subjective elements was not easy, reading the case files. They were real-life detective stories, with gruesome photos of dead bodies and crime scenes and with multiple, often tedious, witness statements. In my early days working at the Prosecutor's Office, I noticed, the news of another murder or robbery shook me to my core, but the more I became accustomed to the work, such reports became my new normal.

When I was moved onto rape cases, I found them especially fascinating. I did not understand how any of those women were brave enough to come forward and tell strangers what had happened to them. The thought of it horrified me because reading the files I learnt the process that took place when someone reported a rape case.

First of all, a medical examiner would examine the woman, from head to toe, looking for signs of struggle, such as any bruises, scratches or lost virginity. All the medical examiners who signed off on the files were men. Then the victim was interviewed by an investigator, also a man. Typical questions included: Where were you? What did you do? What did he do? The questions designed to gather every little detail of the incident were often very explicit. Again, all my colleagues were men. I did not know a single female investigator. Finally, the woman had to appear in front of a court and give an oral statement about the rape. From the files, I gathered that all the judges in the criminal court were men too. Even if the rapist did not bribe his way to freedom, how did these women live with this much exposure, especially in a small town where everyone knew everyone? I knew their chances of marrying someone and leading a normal life again were non-existent. They might be better off dead. I continued to make my way through all the existing files with a mixture of horror and curiosity.

Two weeks later, I realised that Ali *muellim* was still oblivious to my existence. While I dutifully filed the paperwork, following all Masha's instructions, I was able to observe the Prosecutor's calm mannerisms as he walked down the corridor quietly. He did not fit in with my idea of how a Prosecutor should look either, though there was a certain gravity in his measured tones, heavy footsteps and tall, sturdy figure. To my great relief, he also did not have an entourage of bodyguards.

The new Prosecutor was only half of my problem with work. There was a weird tension between Arzu, the receptionist, and me. She was quite competitive, especially when it came to male attention. True, we were both single and on the lookout for an eligible husband, but I felt it went deeper than that with Arzu. She needed to be adored by male colleagues, who paid her a never-ending stream of compliments, to feel worthwhile. She made the efforts that others did not. She always looked impeccable in her white satin shirts and modest but flattering skirts that accentuated her narrow waistline and curvy backside. Was it possible she saw me as a potential threat, even though I did not often dare to venture out of the safety of Masha's kingdom? It turned out there was more to it than that.

Shortly after my return, we sat – Arzu, Masha, Mahir and I – sharing a meal in Masha's office.

'Tell us all about your studies in Baku, Gulush,' said Masha, her eyes twinkling under heavy black eyeliner. Without make-up, I imagined they would be as small as sunflower seeds.

Excited to be the focus of attention at last, I told them, enthusiastically, about the subjects we studied, the eccentric lecturers, my new friend and the sights and sounds of Baku. I didn't mention the meal I had with Mahir. He and Masha seemed very interested, wanting all the details, but Arzu was quiet and soon excused herself.

In the days that followed, I noticed that every time anyone mentioned my studies, she left the room.

'What's up with her?' I asked Masha quietly on one occasion.

'Well,' confided Masha as she dabbed the corners of her mouth free from chicken fat with a handkerchief, 'she can't help it, Gulush. It has always been Arzu's greatest wish to become a lawyer, like her dad. He died in a car accident, may he rest in peace. I remember him very well.' Masha paused and smiled dreamily. 'He was a lovely man. I had just started working here and he was very charming to me. It was so sad when he left us.' Her eyes filled with tears and I worried that her black eyeliner would be ruined if she cried. She sighed, then straightened up, composing herself. 'Anyway,' she continued, 'from what I've heard, Arzu has applied to study law both in Baku and in Moscow, for seven consecutive years, but each time has failed to get in.'

'No wonder she left the room,' I said. I wished I had asked before. I felt so sorry for Arzu. I had obviously opened a wound I did not know existed.

From then on, I tried to be diplomatic and avoid any talk of law school in front of her. Since my own childhood was spent in a house where Nana and Mama often argued and gave each other the silent treatment half the time, any animosity around me felt unsettling. I resolved to charm Arzu because I wanted her on my side, even though it was difficult to build trust with her because I found that, although she was good at asking questions, she seldom disclosed anything about herself.

As the late autumn winds gradually bared the *chinar* tree outside of Arzu's window, I bought her regular 'peace offerings' of Mars and Snickers bars out of my bus money. I learnt to make a frothy coffee for her, mixing instant coffee with a small amount of water and a heaped dessert spoon of sugar into a paste. It felt so satisfying to add boiling water to the mustard-coloured mixture, which transformed it into a delectable drink with a frothy topping. I even went shopping with her in a flea market not far from work on a few occasions. I spent a lot of the Prosecutor's 'gifts' on what Nana considered frivolous purchases, such as costumed dolls, which I had never had as a child, and a fake, plastic palm tree.

As the temperature plummeted outside, Arzu started to thaw. This turned out to be a timely development for me. Masha had kept asking me to type up some of the paperwork for the files. I found this task very daunting since I had never used a typewriter before. Locating each letter took me an excruciatingly long time to start with. There was one electric typewriter in the reception area. While Arzu made tea for the Prosecutor and ushered visitors in and out, I perspired over each page of writing for what seemed like hours. I prayed that the visitors did not notice my shaking hands, especially as I kept hitting the wrong keys. I would often make such a mess with trying to scratch out the wrong letter with a razor and then attempting to hit the right key at the right spot. Each time I had to start all over again. That was usually when Arzu stepped in. As I watched wistfully, her fingers would fly over the keys as if she was playing a piano.

Deep into the cold winter of 1992, my typing skills

had improved so much that I was asked to type up reports and case materials for the investigators. I was still slower than Arzu, but I enjoyed the challenge of learning a new skill and it gave me the opportunity to read case materials. Although there were many distractions in reception, it felt more interesting than being encased in Masha's office. There was a never-ending queue of people wanting to see the Prosecutor. Soon people like the blue-eyed police investigator Tolik were dropping chocolate bars in for me and Arzu too.

Occasionally, when Arzu was in a particularly good mood and the reception was quiet, I tried to learn more about her. She was twenty-five and, according to her, there was no man on the horizon, even though she was quite pretty. Her mother was Russian. I thought the lack of pressure to marry was probably due to her ethnic background because, although I was only seventeen, I was already feeling like I might end up a spinster. A friendship grew tentatively between us.

I had initially loved the safety of Masha's office, but now working in reception felt more dynamic and edgy. Unlike Masha, Arzu flirted with the young investigators, who crowded in from time to time. I found my obsessively competitive nature made me want to shine more than her. I enjoyed being warmly complimented for typing up urgent, extra paperwork in double quick time. Once again, my learnt mistrust of men was in conflict with the part of me that revelled in their attention. Mahir had made himself a new station by the window next to my table and took his tea breaks in our room, frowning at men who lingered unnecessarily.

I was working in reception full time by spring 1993, only seeing Masha during lunch breaks and when it was time to receive my salary and 'gifts'. I still felt reserved around the Prosecutor and other older co-workers, though I was flattered by their praises. When Arzu told me that an office party was being organised to celebrate International Women's Day, I debated making some excuse to get out of it. The idea of Arzu, Masha and I sitting down to eat at a table full of men was daunting.

'I... don't think my family would approve, Arzu. It's one thing to work alongside men but quite another thing to have a meal with them, even in the office,' I was whispering, just as Farid *muellim*, the Prosecutor's assistant walked in.

'Talking about the party?' he asked. A toothy smile lit up his round face. He waved a loaded clipboard around proudly. 'I am in charge of it! Saying 'no' to the invitation is not an option, in fact I'll be deadly offended if you don't come. It is especially to celebrate women, after all,' he finished brightly and marched back to the Prosecutor's room.

'You want me and Masha to be there alone, Gulush? We need you.' Arzu directed the full force of her big, brown eyes at me. How could I refuse?

★★★

Monday the 8th of March arrived all too quickly, three days after my eighteenth birthday. At home, I pretended that we had to attend work as usual, even though International Women's Day was officially a countrywide holiday. I still felt slightly agitated about the forthcoming party. Despite

Arzu's protests, I spent the morning typing up the papers left by investigators in my tray over the weekend.

As I passed down the corridor, en route to the toilet, I noticed that Farid *muellim* had joined several tables together in his office and covered them with a large white tablecloth. The food, from a local restaurant, had not arrived yet, but the middle of the table was crowded with bottles of alcohol, which made me wince. Why did men need so much to drink? When Baba was alive, he and other male family members would drink alcohol often until they got loud and sometimes angry. I didn't want to watch my colleagues getting drunk.

At noon, the clunk of heavy footsteps and the smell of kebabs wafting across the corridor announced the start of the party. When I followed Arzu and Masha to Farid *muellim*'s office, we found the joined tables crammed with lamb and chicken kebabs on skewers, feta cheese, salami, a variety of pâtés and all the usual trimmings, such as flatbreads and pickles. Everyone else, including the Prosecutor, were seated when we arrived. The noise of shuffling chairs as they stood to greet us, along with jovial celebratory remarks about women, made me increasingly uncomfortable.

I sat on the edge of my chair, closest to the door, next to Arzu. I had no appetite for once, but someone picked up my plate and returned it moments later piled high with chunks of well-cooked lamb, a quarter of a chicken and a bit of everything else. Mahir insisted on filling our glasses with champagne and the men opened their bottles of vodka. The Prosecutor stood to speak and give the first toast to honour us, the women of the office. My brain felt foggy with tension. I couldn't absorb a single word of his long speech. I was relieved when everyone started clinking their glasses.

'Gulush,' Mahir nudged me with his foot. He indicated my glass. 'The toast?'

'Oh, no, no, I don't drink,' I protested, but he stared, sticking out his stubbly chin until I felt compelled to pick up the tall flute filled with sparkling, light gold liquid. My glass tinkled when I touched it first to Mahir's and then to Arzu's. I faked taking a sip then sat back watching everyone else emptying their glasses enthusiastically. Despite the occasion – the decorated table and the feast before us – the atmosphere in the room felt as sombre and official to me as ever. I would not have been surprised if my male colleagues suddenly started discussing case details or some other work issue. Apart from Mahir, in his regular white shirt with black trousers that sat below his belly fat, the men were dressed in stern grey suits, starched shirts and formal ties. During the meal, many delivered pompous speeches about 'the role of women in our newly developing society', which were mostly boring and pretentious.

'You should finish your champagne before it goes flat, Gulush,' Mahir said, as a discussion about court procedures broke out at the other end of the table from us.

I felt I had no choice, despite all the talk of equality. I obediently put the glass to my lips. The bubbles tickled. Then I took a couple of large sips. It was a bitter prickle of a taste, not as sweet as I had imagined, but I managed to stop myself showing any reaction. Mahir smiled, satisfied, and started chatting to Masha. I placed the glass down. I fiddled with my lamb rib but could only stomach a mouthful. The temperature in the room seemed to rise as my colleagues refreshed their drinks. The sound of clinking glasses filled the room as a succession of toasts were drunk, to women, the office, the country and other worthy things. Since I kept taking a sip from my glass after each round of cheers and long odes to women, my face grew warmer, but the sense of relaxation spreading across my shoulders and down my arms was counterbalanced by my uncomfortably full bladder. My glass had been refilled several times, but the thought of leaving the room felt unbearable. Everyone would know my destination. I squeezed my legs together, making my face redder. I prayed for the celebration to end.

Eventually, the Prosecutor pushed his chair back, signalling the end of the meal. I was about to get up, but at this point Farid *muellim* presented us three women with bouquets of flowers and some small, red double cassette players from behind his desk. I graciously accepted my crimson roses and gift with a forced smile. I lingered politely, though inwardly desperate, while Arzu and Masha were similarly rewarded and grateful, then I slunk out, dashed down the corridor to Masha's room, left the flowers and my first cassette player on her desk and went to open the nearby toilet door, but it was locked. I cursed as I scurried downstairs to the other toilet, used mainly by the men. I flung the door open heading for the cubicle next to a sink, but to my horror Mahir was there, in mid-flow.

'Just a moment,' he said matter-of-factly.

I hastily shut the door and fled back upstairs. I didn't see his private parts, but I was so shaken I forgot my own pressing need for a moment. I had just seen and heard a man I wasn't related to urinating. Tears of confusion pricked my eyes as I huffed up the stairs and back down the corridor. I had no idea what I was going to do. The upstairs toilet door was ajar. I sighed with relief; I had made it just in time.

I took a few minutes in the clean, white-tiled coolness to calm myself. As I stared in the mirror, smoothing my hair back into place, watching my skin turn from red to pale pink, I realised I had a headache. I splashed water onto my face and straightened my clothes. I was only a short walk and a bus ride from home. I sniffed my top. There was a strong smell of cigarettes, which Nana would expect after work, but no trace of champagne. I made myself smile with the thought of the flowers and the long-coveted cassette player. I didn't have any tapes, but payday wasn't that far away. *You can do this, Gulush*, I told my reflection, although she looked doubtful.

When I emerged from the toilet, I was in for another shock. Mahir was there, leaning against the wall. Treacherous scarlet spread hot across my face. His mouth widened into a smile, revealing short, cigarette-stained teeth under his bushy moustache. I didn't acknowledge him. He was clearly still drunk. I stalked past, eyes facing front, to collect my things.

'Don't make a big deal of this, Gulush. Aren't we friends?'

He followed me into Masha's office and, before I could think, he scooped me up in a bear hug. I flailed against his strong arms. The office was empty. Masha was probably in reception. As much as I tried to pull away, he pushed me closer to him.

'What are you doing, Mahir?' I gasped.

His answer was to press his hot lips to mine,

overwhelming me. He smelt of vodka, smoke and lamb fat. Tight against his fleshy body, I froze. This behaviour was forbidden. Mahir was married, I was a virgin. Why was he doing this? Did he think he loved me? Had I encouraged him? He had been so kind and caring to me, like a brother or a young uncle. So why this and why now? I started to panic. Images from the files I had read poured over and flooded my brain. Was this going to be…?

'Gulush, are you still there?' Arzu's approaching footsteps shattered the moment.

Mahir released me. I shot out of his arms and reached for a tissue to wipe my mouth. Trembling, I gathered up the cassette player and the soft perfumed roses. Mahir's cheerful voice greeted Arzu. They spoke briefly. She was laughing, then I heard him start to whistle as he strode away. Hiding my face behind the flowers, I mumbled that I was going to reception to collect my bag. My knees felt ready to buckle. Again, I worked to calm myself. I couldn't let Arzu know. Mahir was probably so drunk, I reasoned, he will have forgotten all about this in the morning.

I grabbed my handbag, thrust the box with the cassette player under my arm and, hiding my face behind the roses, made to move to the door.

'Gulush, are you OK?' Arzu called after me. Her voice was slightly slurred.

'Yes, yes, just feeling a bit sick,' I replied, without looking back. This was not a lie. My headache had also returned.

'It must be the champagne,' Arzu laughed. 'Me too.' Her voice sounded so relaxed.

'I'd better walk home to sober up,' I called from the corridor. 'See you, Arzu.'

Though Mahir was nowhere to be seen out on the street, I felt like a deer chased by dogs, all the way home, starting at every sound and every movement. When Nana finally opened the door, I dashed past her, saying I thought I had eaten some bad chicken Arzu had brought from home. Nana hurried me to bed with a mug of hot tea and I fell into a deep but dream-filled sleep.

## 3.

# MIXED BAG

The next day, the Prosecutor was called to Baku and apparently left before dawn.

'What was the urgency?' I asked Arzu.

'The Armenians are advancing on Kalbajar.' Her thin mouth tensed up.

The office was quiet, and I was relieved to have space to nurse my thumping headache. I still could not make sense of Mahir's behaviour, but the news about Kalbajar distracted me from my petty worries.

When Arzu went to the toilet, I snuck into the Prosecutor's room to examine the giant map of Azerbaijan. South of Ganja, Kalbajar, one of sixty-six regions, had a direct border with Armenia. I compared the distance between Ganja and Baku and Ganja and Kalbajar. The latter was awfully close. From the map's topography, I could see that Kalbajar had the highest mountains in Azerbaijan and the River Tartar slicing across it.

If Armenia occupied Kalbajar, it would have a direct land link to Nagorno-Karabakh, the disputed area. Suddenly, Mama's concerns all made sense. My anxiety skyrocketed. I could still remember when the Armenian forces were advancing on Ganja, the distant shots growing closer and closer. Back then, I was petrified for days after Nana had declared that she would kill me herself to prevent the Armenian soldiers from taking my 'purity'. Fortunately, the Azerbaijani forces had managed to push the enemy back that time. Now the country was on its knees financially and organisationally. If the Armenians kept advancing, who knew what might happen? I shook my head and returned downcast to my desk.

The atmosphere at work became miserable and tedious. Even the air felt oppressive, as if a heavy blanket hung over the building, making everything grey and lifeless. We didn't joke or eat together as we used to do. I found it hard to think straight. My fingers often drifted, as I tapped out seemingly endless paperwork on the keys of the electric typewriter. Crime did not stop for anything.

It was no better at home, where Nana's fears magnified mine. What if they took over Kalbajar and kept advancing on Ganja again? I knew from past experience that Nana would never consider running away. 'There is nowhere to escape when an enemy knocks on your door,' she would say. She was so worried that she did not even feel motivated to cook up a feast on Novruz, a dearly beloved spring festival in Azerbaijan. Our table used to heave with bowls of steaming *pilav*, succulent lamb mixed with thinly sliced caramelised onions, chestnuts, juicy raisins, sweet apricots, dolma, Russian salad, vinaigrette made of boiled beetroots, potatoes, carrots, kidney beans and sauerkraut, seasoned with oil, salt and pepper. Most importantly, Nana would splurge on overpriced walnuts, hazelnuts, apples, mandarins, and even well-preserved pomegranates. She had made sweet dishes too, including baklava and shekarbura, enough to last a month after the festivities. This Novruz, like for many people, our house felt hollow without the usual family gathering. Nana and I had a quiet meal alone. The contrast made me realise just how much I missed Mama and the rest of the family.

★★★

Throughout March of 1993, I woke up every morning with a sense of dread, heading for the TV before I even used the toilet. Fear hung in the air like a pungent smell. No matter how I tried to distract myself, the thought of advancing Armenian forces kept me restless and anxious. Even when Arzu's birthday arrived, on the 31st of March, we sat quietly in the reception as if we were at a funeral. The Prosecutor was back and an endless procession of men in stern suits or police uniforms had come to visit him all morning. When Mahir delivered a cheerful congratulatory speech to Arzu over a cup of tea, it felt jarring and awkward, for more than one reason.

'You two need to cheer up. What's the matter with you? Our men are fighting out there. We haven't lost yet. It's your birthday, Arzu, how about I take you two out today?'

'Where?' Arzu came alive, like a princess waking from a deep slumber. She sat up in her armchair.

'To have a bite and a drink, up in Hajikand.'

'Well, I'm not allowed,' I said as I slumped back in my chair.

Mahir had never mentioned what had happened on International Women's Day, and neither had I. It was far easier to pretend it never happened. However, it was one thing to go for a meal with him in Baku, where no one knew me; quite another in Ganja: if you spoke to someone for five minutes, you would often find out that you were related in some way. What if he got drunk and tried it on again? I fought off the memory of his hot lips on mine. Nana was right in saying that mixing with men was trouble. I pictured Nana's wrath if she ever found out that I had gone out to a restaurant with a male colleague in attendance, irrespective of the occasion. It wasn't worth it, even to please Arzu. I gazed through the open reception door to where naked trees danced in the bitter wind. There was no sign of spring here, yet.

'Listen, Arzu,' Mahir purred. He leant in closer to her desk and lowered his voice conspiratorially. 'The boss is heading to Baku with his brother, so I'm staying behind. There will be no visitors to see him today, so you might as well pack up early. You'll still get home in time, even if we go and have some fun. It's no different from us having lunch here, together. No harm will come of it.' He glanced at me. 'We'll sit in our own cabin. No one will see us.'

I tried to busy myself with paperwork, but then Arzu said something that drew my attention.

'Life's too short to worry all the time, I suppose.' She paused, as we all thought about that. 'Who knows what's going to happen with this war? They came so close last time. Perhaps we might...'

'What are you three chatting about?' Farid *muellim*'s deep voice startled us. Tall and balding, he usually had a calm, warm presence. As the Prosecutor's assistant, he dealt with complex cases, mostly involving factories and organisations. Unlike investigators, he did not run around crime scenes, but stayed in his office, sifting through paperwork.

'It's Arzu's birthday today,' Mahir said. 'I was trying to cheer these two up by taking them out for lunch.'

'Is that so?' Farid *muellim*'s plump lips stretched into a smile. 'Happy birthday, Arzu. I wouldn't mind joining you. The boss is about to leave, and I'm done with my paperwork. Besides, I could do with a break from the news too.'

'That's decided then.' Mahir pushed his chair back and got up. 'Be ready for 1pm, I'll collect you from the entrance door.'

As soon as the men left the room, anxious words bubbled like soapy water out of my mouth. 'Are you crazy, Arzu? What if someone spots us in his car? Going out for a meal with two married men… If that doesn't kill Nana, nothing will. I can't do it. It's too risky.'

'You're not going alone with a man. There are other people too. No one will see us in the back seat. Come on, Gulush, it's my birthday. Just this once. I'm tired of all this tension, all the depressing news.'

I paced the office for the next hour, unable to relax. I felt excited at the prospect of having a meal out. Eating out with Mahir and Lala, in Baku, had been fun, hadn't it? Somehow the risk added to the sense of adventure I began to feel. With a rush of adrenalin, the dead weight I had been carrying in my heart gave way to a sparkle of aliveness.

The Prosecutor left at midday. Arzu went to Masha's office to deliver a list of reasons as to why we needed to leave early that day. I loitered in the corridor, listening. Every time Arzu lied I felt my own cheeks getting hotter;

but Masha agreed surprisingly quickly. I suspected she planned to skedaddle herself as soon as we had gone.

The last twenty minutes of our shortened day ticked by painfully slowly, but at last it was 1pm. Quivering on the inside, clasping my bag tightly, I followed Arzu and Farid *muellim* to the car. Mahir took off immediately. I pressed myself into the familiar back seat, trying to be as invisible from the outside as possible. He drove as fast as before, weaving skilfully through busy lunchtime traffic. It was easy to see why he had been hired for the job. The further we drove away from central Ganja, the more I relaxed. Once the car started climbing up the mountain roads, I even joined the conversation.

'There's a nice place in Hajikand,' Farid *muellim* was telling Arzu. 'Their food is superb and it's very discreet.'

I rolled down my window to breathe in the crisp mountain air. My family used to come to Hajikand for picnics when Baba was still alive. His idea of a picnic was a whole lamb in the boot of the car, which he cooked to perfection on skewers over amber coals. On those occasions, we brought blankets, lounged on the grass and made tea in a Russian-style samovar. It had been my job to collect the fresh, wild thyme that Nana added to the tea for extra flavour. I had not been back since Baba's death four years ago.

The car pulled up in front of a long row of cabins overlooking a vast bare woods that clung to the side of the valley as far as the eye could see. The men got out of the car and spoke to a waiter, who hastily showed us to a cabin with a stunning view over the mountains. The cabin was essentially a well-built wooden shed with a table and chairs.

A stout puffy faced young man in grey trousers and black jumper had just finished cleaning up a plastic tablecloth after the previous customers. I was struck that at home cleaning was a women's domain, but here... I guessed that no self-respecting man would let his wife, mother, daughter or sister work at a place designed for men's pleasure. Yes, a man could choose to bring female companions here, but a woman could not show up independently in such a place.

I remembered with unease my older uncle's reaction to the news of my job at the Prosecutor's Office. 'It's a brutal place, Mama,' he had pleaded with Nana. 'Gulush is a child, she wouldn't survive a day amongst those wolves!' Somehow his words fell on Nana's deaf ears. She had her heart set on my prestigious career; she herself sacrificed so many opportunities in life, like turning down her factory's initiative to send her to study in Moscow because she had a family to look after. She wanted me to be well-educated and financially independent before I married, so that I was not dependent on any man. Failing to persuade Nana over several phone calls from Moscow, my uncle eventually ended the discussion with: 'Don't come crying to me when things go wrong!'

What if my uncle was right and this was exactly the type of thing he was on about? My conscience momentarily pricked; I sat heavily on one of the four wooden chairs, but as the familiar scent of kebabs wafted in, I suddenly realised I was hungry, and the image of my uncle's worried face faded away.

Within minutes, the waiter came back and covered the table with the starters. There were platters of feta cheese, sliced salami, fresh coriander, basil and spring onions, chopped tomatoes and cucumbers, pickled cabbage and gherkins. Baskets of steaming oven bread and paper-thin flat breads sat in the centre. There was cutlery to transport these delicacies to our plates, but we would eat, as was the tradition, with our fingers.

'No wonder the table is so large!' I said, as the others laughed.

Mahir gave our mains order and the waiter shortly returned with a bottle of vodka, a jug of fruit compote, one of water and a plate of lemons cut in two.

'Is this place good enough?' Mahir asked. We all agreed it was, as he poured vodka into four small glasses.

'Not for me, I don't drink!' I protested.

'You drank champagne the other day,' Arzu reminded me unhelpfully.

'This stuff is cleaner, much better for you.' Mahir distributed the glasses.

'Nana would be furious.' I pushed my glass away.

'Don't worry, it'll wear off by the time you get home,' Arzu said, grinning. 'It always does.' How did she know that? I examined her with renewed curiosity. Had she been somewhere like this before?

'I find it helps me to relax,' said Farid *muellim*, 'and enjoy my food.'

Mahir had now squeezed lemon into a glass of water. I was feeling thirsty.

'I'm going to teach you feather-weights how to drink vodka,' he announced, enjoying everyone's attention. 'Hold your breath and drink the vodka in one go without tasting it, then take a few sips of lemon water. You too, Gulush, don't be a wimp. To Arzu and her many happy returns!'

As Farid and Arzu were smiling encouragingly, holding their glasses ready, I lifted mine and we clinked them together. My gulp of vodka left a burning trail in my throat.

'Now drink the lemon water,' Mahir insisted, ignoring my scrunched-up face. We all did and I discovered that it soothed all the discomfort away, though I still wasn't convinced that vodka was worth the pain.

We had barely had our fill of starters when the mains arrived. The waiter carefully placed the dishes of lamb chops and lamb kofta kebabs in the remaining spaces, then deftly whisked any empty plates away on his huge oval tray. The meats were garnished with thin slices of raw onions, pomegranate seeds and coriander leaves.

'This all looks splendid,' Farid *muellim* said as he offered the plates around. I chose two lamb chops and one long kofta kebab.

Arzu beamed at me and we started eating. For several minutes, everyone was quiet, indulging themselves in the scents and taste of the well-cooked fresh meat, bread and trimmings. Farid *muellim* refilled all the vodka glasses, despite my objections, and raised his glass to toast Arzu, again.

Although I admired Arzu as a colleague, Farid *muellim*'s extended praises of her beauty, her charm and her skill in managing any situation sounded extravagant to me. I had to fight an overwhelming desire to giggle. My glass refilled a third time. I was getting used to the taste, I began to feel joyous and, after any initial hesitation, much to everyone's surprise and delight, I raised my glass and toasted Arzu myself.

The atmosphere in the room seemed lighter, more

spacious and colourful somehow. As the meal progressed, our voices became more animated. I laughed, with Arzu, at the jokes the men made, even if I didn't understand some of them. Through fits of laughter, I managed to tell a joke myself: 'A man boards a big liner to travel across the ocean. Just a day into his journey, Death shows up and says that it's his time to die.

"'How are you going to take my life?" the man asks, resigned.

"'I'll sink the liner."

"'Oh no! I get that it's my time but what about the other 500 innocent passengers? Why do they have to die?"

"'Do you have any idea how long it took me to get you all together on this ship?"'

I seemed to be the one who laughed the hardest at my joke, but I didn't care. By the time Mahir said that it was time to drop us off at our respective homes, I really did not want to go. Walking to the car, I was slightly unsteady on my feet but driving home had a sobering effect, as the wind dashed into my face and whipped up my hair. Mahir's driving did not seem to have been affected by the vodka at all. Despite the speed, he kept a steady course. It seemed unlikely that the police officers would pull over the Prosecutor's chauffeur. Thankfully, the closer we got to town, the clearer my head felt. I insisted Mahir drop me a street away from my house. Once home, I slipped into the garden and entered the house via the kitchen door to brush my teeth before presenting myself to Nana. I could hear a Turkish soap opera tune practically from the outside gates, which meant that Nana was glued to the TV. While avoiding any eye contact with Nana, I breezed in, complaining of stomach ache. I refused dinner, claiming I was too full of Arzu's birthday cake and went to lie down.

The next day, Arzu and I kept chatting about our adventurous outing when the reception was empty; the food, the view, the drive and the jokes. Even the reporters' anxious voices on the radio about the Armenian forces progressing towards Kalbajar seemed to be a step removed from us now, as if they were part of a WWII movie on TV that I had seen before. Though part of me knew it was reckless, there seemed something strangely liberating about going out with my colleagues. My old fears faded away. I craved another excursion to help me feel alive and carefree again; but that feeling was fated to only last another day.

On the 2nd of April 1993, Kalbajar fell. The defeat of our troops was devastating physically, as well as mentally. Tens of thousands of people fled from their homes, thousands were injured and hundreds, including some civilians, were killed. A heavy blanket of despair weighed down on the nation. Once again, I put on hold my desire for more fun and colour in my life and took refuge in my work.

# 4.

# SCANDALS

My impending law exams at Baku State University diverted my attention away from the news for a while. I had to study but had no access to current law books in Ganja. Instead, I had to borrow some old textbooks from the investigators who worked on the ground floor of our office. Trying to learn theory while ignoring all references to the Azerbaijan Soviet Socialist Republic was a challenge, but most laws had remained the same as they were during the Soviet regime. It was not easy to understand the dense legal texts, so every spare moment, including my lunch break, I would sit with my nose in a book, with my colleagues making jokes about my diligence.

My next trip to Baku was a huge relief from all the work and military conflict-related tension, though I still found the hustle and bustle of busy Baku streets so loud as to be overwhelming, at times. Everything in Baku was on a bigger and brighter scale than in provincial Ganja. I watched other women from my bus window, on the way to Azad's flat. They even seemed to look freer than me. Maybe it was the way they dressed or held themselves, but I was convinced that a woman's lot was easier in Baku than in my hometown of Ganja, where your main function was to marry, keep house and produce many children, preferably male.

Nana delivered me to Azad's flat with the usual gifts, including half a lamb, clotted cream, feta cheese and several large bunches of fresh herbs. Despite originating from Baku, Nana did not like lingering there. She didn't even go to see Mama as it would have added a day to her stay, and she was anxious not to outstay her welcome in the crowded flat. She also much preferred her own bed.

As soon as Nana left, I threw myself into my studies and enjoying student life. Lala was delighted to see me again. We spent our days traipsing between the Akhundov library and our favourite Presto café. I had been saving up for this trip for months by hiding some of the Prosecutor's 'gifts' from Nana. I now had enough money to buy myself a tight black top and a pair of blue jeans, clothes I was definitely not allowed to wear in Ganja. I had always yearned to wear proper fitted trousers, so I did not begrudge the money they cost. I even treated Lala to a fashionable sweater. She clearly could not afford to buy any new clothes. She always wore the same short, tight black skirt and a collection of cheap synthetic tops. After paying for our meal one day, I passed the sweater, hidden in its carrier bag, to Lala and waited for her reaction. She was very affected by the present. Her slim shoulders hunched down, her green eyes filled with tears and she curled into herself.

'It's nothing, Lala. Come on, don't cry,' I said, panic rising. I did not understand her reaction.

'It's not about this. Thank you so much, Gulya.' She hugged the soft sweater to her belly. Her long curly hair hung over her face, obscuring her expression. 'It's just… If you wanted to spend money on me, I have a more pressing issue I need help with.'

'What's the matter, Lala?' I asked.

She hesitated, looking up at me. I could see she was chewing on her pale-glossed lower lip, as she always did when she was worried. She dropped her head and whispered to the sweater on her lap.

'I am pregnant.'

We sat in silence as our coffees chilled. Strange waves of emotion passed through me, from shock to helplessness. For once, I had no idea what to say. This situation was too huge. I would be literally facing death if that was me. I had no doubt in my mind about that. A pregnancy outside of a marriage was seen as bringing unforgivable shame on the whole family. Then my mind whirled with the realisation that Lala was no longer a virgin. She had had sex! When did she manage that? She was Lezgi by birth, maybe they were more lenient about sex outside of wedlock, like the Russians? Wait, were Lezgis Muslim like us? I didn't know for sure. My head was full of questions, but I tried to choose the first one carefully.

'What about the baby's father?' *Does she even know who he is?* I could hear Nana's voice enter my thoughts. In her view, only the loosest of girls ever got pregnant.

'What about him?' Lala sighed. 'We were at a party. Remember that friend I was telling you about? Well, we smoked something and… it happened. It was all over in minutes. I can't remember the details, but we started meeting up regularly. We have been, ever since our last study session. He can't afford to pay for an abortion, and I can't tell my parents. There's no point. They'll get angry, then upset, but they have no spare money. So, I'm stuck with it. I don't know what to do.'

Her green eyes filled with tears as she wept quietly. I shifted uncomfortably on my chair fearing someone would notice. Luckily, the lunchtime rush had now died down. I leant into her and patted her hand.

'You need to stay calm,' I said, the way Mama would. 'Do you want the baby?'

'Now? Of course not. If I did, I'd never be able to finish university and my family would… They wouldn't reject me, but they wouldn't be at all happy. No, I've got to find a way to get an abortion. I have asked around. My cousin said it probably costs fifty dollars.' She looked down at the sweater again.

It took me only a moment to decide. Fifty dollars was quite a lot of money, but if the tables were turned, I believed she would have done the same for me. What were friends for?

'I'll pay for it.'

'What?' She looked up in surprise.

'I'll pay for you to… And I'll come with you,' I said firmly.

It all felt very awkward. Lala began to cry even harder, her round, slightly blemished face scrunched up with emotion. The girl at the far-end table had started to stare at us, I was certain. I had thought my offer would make Lala happy, but it seemed to have done the opposite. My coffee was hopelessly cold, so I finished off my cola instead. A childish pleasure in an adult world.

The next week, Lala and I travelled secretly to a local clinic, after our classes. Outside, the weather was warm. I enjoyed the sensation of sunlight on my pale skin. Inside the clinic, a large building with marble floors and stark, unfriendly walls, it was as cold as a fridge. We shivered in our fashionable clothes. I wished I had brought my cardigan.

'Name please,' the receptionist asked curtly.

'Sakina,' Lala lied. The receptionist did not ask for any ID; she didn't even look up to see which one of us had spoken. I got the impression, based on my own experience, that hers was a job that was too busy for any sort of interaction. She simply stamped 'Sakina's' papers, tossed them in a tray and pointed to the waiting area. That's where I sat, in tense anticipation, when Lala was taken for the procedure. I watched a number of women come and go during that time. I could only assess them by their clothes, but I was surprised at the variety. An unwanted pregnancy, it appeared, was not just an issue for the poor or sinful, contrary to what I had been told. Was I doing the right thing by paying for Lala's abortion? Many would have said not, but I looked at it in a practical way, as a friend. Her parents could hardly support Lala herself. Another mouth to feed would have been a disaster for them, to say nothing of how the community might react.

Lala emerged, pale and trembling, over an hour later. She had been told what to expect and what to look for in the next couple of days. I was so glad to be there for her. I insisted on taking her for a meal to give her some energy and time to adjust to the situation. In her current state, I was sure that even her busy family would notice. Neither of us would want them to ask questions. She mostly ate her food in silence, while I rattled on about my plans and my family. It wasn't until she lit a cigarette that she spoke.

'I feel so empty,' she whispered through the veil of smoke that hung about her and twisted into the corners of the deserted café. Again, I did not know what to say, but held her as she collapsed into my arms.

★★★

Having to have an abortion hit Lala hard. She was no longer the bright spark I had first met. She missed many of her classes and most of our study sessions at the library. When she did turn up, she found it hard to concentrate on anything. I had no means of reaching her, so I decided that the best thing I could do was to make sure I attended everything myself, so I could help her out with the notes when she got better. Although I was on speaking terms with my fellow students, I didn't have any other friends. The days without Lala were lonely. I felt lost and was worried about her, but unable to share my concerns with anyone else. I always looked out for her on my way to class. One morning, instead of Lala, I spotted Mahir attempting to stand casually by his car.

'Hello you!' he said, waving a cigarette in his hand.

'The Prosecutor is here in Baku again?' I asked, staying where I was. The memory of the illicit kiss flicked through my head. It seemed so long ago now and so irrelevant compared to what Lala had just gone through.

'Yes, of course. Jump in and we can catch up. New car, see? She runs like a racehorse.' He pointed at the car. It looked the same to me.

'Sorry, Mahir, I'm too busy,' I said, clutching my files to

me. I was suddenly aware of the tightness of my black top and blue jeans.

'Busy, busy, you are always busy, Gulush. That's why Masha and Arzu miss you so much. You do so much work. But I am concerned about you. You are looking so pale and I'm sure you are losing weight. Even your Nana wouldn't mind if big brother Mahir took you for a treat. She likes me, you know.'

Still, I hesitated, but then a snapshot of Arzu's birthday feast slipped into my mind. We'd all had such fun and, to be truthful, I had enjoyed being tipsy, until I got home. The prospect of getting away from my sad day and seeing someone I could really talk to kicked in and I trotted eagerly to the car.

'Best to get in the front seat. It's hard to talk when you're in the back.' I paused by the back door. 'Come on, Gulush, no one else from Ganja comes here.'

'It's just me, though. Lala isn't here, today.' I didn't want him to know everything.

'What? You don't eat without Lala?' He chortled. 'When does your next class start?'

'In an hour.'

'I'll make sure you're back for then. Come on. You can set your Nana on me if I'm wrong.'

I smiled at the thought of that, though, of course, I would never tell her. I got into the car and, after overtaking a few cars, he surprised me by pulling up outside a quiet café not far from the university, where we had a private room at the back and tasty food that made my eyes water with delight. I had refused to drink alcohol but, after the meal, Mahir offered me a drag on his cigarette.

Curiosity fought with my common sense; I hesitated. I had sat in Nana's dark bedroom as she smoked her way through disasters and celebrations so many times. I held the cigarette carefully and tentatively inhaled. It tasted disgusting. I choked on the smoke, much to Mahir's amusement, and felt a little sick.

'You'll live, Gulush. The first time is always horrible,' Mahir said. Grinning, he took the cigarette back and popped it between his teeth before getting up to pay the bill.

When it was time to leave, I felt sad given how lonely I'd been without Lala, so even when Mahir gathered me in his arms, I did not resist. I wasn't even bothered when he kissed me on the lips, but when his hands started to caress the contours of my body, I squirmed with a surge of excitement that felt as pleasurable as it felt dangerous.

I didn't even fancy him. He was fat and nearly twice my age, but strangely, my body responded to his touch and the now familiar rush of adrenalin woke something inside me that I did not yet fully understand. Culturally, I was expected to know nothing about these matters till my wedding night, when an assigned female relative was meant to fill me in on what exactly happens between a man and a woman. However, like most of my peers, I had already gleaned some basics, from eavesdropping on adults' conversations and a rare erotic scene on Russian TV.

I felt patches of rose blooming on my cheeks as my breath grew shorter. It was not like I wanted to go all the way with Mahir. That was completely out of the question. I just wanted to play a little bit... I felt like I could trust him, that he cared enough about me that he would not compromise my well-being and put me in danger.

'Don't worry,' he sighed, his hot breath tickling my neck, 'I won't touch your virginity. This is just a little bit of fun, for us both.'

His words and touch felt almost beautiful, until his roving hands reached my breasts. My bubble of pleasure burst as Lala's sorrowful face started from my memory. I instantly sobered up. I pushed Mahir away. I knew this sort of fun could end badly and I could not take the risk. Perhaps he knew that too, because when I croaked that I had to go, he nodded solemnly and drove me back to the university. We were quiet on the drive, and only exchanged hurried goodbyes before I scurried off to the safety of the law school.

Still feeling a little stirred up, I made it to the next class, but my notes suffered as I sifted through my thoughts. Like all females in my community, I had to pretend to be an 'innocent', someone who knew nothing about sexual arousal. The truth was I had already discovered the joys of masturbation, though by accident. I was fifteen. Nana had sent me into my uncle's bedroom to empty his pockets and bring his clothes for her to launder. I was surprised to find a folded piece of paper in an inside pocket. He was not the type who ever made notes. Was it a love letter? Or something more sinister? I knew it was probably private, so it took me several minutes before I plucked up the courage to unfold it. There were two pages of typed writing. The first was a poem. The contents made me blush. It was about a whore who was looking for the right penis. The writing was extremely explicit but while my mind was shocked, strange sensations had started up within my body that I had never felt before. I failed to talk myself out of reading the second page, the temptation was too strong. It was a pornographic horror story about a woman who involved her son in threesomes. He was instructed to just 'accidentally turn up' at the right moment. However, when she found a man so wild in bed that she did not want any distractions, she shut her son out and he could only watch them, in anguish through the keyhole. He felt incredible jealousy, which turned to rage. He killed his mother, sliced her breasts off and filled her vagina with broken glass.

Initially, I could not understand why my uncle would read something so violent and even carry it round with him, but the images the words conjured stayed with me. As I lay in bed that night, they made my body feel restless and hot. Between my legs my genitals seemed to ache. I instinctively reached down and found I could relieve the unfamiliar tension and bring myself to an intense pleasure of release, without any real comprehension of what my fingers were doing.

Even though I had vowed not to, I found myself reading those pages again and again, each time repeating my secret night-time routine, allowing my hands to explore me. When the pages disappeared from my uncle's room, I found I could replace them with my own fantasies, those stories that had haunted and excited me in equal measure. In the dusty depths of a large lecture room, the recall stirred something in me. After the class, I tidied up my notes and headed back home.

★★★

The next day, we had an unexpected visitor during our criminal law lecture, the law faculty's bald-headed dean. He had come to introduce a new student who was transferring from a different department.

'This is Amina, your new classmate,' he announced loudly, as if she were about to start singing on the stage.

I thought she looked as if she could. Amina was dazzlingly beautiful. She had long, straightened, platinum hair, painted nails, impeccable make-up. She could have been a photographic model in her fashionably tailored and expensive suit. I was smitten. With a charming smile, Amina took a look around the room then headed straight for my table.

'Is this seat taken?' she asked. Her voice was so smooth.

'No,' I lied effortlessly. Lala was not in that day, so technically, I reasoned, the seat was empty.

I could feel her warmth next to me as she sat down, and her perfume smelled divine. I stole a sideways glance at her straight nose and clear skin. Her caramel, cat-like eyes met mine, as her lips, precisely outlined in smooth, matte, nude lipstick stretched into a wider smile, revealing her pearl-like teeth. I gulped and looked away.

Now it was even more difficult to concentrate on 'the subjective elements of crime'. The gaunt female lecturer, with short, henna-orange hair, spoke in short staccato sentences. It was hard to grasp what she was saying and make notes. Amina, in contrast to the rest of us, was doodling pretty patterns on her notepad, making no attempt to capture the woman's words. Did she know how challenging it was to get textbooks and that this could be all we got to base our exam answers on? I felt I was letting

Lala down with my lack of concentration. I was thankful when the bell rang and we were released. I needed fresh air to clear my head. Standing up, Amina packed away her notebook and said: 'Where now, um… sorry, I don't know your name.'

'It's Gulya. This is the last lecture today.'

'Oh, that's great! Do you fancy a lift home?'

I was excited that this glamorous new student wanted to spend time with me. I explained where I was living, and Amina said that was fine. As I trotted next to her, I was conscious of my plain blue jeans and black sweater beside her fashionable chic. All eyes, male and female, were on her. I knew they would hardly notice me.

I expected Amina's husband, father or brother to be waiting for her, but to my astonishment, she pulled out her own car keys and a flashy white Hyundai Sonata winked its bright lights at us.

'Wow, you drive!' I could not keep the words back.

'I do,' Amina said, exuding confidence. We slid into the car's soft leatherette seats. 'Are you in a rush?' she said as she touched up her make-up in the car's flip-down mirror.

'Not at all. Lala and I – she's another girl from our class – normally eat out then go to the library, but she's not in today,' I said.

'No studying for me,' Amina smiled. 'I don't bother.'

I wanted to quiz her about how she managed to get admitted, but decided not to, yet.

'Let's see.' She checked the time on her mobile phone. I felt envious, no one I knew had one of those. 'Do you want to come to an aerobics class with me?'

'Now? Sure, I would,' I gushed, 'but I don't have

anything to wear with me.' Or anywhere, I thought grimly.

'We'll pick something up on the way,' she said casually. I should have been honest, I should have admitted I didn't have any spare cash for something like sportswear, but to be with Amina already felt as smooth and soothing as a warm honey drink, one that I didn't want to finish. I needn't have worried because she insisted on treating me to some gorgeous black Lycra leggings and a loose grey top.

'It's a treat for me too,' she said. 'I hate shopping alone.'

***

That whole week was what Amina called 'a blast!' She knew how to have fun and, for some inexplicable reason, she liked to share it with me. Every day, instead of going to the library, I went to aerobics classes with Amina, as her guest, in an exclusive city centre gym. Once we had finished sweating to Dr Alban's 'It's My Life' in the high intensity aerobics class, all the women congregated in a hot sauna, sipping freshly brewed herbal teas. While some complained about their cellulite and their lovers, I kept quiet, soaking up the luxurious and utterly unfamiliar atmosphere. I always left the gym feeling refreshed.

'Fancy joining us for dinner?' Amina asked one afternoon. 'I don't know what the girls have cooked today but I'm sure there's plenty.'

'Sure, thanks,' I said. As long as we phoned Yasmin first, I was sure the couple would enjoy an evening without me. 'What girls?' Could Amina be a mother?

'My two, um, cousins live with me. They are great. You'll love them.'

She was right, I did. Irada and Nargiz were very friendly and laid a table for four of us in no time. Younger than me, mid-teens I guessed, they were slim and pretty with long, curled eyelashes and pale, delicate features. They wore expensive tracksuits and seemed utterly comfortable and at ease in the spacious, clean flat with its expensive gadgets and décor. This family must have a lot of money, I thought. I had spent much of my childhood envying those at school whose families were loaded, but this was different somehow. Amina appeared so independent. How come she had her own place? Had she a husband? When I plucked up the courage to ask her a couple of questions, she said she understood my curiosity.

'I did have a husband once, but not any more. I got married early, at sixteen. He was kind, a bit older than me. It was all right, to start with, but…' her voice faltered. She drew in a deep breath. 'I had a stillbirth, the baby was perfect, but dead. Things were never the same between us after that, so eventually I left. It happens,' she said, touching my arm.

She started to quiz her cousins about their day. As we stretched out, on the huge cosy cream sofa in front of a giant TV set in the living room, I wondered if, one day, when I was qualified in law, I would be able to afford a lifestyle like Amina's.

★★★

The pleasures of having a new friend and enjoying novel things from aerobics to sliced supermarket cheese and salami sandwiches, were rudely interrupted one hot June morning.

'Have you heard the news?' Vugar, a classmate, stopped me at the university entrance.

'What news?' I said dozily. I had been up late, doing some exam revision. I was still groggy from waking up five minutes before I had to leave the flat. The gentle breeze that was stroking past my bare arms had also blown my hair into my eyes. I blinked at Vugar through it.

'There's been a coup, in Ganja,' he said bleakly.

'What?' I couldn't believe it. I wanted to sink on the steps; my legs seemed unable to hold my weight.

Without pausing for breath, Vugar fired a barrage of words at me. 'Suret Huseynov – the one who made such catastrophic losses in Nagorno-Karabakh that the president had him disarmed – has apparently got hold of an arsenal of weapons left by the departing Russian military. He's gathered some troops in Ganja. The government sent in the army, but he defeated them. It's rumoured he's now marching to Baku with several thousand soldiers in his support.'

'Why?' I squealed, panic tightening my chest.

'I don't know, Gulya. Perhaps he thinks he can overthrow President Elchibey.'

I couldn't listen any more, I turned around and ran towards the nearest group of phone booths. All I could think of was what might be happening to my family in Ganja. Vugar called after me, but I didn't look back. I needed to know that Nana was safe. I wasn't the only one who wanted to call, but I managed to slip into the last free booth.

I couldn't believe it when the phone call wouldn't go through, though time after time I tried. Either all lines were down, or the phones were no longer working. I trembled with fear as I kept imagining the worst: Nana dead, our home wrecked. What about the Prosecutor's Office? What side was he on? Would I have a job to go back to? What about my friends, Masha, Arzu, even Mahir? Where would I go? What would I do? I did not want to be a burden on Mama's new family. Her political activism barely paid for her own bills.

I stood in my booth long after the others had given up, so desperate to hear Nana's voice. When I finally replaced the receiver, I dragged myself mechanically to the next lecture. I didn't know what else to do. Several people were absent, including Amina, but the lecturer droned on monotonously as if that were perfectly normal. My tears dripped silently onto my notebook, leaving little blurred pools amongst the few words I could take in. I couldn't even remember what subject the lecture was supposed to be about. When break-time came, I didn't stop to see who had tried to catch hold of my arm as I sprinted back to the phone booths to make more unsuccessful attempts at reaching Nana.

When I turned up to the next lecture, Amina quizzed me about my puffy red eyes. Vugar and Nahid flocked around me too, as the lecturer hadn't shown up yet.

'You know, Gulya, they are probably all fine,' Amina said, stroking my shoulder with her manicured hand.

'I know 'probably' doesn't sound good enough, Gulya, but it is better to be hopeful than hopeless,' Vugar said. 'I tried to follow the news to get my head around the situation in Ganja, but it was just snippets of information. People are saying different things.'

I felt blank, unable to take their words in, but when Vugar attempted a joke, weirdly it made me smile for the first time all day, though my body still felt tense and exhausted: 'See what happens when you leave Ganja, Gulya? I think in the interests of national security, you should get an automatic pass for all your exams.'

Encouraged by my smile, Amina spoke more urgently: 'I really don't want to leave you alone, in this state, but… I have an appointment to go to. Please come with me. You could use my mobile phone to keep calling home.'

I gratefully agreed. We drove to the city centre, chatting in between my attempts to contact Nana, but as soon as we pulled up by a grand, modern building, I regretted my decision to come along. I was sure I would look out of place in such a glamorous environment. Through its huge downstairs windows, I could see sparkling chandeliers illuminating spacious rooms and well-dressed staff. Amina sensed I was worried.

'You don't need to do a thing when we get inside. Just relax, have some food and keep calling your family.' She handed me her mobile phone then guided me, head held high, into an expansive foyer edged with luxurious sofas.

A tall man came to meet us. He kissed Amina on both cheeks. He smelt like he had money; an intoxicating mix of classic cologne, a new suit and shiny shoes. He was charming, confident and at least twenty years older than Amina. He led us to a private area, where a long table groaned under the weight of large vases of flowers and enough food to feed ten people. Next to it there was a swimming pool full of clear, bright water. Through two open doors, I glimpsed other rooms beyond.

I sat awkwardly on the edge of my seat. I didn't have any swimwear with me. Even if I did, mixed bathing with a stranger was unthinkable, far too intimate for me. Unexpectedly, I found myself longing for my times with Lala. Life had been so uncomplicated going to the cheap Presto café, where we relaxed, shared our day and exchanged jokes, some of them quite dodgy. I felt simple and unsophisticated in this new place. What could I possibly contribute to a conversation? I listened to Amina chatting with a frozen smile on my face, nodding in some places, but feeling unable to participate. She encouraged me to eat. A well-cooked piece of lamb and its accompaniments kept me occupied, while sipping champagne helped me relax. The man, I will call him Mr A, seemed so enchanted by Amina that he hardly paid me any attention, even when prompted by Amina: 'Gulya is a bit upset,' she said kindly. 'Her family is in Ganja and she hasn't been able to reach them yet. She'll make some phone calls, while we...' she smiled. Mr A pushed his chair back and took Amina's delicate ivory hand in his own large paw-like one. His had two rings, thick and gold. One was a chunky signet ring and the other was a wedding band.

'Please excuse us, Gulya,' he said, bowing slightly. 'I would like to have a private moment with Amina.'

I made to leave the room, but he protested: 'No, no, you stay. Please enjoy the food. We'll be back... shortly.' He winked at Amina, then led her into one of the other rooms and closed the door.

I sat with the phone on autodial, sipping champagne and trying out the various foods. As I enjoyed some black caviar on a piece of crusty bread, I debated with myself.

I was not a fool. Were they having sex next door? That thought made me squirm. Should I leave? It felt wrong to be so close by if they were, but I could not will myself to go. Here, I had the phone, food, comfort and the promise of a lift home. Out there, I had no idea where we were and probably not enough money to pay for a taxi. Amina wouldn't let me down. Was Mr A some sort of benefactor who helped Amina to afford her lifestyle? If that was really a wedding ring on his hand, it would imply she was his mistress. This conclusion didn't shock or even surprise me. I knew full well that normally, in our country, if a woman was a divorcee, her chances of remarriage were slim and perhaps the best she could hope for was to be part of someone else's second, unofficial, family. I didn't think this should apply to Amina. She was so beautiful and elegant. Who would not want to marry her, whether it was a second, third or fourth time?

When I heard groans coming from the room, I tried to ignore them. I went to sit by the pool, looking out through French windows onto a garden patio. Amina had left her pack of cigarettes, so I helped myself to one. It was long, slim and feminine, just like her. I lit it with her expensive lighter and drew the smoke into my mouth. It was not as bad as that first time with Mahir. I found I quite liked the taste. I had no idea there were variations, but it made my head spin a little bit. I spent little time inhaling but instead tried to produce smoke rings like my uncles could. I still couldn't get through to Nana. Time started to drag as I walked myself round the pool, longing to jump into the warm water.

I had just started to get bored with the room and its

luxuries, when Amina and Mr A emerged, arm in arm, relaxed and happy. I had expected Amina to look dishevelled, but her make-up was fresh, her manner confident and matter of fact.

'Shall we be off?' She beamed at me. I noticed her place a white envelope into her handbag.

'Yes, yes, of course,' I said, springing to my feet a little too enthusiastically.

'Thank you for your patience and discretion,' said Mr A. He and Amina exchanged amused glances, as he walked us to the door. I was not entirely sure what he was on about.

It was a relief to be leaving a world so different from my own. It had been a fascinating experience but way beyond my comfort zone. Amina smiled benignly as we walked to the car, but I felt I couldn't talk about what she had been doing. Once on our way, we relaxed into chatting about our last aerobics class and our studies, as if the meal had never happened.

'Do you want to stop off at mine before I take you back?' she asked, skilfully negotiating a roundabout.

'I can't. We've got exams tomorrow morning, remember?' I had been staying up late every night, once the others had gone to bed, poring over the notes I had made during lectures and in the library, praying that I had learnt enough to get through. 'Aren't you worried about the exams?' I never had seen Amina studying.

'Not really,' she shrugged. 'My friend of today is well connected. He'll make some calls in the morning and I'll most likely pass. Even if I don't, for whatever reason, I've got the means to change that.'

Bribes and favours; I was familiar with them. I had

been lucky enough to have the chance to enter university by passing written tests, but the education system had not completely changed since the collapse of the Soviet Union. Success could be gained in many ways. I was grateful that President Elchibay had insisted on education reforms, but unfortunately, he was the same president everyone now blamed for the loss of Kalbajar and the same president that Suret Husseynov was trying to overthrow. Thinking of that reminded me of Nana. I tried one last call before parting with Amina, but the line was still dead.

When we stopped, near Azad's, I kissed Amina's pearly cheek, inhaling her sweet, signature perfume Issey Myake one more time. I swayed onto the pavement, still a bit fazed by the day's events. Amina rolled her window down. 'Don't worry about your family. If anything ever happens to them, remember you have a new family now: me and the girls!'

I was touched by her care, but if I were honest, in my heart it didn't yet feel like the friendship I had with Lala. It was an unequal relationship. I was in awe of Amina, almost willing to follow her anywhere. What she wanted from me I wasn't sure. Perhaps just someone to shop with? My instincts told me that she was likely to be trouble and I knew she did not fit in with Nana's standards, but as I climbed up the stairs to Azad's flat, I decided that Amina's personal life was none of my business and the less I knew, the more I could enjoy my connection with her.

\*\*\*

Lala surprised us all by finally turning up at university the next day, to take her exams. She looked as pale, withdrawn and depressed as I did after a sleep-deprived night and no news from Ganja. The contrast between Amina and Lala could not have been greater, especially on a day when I needed some reassurance myself. I found Lala's company unbearably heavy as I patiently shared all my notes with her, in the hope that it would help her scrape through the exam. She was so wrapped up in her own troubles that she didn't ask how I was feeling, even when Amina made a point of doing so. I could only pray that I could concentrate enough during the exam to pass myself. I wished I had Amina's 'friends' because she was the only person who was calm and smiling.

The exam proved to be more stressful than even I had anticipated. When I walked into the room there was not one, but three lecturers sitting at a desk. Trembling, I approached them and took the next 'ballot' paper with three random questions on it, based on modules we had studied. I knew I would have to answer them orally in front of this panel. I had a maximum of ten minutes to sit at a side table and prepare my answers. Two of my classmates were already sitting and perspiring over their answers.

Though painfully weary, I followed the pattern drummed into me from school onwards. First, I skimmed through the questions. I quickly realised I knew the answers to two of them reasonably well but couldn't yet remember anything relevant to the third one. I struggled to concentrate. Vugar's loud voice as he answered his questions and my worries about Ganja fogged my brain. When my name was called out, ten short minutes later, I had barely sketched out a plan for my answers. As I walked unsteadily to stand in front of the panel, I felt like I was about to face a firing squad. Though the lecturers were neither outwardly friendly nor hostile in their manners, I knew I was at their mercy. Senior students had warned me not to object to anything the panel said. Their word was final, whether I thought I had answered the questions correctly or not.

I forced a polite smile and started to speak as fast and clearly as I could on the first question. One of the lecturers stopped me mid-flow. Peering over his wire-framed glasses, he asked about 'the grounds of criminal liability'. I answered with feigned confidence. He ticked something off on his clipboard. I moved to the second question. They seemed satisfied with my answers until I reached my third answer. I stumbled over my words as I rehashed the same argument twice. Dr B, the lecturer with henna-coloured hair, scribbled something in my *zachetka* – passbook – and handed it to me. 'Dismissed,' she said, without looking up.

Checking my *zachetka* outside, adrenalin still coursing through me, I discovered I had been awarded four points, which meant 'good'. It was not the 'excellent' that I usually received at school, but in the circumstances, I was relieved that I had passed at all. I walked slowly up and down through the crush of students in the corridor looking for Amina, but it seemed she had already left. Instead, I found Lala crying quietly by a window overlooking the university courtyard.

'I failed!' she cried, as soon as she saw me.

'Oh no!' I said, sitting down beside her. I wasn't surprised given her recent mental state, but it was one of the subjects we had studied at the library together before her pregnancy. I tried to reassure Lala that she would pass the resit in the summer, but she wouldn't believe me and walked away hunched up in her own despair, leaving me to deal with my own fears.

I decided to go straight back to the flat because, to me, the city centre felt too unsafe even for a visit to the library. The university corridors were full of rumours about how several top government officials were being fired or had resigned that day and how a large number of demonstrators had gathered to demand a change in the government. President Elchibey, it was said, had endorsed Heydar Aliyev's election as chairman of the *Milli-Majlis*, the state legislature of MPs.

'Wasn't Aliyev once head of the Azerbaijani KGB?' I heard one student's worried voice say.

'What we need is "a man of steel", like Stalin was,' another replied.

Tears suddenly threatened to flood my eyes because that was exactly the kind of thing Nana would say. I still didn't know if she was safe. Again, I hurried to a phone booth, but there were still no lines to Ganja. I ached to sit, like Lala, and weep, but Nana's fierce face filled my mind. She had survived far worse. I knew I had to push the fear from my head and do my best in the remaining exams.

Once I got into a rhythm, despite my distress, the exam period passed smoothly. I managed to get some decent results, until my last exam in the theory of state and law. I had been forewarned that Salima *khanim* was in an impatient and unfriendly mood that day. She clearly did not think my answers were specific enough, even though I was quoting her verbatim from her textbook and lecture notes. After a brief whispered consultation with the other panel

GULARA VINCENT

members, she beckoned me forward. 'You passed, young lady,' she drawled. 'By a whisker,' she added, pushing my open *zachetka* towards me. I gasped because the three points out of five written there was the lowest grade I had ever been given, in all my years of studying. Only by getting the highest grades could I hope to feel good enough.

When I came out of the exam room crying, Vugar towered over me to see if I had failed. I showed him my *zachetka*. He startled me with booming laughter, then said, 'It's a miracle that you survived her.'

It turned out that only five of us had passed this exam, including Amina, who no doubt had paid a hefty bribe. The remaining twenty-five students would have to retake it in the summer.

When I returned to the flat, I was in for more good news. The phone lines to Ganja were restored and Nana had called Azad's family earlier that day to say that all was well. Azad kindly let me call her back.

'Nana, Nana, can you hear me?' I could not help crying.

'Gulush, is that you? I am OK, we all are. Don't worry, it's just the lines were cut off and people are so restless. Your mother called just now. She says it's not safe for her to come see you tomorrow. She says there is too much unrest. Is that true?'

'Yes, I know, Nana,' I said. 'I'm so happy to hear your voice.' There wasn't time to tell her about my exam results.

'Come home safely, child.' The phone line crackled. 'When you return, I'll pay Mullah to read some Quran verses to thank Allah for protecting you,' she said and rang off.

87

★★★

The next day, I said my goodbyes to everyone and headed for the central bus station to start my eight-hour journey home. As I got on to the rickety bus, for the first time in my life, I found I was not sorry to leave Baku, which now resembled a disturbed hornets' nest. I was relieved to know that I could progress into my second year of study, so I would return to Baku, but not for six months, by which time, hopefully, things would be peaceful again.

'President Elchibey has fled!' I heard someone shouting in the bus station. 'He's gone! Heydar Aliyev is taking charge! We have a new president.'

Inside and outside the bus, some groups erupted into a mix of cheers or heated debate, while others, including me, kept their own counsel. I wondered where President Elchibey had gone and why. I thought he was one of those rare politicians who was not money and power hungry; a true reformist who valued education and talent. His higher education reforms were the main reason I was a law student now. Personally, I was sad to see him go, but realised that the military defeat in Kalbajar, which had allowed Armenia to access Nagorno-Karabakh, was too devastating for people to accept. Someone had to take the blame.

On my journey home, I thought about Lala, who had failed three exams, which she would have to retake. I genuinely hoped that she would get into the next year, so we would meet again. Amina, of course, would be there. Who knew where my friendship with her would take me? I was sad to have missed seeing Mama this trip, but such were the times.

# 5.

# DRIVING CHANGE

Transitioning to life in Ganja was not easy, especially after the vibrancy of life in Baku had been amplified with Amina around. The atmosphere in the Prosecutors' Office was subdued, as we watched events unfurl. Taking advantage of the coup in our country, the Armenian forces were now advancing on Agdam, another region of Azerbaijan adjacent to Nagorno-Karabakh. Preoccupied by the change of the presidency, our government seemed too split and depleted to put any appropriate defences in place.

The people of Agdam, alongside the military forces, fought valiantly, while the rest of us held our breath. On the fortieth day of the campaign, the 23rd of July 1993, Agdam fell and, with it, the spirit of the country plummeted. As I headed to work every day, in the scorching heat, I stole glances at people on the bus. Their empty eyes were devoid of hope.

Mahir, Masha and Arzu's friendship was all that kept me going in those days. They were concerned and anxious about the conflict too, but they also took time to chat about other, more trivial things and share silly, sometimes rude, jokes. They brightened the long summer days. I felt I could share some of my thoughts with them, things that I would not dare reveal at home. We had kept up the habit of sharing lunch. I would rattle on about my other life in Baku as they ate. 'I'm not envious of Amina,' I would say. 'I guess I'm just inspired by her, seeing her driving in Baku, seeing her lifestyle. If I could drive… Well, that would be real freedom, right? But my family are never going to allow me to own a car, or use someone else's, for that matter. Still, with girls like Amina around, it gives me hope.'

One lunchbreak, when Arzu nipped to the toilet, and Masha was rummaging in the back room for some alcohol, Mahir leant over and said quietly, 'I can teach you to drive, Gulush.'

My eyes lit up. Despite my logical mind saying, 'No you don't,' all the cells in my body sang a resounding, 'Yes, do!' I nodded enthusiastically. It was hard to hide my excitement when the others returned.

'Tomorrow, lunchtime, out front,' Mahir whispered to me on his way out later.

★★★

For my first lesson, Mahir took me to a virtually deserted road on the edge of Ganja. I had to watch him drive slowly up and down, his left arm hanging out of the open window to cool himself down. Finally, he stopped and motioned for me to sit behind the steering wheel, while he walked around the car and plonked himself into the passenger seat. Since I was shorter than him, I sank into the black leather driver's seat of the powerful car and squinted over the wheel at the bright sun. There were no trees on the seemingly endless road, no buildings nearby, not even a stray dog. The orange-red terrain looked as desolate as a desert.

I was so sweaty that my grey short-sleeved dress was sticking to my back, but thankfully my armpits were smooth and perfumed now, I thought, as Mahir placed his hands over mine to show me the car's controls. After an embarrassing hug, on a hot day, with my neighbour Amaliya *khala*, she had had a discreet word with Nana about the state of my armpits and, much to my amazement, Nana had subsequently given me a rusty razor, with a fresh blade, to shave them.

'Why is the earth all red here?' I asked Mahir.

'That's a brick factory out there,' Mahir pointed to a distant, long building. 'All the waste and dust from the factory saturates the land and the air around here. Don't get distracted, Gulush. Let's begin.'

I sat up as straight as I could and tried to copy Mahir's actions but simply managed to create some strange scraping noises in the engine.

'No, no, no,' he said, putting a restraining hand on mine. 'It's already on. Don't do that again, Gulush, it hurts the car.'

Judging by his facial expression, it was as if I had hurt him personally, but he managed to keep his voice calm. I nodded emphatically, ignoring the fact that it took him a moment too long to withdraw his hand. His physical proximity was unsettling, as he showed me how to coordinate pressing pedals and using the clutch, but I refused to let myself lose concentration. I wanted to learn to drive, and this was probably my only chance. After stalling more times than I care to recall, I managed to drive a short distance up and down the empty road. I was so proud.

'To be continued,' Mahir announced. 'You did well,' he said as he waited for me to climb out of his seat. He was in my way for a moment; I remembered our drunken kiss; but he stepped aside to let me pass. I took extra care to avoid brushing against him but realised that there was a part of me that was tantalised by being so close to him. I was confused by my reaction. I couldn't speak on the way back to the office. I was lost in my thoughts. I didn't think Mahir even noticed, he was too busy dealing with other drivers driving like the heat had addled their brains. One part of me, sensible but prudish, rejected any idea of fraternising with a married, older, not particularly attractive man; but the other part, outrageous and egotistical, wanted to flirt, to drive him crazy, then command him to stop, just in time, and watch him squirm with sexual desire for me – like the women in my fantasies.

The secret lessons continued and, at the end of the week when I had just finished a perfect practice drive on the now familiar stretch of empty road, Mahir said, 'Well done, Gulush! You're definitely a fast learner.'

I beamed gratefully at him and sighed in satisfaction. As usual, when I got out, he was already waiting by the door. Before I could react, he pulled me to him, his heated breath tickling my neck as he kissed it. My heart pounded with a bewildering mix of fear and excitement. Not knowing what to do, I waited for him to release me, but soon his hungry wet mouth pulsed on mine and I found my lips responding.

There was something about these forbidden actions that made them intoxicating. When his hands reached to cup my breasts, I was curious to find I didn't flinch, instead my back arched spontaneously. My mind seemed to detach itself from my body, like it was watching this happen to someone else, but I managed to come to my senses and pull away.

'We'd better go back,' I said breathlessly.

Sweat pooling on his round face, he nodded, before adjusting a bulge in his trousers. I didn't know where to look or what to say. I was embarrassed, but also deeply aroused. Was this the price of learning to drive? Was I like Amina now?

Mahir didn't speak to me on the way back, or for the rest of the day, and he chose to have tea in Masha's room that afternoon. I was relieved. I spent the afternoon typing up the usual handwritten reports, making many basic mistakes.

'You seem distracted,' Arzu observed. She was making tea for the Prosecutor.

'Just another one of my headaches,' I told her.

I had no intention of sharing my encounter with anyone in Ganja. I had seen false rumours rob other girls of any chance of a happy marriage. As a virgin, you were expected to be pure in mind as well as body and, right then, my mind was far from pure, crammed with exhilarating images: Mahir's hands cupping my breasts; his lips on mine; even the bulge… I grew so hot thinking of them that finally I had to excuse myself and go slip into a cool toilet cubicle where my hands could give me release.

Afterwards, I felt calmer. The sensible voice in my head spoke, as I took time to wash my hands and splash cold water on my flushed face. It told me to stop all the lessons immediately and not to see Mahir outside of work ever again. This wasn't the first time he had crossed the line, it reminded me, and resuming driving lessons would only give him the message that I was on board with his behaviour. I stared at my reflection. *This has to stop*, I told it firmly. Nana was right, men were not to be trusted.

Mahir and I avoided each other over the next few days. I found endless reasons for leaving the room every time he came into reception. When I heard he was driving the Prosecutor to Baku for several days, I initially felt a huge relief.

While he was gone, the 'purity guard' in my head gradually lost her power over me. Nothing that bad had happened, I told myself. What did it matter that he kissed me? We were on an empty road, no one saw us and, since he was a married man, he wouldn't divulge that information to anyone else. All was well.

By the time Mahir returned from Baku, everyone, especially me, was bored of the long too-hot summer days that dragged on and on. There was nothing to distract me from the brain-numbing typing at work, dull chores at home and the depressing news about Nagorno-Karabakh everywhere. The level of disconnect I felt was deadening. I ached for any stimulation to bring me back to life.

I was alone in the reception when Mahir strode in, heading for the kettle. I shuffled piles of paper on my table to make out I was occupied, while all the cells of my body followed his every move.

'Want a driving lesson today?' he asked cautiously.

I looked up and met his searching eyes. I nodded,

ignoring all the warning screams from my internal guard. Mahir nearly dropped the kettle. 'Right. I'd better run my errands before lunch then,' he said, puffing out of the door.

As soon as the clock struck one, I made my, 'have to get things for Nana' excuses and snuck downstairs to where Mahir's car was parked out of sight, behind the blocks of flats. I jumped quickly into the back seat and we took off.

I knew I had more than driving on my mind that day, but it was as if I had forgotten everything Mahir had taught me about driving the week before. When he tried to correct me, I could not take in a word of what he was saying. I felt very frustrated and disappointed with myself by the end of the lesson.

I made a half-hearted attempt to get around to the other side of the car before he reached me, but I think we both had some idea what was going to happen next. He held my face, pulled me close to him and kissed me. While Purity wailed in my head, my body responded with a sensation of intense heat between my legs. I let Mahir's hands wander all over my still-clothed body. It was only when he tried to pull my dress up that I pushed him away.

'Are you crazy?' I croaked.

He didn't seem to hear me. To my horror, I saw that he was unbuttoning the front of his trousers. As he released his hot, red genitals, he purred, 'I won't touch your virginity, Gulush. We'll just have a tiny little play. I know what I'm doing. It'll be safe, I promise.'

'No, Mahir!' I said, trying to control my panting breath. 'My family will…'

'… Never find out anything. There are only crows here and they aren't going to tell them.' He smiled. 'I think

95

you'll like it. I'll just rub it gently against you, it won't hurt you, I promise, and your virginity will stay intact,' he said, pushing me against the car. I didn't even have time to worry that the side of the car may be dusty and stain my dress.

My face, squashed against his sweaty neck, flamed scarlet as he hitched my dress up and pulled my pants to one side. I felt his hardness against my labia, so forbidden, but so stimulating. As he moved himself back and forth between my legs, I could barely hear Purity in my head, as she screamed: 'No marriage, shame and disgrace!' Mahir's movements became faster and more thrusting as his breathing quickened, then suddenly his face twisted, he gasped, shuddering and my legs and pants were drenched with a warm, pungent liquid.

'What the f★★k!' I exclaimed.

Mahir buttoned himself up quickly and tossed me an old towel from the boot. 'See, no harm done. You'll soon dry off.'

I mopped my underwear and legs, as well as I could. Luckily, my dress had been pulled up away from the mess. He smoked a cigarette as he drove, one hand on the wheel, flicking ash out the window. I couldn't bring myself to ask for one. My heart raced as my mind tried to make sense of the experience. *Never again*, I vowed, as the reds and greens gave way to the sparkling windows and pavements of the city. *Never again*, I repeated, as we arrived back behind the flats. *Never again?* I thought, as we parted without another touch. A part of me already knew, I had lied.

★★★

As the war in Nagorno-Karabakh raged on, my clandestine meetings with Mahir continued to relieve our tension. The original premise, the driving lessons, started to take second place to Mahir's 'little plays' with me. We even risked 'playing' in the upstairs toilet, when my colleagues were out shopping. These encounters followed the now familiar script, of me resisting, then Mahir overcoming my objections to the forbidden, but strictly exterior, pleasure for us both. Young and inexperienced, I revelled in the attention I was getting from him. The anticipation and stimulation of those snatched moments of intimacy, the touches and the kisses, outweighed all my fears. Nana may have primed me for marriage ever since I was little, but there were no eligible candidates around. No one ticked all the boxes: educated, good-looking, own car, own house, excellent job, begging me to marry him. So, I was happy to settle for Mahir until something better appeared.

# 6.

# HATE

The scorching late summer of 1993 was full of grief and turmoil for my country. Between the 22nd and the 31st of August, Azerbaijan lost three more of its regions to the Armenians: Fizuli, Jabrayil and Gubadli. Fizuli was east of Nagorno-Karabakh, next to Agdam. Jabrayil and Gubadli were to the south. The four regions had effectively created a cocoon around Nagorno-Karabakh, buffering it from the rest of Azerbaijan. Amidst rising political mayhem, the *Milli Mejlis*, the National Parliament, announced there would be presidential elections on the 3rd of October 1993.

It came as no surprise to anyone that Heydar Aliyev won and was inaugurated as president shortly after. In the past, a change of president had been of little consequence in Ganja, but this time, the effect on day-to-day life felt almost seismic. As soon as his presidency was officially confirmed, Heydar Aliyev replaced virtually all the staff in the law enforcement agencies in Ganja. Suret Huseynov's attempted coup earlier in the summer was neither forgotten nor forgiven. The new authorities did not want to take any chances in case some law enforcement agents were still under the influence of the rebels. Within a week, most of the Prosecutor's Office's staff were reassigned to other regions of the country, some of them to remote areas. We, the support staff, remained, and miraculously, so did Farid *muellim*, who remained as the Prosecutor's assistant.

It was very unsettling having so many brand-new colleagues. The in-jokes disappeared. The atmosphere became grave and heavy. Everyone wanted to make their best impression on the new Prosecutor, Kamal *muellim*. He seemed distant and arrogant. Although his brother lived in Ganja, Kamal *muellim* had worked in Baku for years and had a certain flare that felt unfamiliar. He refused to drink black tea, so Arzu and I had to learn to make up brews from fresh herbs and flowers, which Mahir bought every two days. Kamal *muellim* also installed a camera in the reception room, so that he could see who was waiting and what was going on. Arzu and I could no longer relax or chat with anyone. Our days became tense and lonely.

This was only a start. The punishment of Ganja for supporting Suret continued in unprecedented ways. Initially, our gas pressure started getting lower every day, to the point that it could take over an hour to boil a kettle.

'It might be quicker to use a candle,' Nana said when I checked our kettle for the tenth time one evening. 'For a country that produces and sells gas, this is disgraceful!'

As autumn deepened, the gas was cut off completely. Nana and I had to wrap up in all the layers we had and huddle by an electric heater. This too did not last long. The electricity started waning next; to the point where there was not enough voltage for us to watch TV. Now we were cut off from what was going on in the world outside Ganja.

Electricity cuts became commonplace at work. I was

forced to type up documents on a much stiffer manual typewriter a lot of the time, which made my fingers ache to start with. Thankfully, Mahir managed to connect the Prosecutor's Office to an old generator, so we had enough light and heat. It gave escaping to work a whole new layer of appeal. At home, Nana struggled to figure out how to cook our food and stay warm. As the temperature dropped, there was little need for a fridge.

The new Prosecutor took his time settling into his new role. His family was still in Baku, so he was back and forth. Mahir, left to his own devices, suggested Arzu and I go on another outing with him. We both jumped at the opportunity to have some fun and we headed for the Hajikand mountains surrounding Ganja, only a thirty-minute drive away. Again, Farid *muellim* joined us, smiling like a Cheshire cat as we sped along.

The mountains greeted us with gorgeous leafy, autumnal displays of colour, from golden-yellow, through fiery orange to deepest red; sights that melted our troubles away. The views became even more breathtaking as the car climbed the steep winding roads to the top of the mountains. I felt as excited as I had been when Baba had driven me there years before. However, as we approached the nearest village, I noticed that things had changed.

'What's happened to the woods? They look like a child's given them a haircut! There are clumps of trees missing everywhere, and look at the state of the Pioneer camp. I stayed there for a month when I was twelve.'

Once smart and vibrant, the summer camp for members of the Soviet Young Pioneers now looked dilapidated. Its painted wooden cabins peeling, with broken windows and holes in their roofs. Chickens ran about in the yard we used to practice marching on. A number of dishevelled women were cooking on open fires outside, their children chasing round and about them.

'Those are the refugees from Karabakh,' Farid *muellim* informed us. 'They've been cutting trees down to keep warm. Our government is in too much chaos to offer them any support, so they are surviving however they can.'

Arzu and I were shocked to see them there, living in such dire conditions. I felt ashamed of my moaning at home about the power cuts. This could have been me, I thought, remembering how close the Armenian forces had advanced on Ganja, only a couple of years ago.

'It's not over,' Mahir said. 'I heard Zangalan is fighting hard right now but the outcome is still uncertain.' He shook his head. 'There will be more like these coming, I think, but… I hope I'm wrong.' He mumbled this last observation and hit the accelerator to climb the next rise.

We arrived at the restaurant temporarily subdued, but eager to eat. We all wanted to forget about the war. After drinking two shots of vodka, I was ready to let go of my usual self-consciousness, and lap up all the attention I could get, even by telling some jokes I had learnt from Amina and Lala in Baku. 'A man is walking in the woods. Suddenly he hears a woman's voice screaming, "Help! Help! Rape! Rape!" He runs towards the voice only to find the ugly witch, *Baba Yaga*, sitting up a tree all alone, but shouting her head off. "Oi, Baba Yaga, what's this fuss about?" he demands, all hot and bothered. "Damn," she cries, "won't you even let an old woman dream?"'

After a pause, they all laughed, even Arzu. She was

usually more reserved in speaking up than me, but I had started to notice that she did not hold back in Farid's company. She seemed to have some affection for him. *Are they carrying on like Mahir and me, or is it just a friendship?* I wondered, without daring to ask, while I decided which of my arsenal of thirty jokes I should try next. The vodka gave me an excuse to use them all, eventually.

★★★

On the 29th of October 1993, Armenian forces occupied Zangilan. Its inhabitants fled their homes, raising the number of refugees and internally displaced people in Azerbaijan to over a million people. Our total population at that time was eight million. One in eight people had lost their homes. The hope that the new president could magically stop the war did not materialise. There was desperation all around me.

The Ganja winter of 1993 was brutal, with no gas and little electricity. At home, I kept my blue wool coat with its fake fur lining on all day and night, even in bed. Nana and I only had each other, no other distractions or entertainment, like reading or watching TV. Nana's old kerosine lamp stank and cast long shadows, creating a spooky atmosphere, with only just enough light for us to see each other by. We could not cook meals, so survived on bread and cheese. Electric heaters stood gathering dust. Ironing clothes was a thing of the past.

Alone in my cold, damp bed at night, I dreamt of the days when we had sat around the gas heater in the living room, with full bellies, Nana sewing, me reading.

Sometimes the cast iron heater, which heated most of the house, had been up so high that my skin turned a fiery red in its radiating heat. I had enjoyed watching the silent fat snowflakes floating outside or clinging to the branches of the naked persimmon trees. I would help Nana roast the hazelnuts she would line up on the top of the heater, turning them around at equal intervals, until their delicate skins crumbled away to reveal their brown cheeks.

No gas also meant no hot water, which in turn led to the pipes freezing on the coldest nights. Then we would have no water in the house at all to wash our hands or flush down the outside toilet. Bathing turned into an occasional clean with a sponge and, after years of washing dishes under a running tap, using a small bowl seemed to make them dirtier, not cleaner.

Nana was listless and miserable. She missed bustling about the kitchen preparing food. In our family, Nana showed her love for us through her cooking. Now I felt like I was starving emotionally as well as physically. I even craved for the times when she had bossed me around in the kitchen: chop that up, stir this, pluck that chicken, roll the dough. The most tedious job used to be carefully packing as many little gherkins as possible into three-litre preserving jars. Strangely, I missed even that.

It was not just physical heat that was gone from our lives, but also the human warmth and connection. Mama could only call occasionally. It sounded like her family were having a hard time financially, although Baku's power supplies were secure. I was worried and upset for her and my siblings. I yearned for when we had all lived together. There had been fifteen people in our household then:

Mama's new family of four, in the basement; my uncle's family of four in the garden bungalow; the four of us upstairs – my younger uncle, Nana and Baba and I; and a young family of three who rented a room in the basement.

The only thing that relieved our inertia was the little red tape player that my colleagues had given me on the 8th of March. It managed to play even when the voltage was so low you could see the filament on a light bulb looking like a delicate amber thread. We only had two cassettes of folk songs. On the longest, darkest nights when we ran out of conversation, I would play them and dance for Nana in the dark as she clapped from under her duvet.

Some nights it was so cold that the only way to stay vaguely warm was to sleep fully clothed, pressed against Nana in the same bed, under both our duvets. I often woke up to find my face still painfully cold and sometimes I would wonder what the point of this existence was.

When my younger uncle, Salman, came to visit from Moscow for a week, he deeply regretted it. I think he thought Nana had been exaggerating about how we were living. Sitting with us in the drawing room one day, all huddled up in blankets, he said: 'Gulush, do me a favour. Please open that window.'

We stared at him in disbelief. Had he gone mad? The room was already freezing.

'Some warmth may come in from the outside,' he said as a way of explanation. Nana and I started to laugh hysterically.

He soon departed to his rented accommodation in Moscow with its central heating and uninterrupted electricity and water. When he had gone, Nana and I decided to sleep in the basement, which though pitch black at night, was easier to keep warm in.

***

The deprivation of Ganja continued into 1994, so going to Baku for my next study session in January gave me a mixed bag of emotions. I worried about leaving Nana, although she was well supported by her neighbours. I was apprehensive about the war and about my continued studies, but looking forward to reconnecting with my friends and the benefits of a modern city.

I found it even harder to concentrate on the content of my lectures this time, whether because they were at a higher level, or simply because I was still exhausted from the lean times in Ganja, I didn't know, but I often struggled not to nod off. Duman *muellim*, our Atheism lecturer, made it even harder. He was an old man who ironically reminded me of my Great-Uncle Hussein, who was a *mullah*. His delivery was long-winded and very technical. The module seemed to me to be a relic of the Soviet Union, given that in independent Azerbaijan, Islam was no longer something people practised behind closed doors. I thought that either he had connections that prevented the university from ousting him from his job, or the university authorities had been slow to update their curriculum. I also disliked the lectures given on logic, as well as Latin. I could not see any direct connection those subjects might have with law. On top of all this, the broken windows in the lecture hall had not been repaired, so there was always a rush at the start of each session to get a place on the warmer side. Despite wearing my trusty blue coat, one morning, my right hand went numb and blue with cold while taking notes.

In contrast, my time after classes was luxurious and fun. I loved the warmth of Amina's car and flat. She talked openly about her 'business' these days: including how much money she was making. She had one guy who 'absolutely adored' her and had taken her with him on a work trip to France. Another of her regulars had paid her one thousand US dollars for a pleasant evening out. She hadn't even had to have sex with him. One client's wife had felt so threatened by her husband seeing Amina that she had decided to have another baby in an attempt to save their marriage. Amina thought she was 'an idiot' for thinking that would work.

I tried to listen without judgement, but I was very curious. I didn't fully understand her choices in life. There was a young man on our course who was so smitten with Amina that he wanted to marry her. She even told him about her lifestyle to put him off, but he was adamant that none of it mattered, and he was still willing to make an honest woman of her. I thought that this was the ultimate dream of most women, especially those like Amina, but she still turned him down. Did she enjoy all her encounters with men? I was too scared to ask. Instead, I accompanied her on many of her outings, where she introduced me as a virgin friend who was absolutely off-limits. Soon I was going out every other day, so I bought myself a beautiful, figure-hugging, turquoise shirt and some wide chocolate-coloured satin trousers, with folds at the front, which looked almost like a skirt. With the warmth of fine food and fun, my skin recovered its pinkness and my heart its vivacity. I worked hard during the day at my studies and on my social skills in the evenings.

I enjoyed my leisure time in Baku so much that I dreaded returning to the drudgery, greyness and cold at home in Ganja, where boiling a kettle still felt like a major achievement. When I did, I found that my kisses and 'play' with Mahir were no longer enough to alleviate my misery and boredom.

Novruz, the dearly beloved spring festival, which was normally celebrated with flair, seemed set to be even worse than the previous year. Nana was determined to cook her famous *pilav* on an open fire in the garden, but I thought it wasn't worth the effort. What was the point? My mood plummeted further following the March metro bombings in Baku two days before Novruz itself. Armenian terrorists planted bombs in several metro stations, killing twenty-seven people and wounding ninety-one others. How could people possibly find joy at a time like this? Despite the warmth of the fires on the street, I stayed most of the evening of Novruz at home, listening to the laughter and singing outside. Tears rolled onto my blue coat as I realised that now even Baku did not feel safe, closing off my only imaginary escape route from the war.

By the late spring of 1994, the Azerbaijani forces still hadn't reclaimed the Nagorno-Karabakh enclave, or the Lachin corridor, a mountain pass spanning seven regions, which linked mainland Armenia to Nagorno-Karabakh. No more regions were lost but it was generally thought that the ones the Armenian forces had already occupied were gone for good. Since we could still rarely watch TV at home due to the power outages, Nana and I often felt cut off from the world, especially at weekends. For all we knew, the Armenians could be advancing on Ganja again. My main source of news was people discussing it at work. I would surreptitiously tune in to their conversations whenever I could.

'They are trying to mediate a ceasefire,' I heard Farid *muellim* saying to another person one afternoon, through his open office door as I was passing. I stopped unseen outside, trying to make sense of what was going on.

'I hear the president is in Bishkek right now,' the other man said.

Why was our president in Kyrgyzstan? That didn't sound right. I decided I would ask Farid *muellim* if I got the chance later. There was only one thing he liked more than displaying his knowledge of politics to me, and that was having an excuse to be in Arzu's company. She called him 'the back-up receptionist' he was there so often.

★★★

One afternoon, Mahir was gathering the water containers to refill.

'Want to come along and help me at the springs, Gulush?' he asked.

I looked at Arzu, my eyes pleading.

'You're up to date with your work and no one is going to visit while the boss is in Baku, so go get yourself some fresh air, and me some chocolate on the way back,' she said. I knew she'd be chatting with Farid before we had even left the building.

I followed Mahir to the car. It was no longer 'blue

coat' weather. The air was warm with a hint of blossom. Mahir seemed in a buoyant mood. He chatted away about his four-year-old son and the younger one, who had just started to talk. Then he spoke about his mum's deteriorating health and the shop he had just opened close to his home. I watched the cars as we whizzed past the Soviet multistorey buildings. I was only half listening and I didn't know what to say in response anyway. I was pleased when Mahir's fiddling with the radio finally bore fruit and the commanding voice of a newsreader cut in. After a detailed backstory, the man announced: 'Let all listeners be aware that today, the 5th of May 1994, the Bishkek Protocol has been signed, officially declaring a ceasefire between Armenia and Azerbaijan.' Mahir turned the volume up as the man elaborated on the circumstances of the meeting at which the official delegates from Azerbaijan, Nagorno-Karabakh and Armenia negotiated the agreement. Then a lot of experts debated what this might mean for everyone now and in the future.

'That's something to celebrate, Gulush,' Mahir said.

'It doesn't mean the war is over, they've just paused it,' I told him. 'It's like a storm cloud promising not to rain.'

'Always the optimist, Gulush!' He grinned, catching my eye in the mirror. 'Listen, the boss has had to dash to Baku, some sort of family emergency, and I have to drop some stuff off at his house on the way back. Do you fancy checking it out?'

I knew it was wrong to nose around someone's house uninvited, but I had to admit to myself that I was curious. I had never been to a Prosecutor's house before. I imagined it would be huge and grand.

'Won't Arzu wonder why we've been gone so long?' I cautioned.

'She won't even notice. It won't take that long. Think about it while I fill up,' he said, getting out of the car. Our tap water was not safe for drinking. At work, it was one of Mahir's chores to collect the water, at home it was mine. Once a week, for as long as I could remember, a truck with a big cistern full of spring water from the mountains had arrived near our house and I had to fill two large black containers from it. We always had to make sure we did not miss the delivery.

As I watched Mahir filling work's white containers, one at a time, I tried to decide what to do. What if someone spotted me going into the house and told the boss or even my family? It was too risky. I said no. Mahir could make his delivery and I would stay in the car.

'Your loss,' Mahir shrugged when I told him.

When we reached a part of Ganja unknown to me, the boss's house, as I had anticipated, was huge, half-hidden behind tall, white walls.

'Stay in the car,' Mahir said, climbing out. I relaxed on the back seat as he opened the large iron road gates, but instead of opening the boot, he got back into the driver's seat.

'What are you doing?' I asked, suddenly uneasy.

'Shush…' he said, driving into a paved courtyard. Then he got out and opened my car door. 'Why do you always have to act as if you've never been alone with me before?' he said, beckoning me out of the car. 'Come on! I may kiss you, but if I do, so what?'

I climbed out, though my arms and legs felt like they were weighted down with lead. What if a housekeeper or a relative should appear? However, as we looked round the house, my curiosity silenced such voices of reason in my head. There was a stunning kitchen with all mod cons and sparkly surfaces. There were spacious reception rooms and a sitting room full of ornaments and the largest television I had ever seen. Upstairs, there were numerous impeccably tidy bedrooms, a study and a children's room, which was full of toys. As I entered the master bedroom, which had a vast silk-decked bed, Mahir was suddenly right next to me.

'Nice big bed,' he said, wrapping his arms round me.

'Let's go. Later,' I said as I tried to pull away. I was still worried that someone might discover us there.

'I can't wait. It has to be now,' he said as he fumbled with the buttons of my shirt to reveal my lacy bra, which he flipped up to grasp my breasts.

'Someone might come,' I said as I squirmed, trying to free myself.

His only reply was to pull my skirt up. He had a look on his face that I recognised. There would be no reasoning with him now. He unbuttoned his trousers as I tried to relax and waited for him to rub himself against me. Instead, to my surprise, he turned me over, pushed me down against the bed and stood behind me.

'What are you doing Mahir?' I tried to get up, but he had pulled my pants right down, so they acted like shackles on my legs.

'I told you; I won't take your virginity, but you need to relax now.' His voice was hoarse and impatient.

Reassured, but self-consciously aware that my backside was fully exposed, I tried to reach up to pull my skirt down, but he pinned me down with his bulky body.

'I promised you would not lose your virginity,' he said while starting to force himself inside me.

'Stop, that hurts,' I shouted, struggling for a foothold on the deep-pile carpet.

'Shush! Do you want someone to hear you?' he grumbled, pushing on in.

'It hurts! It hurts!' I screamed. I felt as if my body was being ripped apart as he forced my head into the bedspread. 'I hate you! I hate you! I HATE you!'

The sound of my shattering heart was louder in my head than the sound of my stifled screams. I had trusted him. 'Idiot!' Purity roared. As he continued to thrust harder and harder into me, I found myself temporarily in a place beyond pain, as if I were watching the scene, not a part of it. I wondered if my make-up would leave a stain on this beautiful fabric and if I was going to die.

Mahir groaned as he reached his climax, shuddering, breathing heavily and then finally releasing me from his iron grip. I dragged myself up from the bed, pulling my pants up and my skirt down. I wanted to spit at him, claw his face, rage at him, but what was the point? I couldn't undo the damage now.

'I kept my promise. I didn't touch your virginity,' he grunted, rebuttoning his fly. 'You can still marry and live happily ever after. No harm done,' he added, somewhat nervous.

'Toilet,' was all I said. I did not recognise my own icy voice.

He waved at the door and mumbled, 'Downstairs.'

I hobbled down the stairs to the toilet, then released my urine, bloody faeces and grief into the pristine white toilet bowl. My whole body shook with the shock of betrayal and invasion, my face swollen with tears. How was I going to hide this from Arzu's shrewd eyes? She would surely spot that I had been crying, but I could not go back home either. As I cleaned myself with hot water, I knew there was no one in the world I could confide in. Even if my virginity was still intact, my purity was truly gone now. Killing myself was no solution either, because, I had learnt from my studies, there would then be a medical examination, which would reveal to everyone any sexual activity I had had.

'Gulush?' Mahir's voice jolted me into the now. 'Hurry up! We have to go back to work now.' He spoke as if everything was normal.

I willed myself to stand straight, though my whole body felt numb. I clicked open the solid door and stalked out straight past him. Like a plane on automatic pilot, I found my way to the car through the maze of rooms. It was unlocked so I climbed painfully in and sat like a statue, dead inside. Neither of us said a word to each other as Mahir drove us back to the work car park.

Though I had to make a conscious effort to walk normally, I managed to reach the relative haven of reception, before he had even locked the car. Trying to keep my gait as straight as I could to mask a slight limp in my right side caused by a weird pulling sensation in my right hip, I quickly sat at my desk, and I arranged my face into what I hoped was a neutral expression.

'Oh, it's you, finally,' Arzu said, finishing a call. 'What took you so long? Roadworks, I suppose.' She liked to answer her own questions. 'So, where's my chocolate?' She smacked her lips expectantly.

'I forgot, I'm sorry. You're right, the traffic was awful.' I was finding it hard to speak with a clenched jaw. I think my words sounded slurred to Arzu. She arched an eyebrow.

'You didn't go somewhere else, did you?' she said, mischievously.

I tensed up so much I thought I was going to vomit.

'Was it that restaurant again?' Arzu continued, unaware of my internal struggle. 'What were you thinking?'

'No, no, of course not. Not without you.' I shook my head vigorously. Then I noticed the clock. It had been two hours since I had fluttered out. 'There was this road accident, traffic jams everywhere.' I knew I was gabbling but couldn't stop myself. 'Then Mahir had to drop something off at the boss's. I didn't ask what. I waited in the car, for ages.' It occurred to me at that moment; Mahir had not even opened the boot. Had he planned the whole thing?

'Oh right, that sounds like Mahir.' Arzu chuckled. 'Don't worry about the chocolate, Gulush. I'm not going to fade away.' She patted her belly and turned back to her work. 'You don't look so good yourself. If you're expecting your time of the month, don't forget I've got pads in my desk.'

'Thank you, Arzu,' I said. I was truly grateful that she had given me a reason to go to the toilet again, so I could check myself over. I accepted a pad and slipped into the empty corridor.

I still felt uncomfortable when I returned, so I attempted to silence my thoughts by attacking my work. As my fingers rattled over the keys of the heavy manual typewriter, I stared at the black stains of the words forming on the cheap grey A4 paper. The monotony of the sound and motion was strangely soothing. It helped take the edge off the pain. Although images and feelings continued to flash through my tortured mind, I managed to get through the rest of the afternoon, blinking them away along with the occasional tear, which I prayed Arzu did not see.

I journeyed home on the bus, wrapped in a heavy cloud of misery, unable to speak to anyone. When Nana greeted me with the promise of 'good cheese and fresh bread' for my dinner, I almost broke down. Instead, I gave her a warm hug, burying my face momentarily in her housecoat, so she couldn't see my eyes.

'I think it's my time, Nana,' I lied, using Arzu's cue. 'I don't feel like eating just now. My belly is hurting. I need to rest. Maybe later.'

'Of course, of course,' she said, patting me on my back before bustling off to some corner of the house.

As I put myself to bed, I imagined telling her what had really happened. Weirdly, I found myself laughing out loud at a spectre of Nana, furious, pointing her finger, scolding me, like a little Baba Yaga. All those years she'd spent warning me against men and their ways, and here I was, I could finally accept the word: raped. I had been raped, in the most brutal and undignified way I thought possible and if anyone found out, it would be me, not Mahir, that would face shame and certain death. It was me that had lost my honour. These, I thought, were the cold, hard facts. With no energy left, even for tears, I submerged myself in the damp bedsheets, fully clothed, and fell into the oblivion of sleep.

# 7.

# BLOODY SHEETS

Mahir was not in the office for several days after his assault on me. I was thankful for the time to rehearse how I would respond to him next time we met.

'Hello all,' he said, greeting us with an uncertain smile as he walked quickly through reception, on his way to the Prosecutor's door.

'Hi, Mahir.' I smiled. It gave me great satisfaction to see him stop in his tracks.

Arzu's watchful eyes were on both of us.

'Great,' he said. A trace of confusion flickered in his eyes.

I held my breath and pursed my lips to stop my face from twitching, as long as I could, then as calmly as possible, I got up and made some excuse about checking something with Masha and trotted out, conscious of two pairs of eyes on my rigid body. Once in the toilet cubicle, I broke down and collapsed onto the dry, worn floor, hugging myself, trying to tame my silent tears. I allowed myself only the usual number of minutes, then splashed cold water on my puffy eyes and opened the small window and let the fresh air dry my face, so Arzu wouldn't have cause to quiz me about my appearance.

116

I was initially pleased, when I returned to reception some fifteen minutes later, to find her gone out, but soon the Prosecutor's door opened and Mahir rushed out carrying several folders. He paused, craning his neck to listen for Arzu's footsteps, but all was quiet.

'I thought you were serious when you said you hate me,' he said, coming closer. 'I'm so relieved you're talking to me.' For a moment, I thought he was going to try and kiss me. I sat bolt upright and stared at him in disgust.

'Of course I hate you!' I hissed. 'What do you expect me to do? Tell Arzu? Don't you think she'll ask questions if I stop talking to you altogether? I still don't understand how you could do that to me, to anyone,' I raged through my tears. 'I hate you now and I will hate and curse you forever!'

Mahir involuntarily stepped back. I think he realised that at that moment I no longer cared if someone walked in on us. His face paled under his stubble as he stared back, unmoving, as if seeing me for the first time. Then he said seriously: 'You can report me, if you want, Gulush, but remember your work here. You know the drill.'

I certainly did, from all the rape case files I had studied: the long process, the allegations I might face, the shame on my family and the lack of successful convictions. The prospect of becoming one of those lost souls destroyed my anger.

'Just stay away from me,' I said, as Arzu's footsteps approached down the corridor. 'Do you fancy a cup of tea, Arzu?' I said brightly as she entered the room, carrying more work for us both. 'Mahir can't stop. He's got important deliveries to do.' I turned my back on him and switched on the kettle.

'Gulush, you'll be late for work.' Nana was shaking me by my shoulders, as I woke to another workday morning.

'I'm getting up now,' I said, but lay in bed for several more minutes, before forcing myself up, taking off my pyjamas and pulling on my clothes, which included the turquoise shirt I had bought in Baku. Wearing it always reminded me of the other life I had waiting for me. An extra boost to get me through another day.

'The kettle hasn't boiled yet,' Nana said, getting out butter and cheese and placing them next to a plate of bread on the table.

I sat down and picked up a knife. I found it easier to do what she wanted to avoid any questions about my lack of appetite. While Nana checked on the old red enamel kettle she was trying to get to boil on a portable bottled gas heater, I clattered the cutlery, pretending to make myself a sandwich.

'I'll have it at work, Nana,' I said, grabbing my handbag and giving her a kiss on the way out.

Once I was outside, I walked slowly, hoping to miss the bus and further delay getting to work. Every morning, I would contemplate quitting my job, but knew I couldn't put more pressure on Nana's limited resources. The Prosecutor's 'gifts' paid for my studies in Baku and our bills. Besides, what reason could I give for wanting to leave? I didn't want anyone, at work or at home, to suspect the real cause of my desire to move on.

I was finding it harder to hide my feelings. I hated every encounter I had with Mahir. Watching him laughing and talking with others, as if nothing had happened, was driving me crazy. My rage was increasingly bitter. I stung him with my supposedly unintentional sarcasm every time I had an opportunity. I would say things like: 'Oh, Arzu, Mahir does not need any chocolate with his tea.' She had just offered him a Snickers bar. 'He's quite enough of a man already. Only joking,' I said, with a honeyed smile, as I patted my tummy. I felt a deep satisfaction seeing how deflated he had looked.

My feelings of hurt and injustice were further fuelled when I overheard my boss's nephew gossiping about Mahir, who apparently regularly visited prostitutes. Despite what had happened between us, a naïve bit of me had still wanted to believe that Mahir had had some genuine affection for me. Now I knew for certain he had just been playing with me.

Speaking to Arzu one day, knowing that Mahir could hear us from the corridor, where he was choosing to wait for the Prosecutor, I said: 'Some people pretend to be so saintly while all the time they are up to no good. I've heard rumours that one of our most trusted colleagues is going to see prostitutes, while his wife is sitting all faithful at home, waiting for him. I don't know exactly who it is but imagine how his family would feel if they found out?'

I could only reckon how he looked when he heard that, but I was sure he had because a fit of coughing erupted outside our door.

Whereas before I had looked for every opportunity to linger at work, now I was first out of what I called 'the prison door'. I was exhausted from the constant effort of keeping my secret. When Arzu said we could leave after lunch one day, as the Prosecutor was out, I took the time to walk home in the early summer sunshine. Watching everyone enjoying their day, shopping, playing in the park, chatting at the cafés, made me feel a sense of normality. As I approached our iron gate, I heard voices. Nana was obviously out in the garden, making tea in her Russian-style samovar, for a visitor. This was a rare occurrence these days, so I paused to eavesdrop, trying to make out who it was. Judging by the conversation, it was a neighbour who had just given birth to a baby; Nana's young friend, Shafiga.

'It was absolutely awful! Terrifying! I never thought it would be that bad,' she was saying. 'It was like I birthed him through my bum!'

I froze inside. I had never heard of such a thing before. If you could birth a baby through your bum, did that mean you could get pregnant that way too? I was so worried by that thought that I had to walk around the block for another half an hour before I could face going home. By that time, Shafiga had gone, leaving only a bright pink lipstick trace on her glass. I sat in the garden for a while, staring at it, wishing, again, that I had someone I could talk to about such things as she had so easily shared with Nana.

The next day, I decided I had to speak to Mahir. I eventually managed catch him alone, polishing the car. I didn't mince my words but started in with: 'Did you ever consider what would happen to me if I got pregnant?'

He blinked at me in the sunlight and frowned. 'What?' His black eyebrows shot up. 'What are you on about now, Gulush?'

'My neighbour just gave birth through her bum. What

if you've got me pregnant like that? You never cared about me!' I squealed.

Mahir sighed and shook his head. 'You cannot get pregnant that way, I know this,' he said. His voice was weary, and his shoulders slouched. 'Please keep your voice down.'

'I don't believe you!' I retorted and walked away, my blood boiling.

Who could tell me the truth? Virgins were not supposed to know anything about procreation. Intercourse was, traditionally, something a trusted female family member would tell you about on your wedding night. The little I did know came from things I had heard older people saying, my uncle's disturbing typed story and my own limited experiences with Mahir and by myself. I didn't think there were any books I could read about it. Even if they existed, I knew I wouldn't dare to buy one; it was too exposing and where would I hide it anyway, while sharing a house with Nana who poked into everything? There had been the two chapters in our year eight anatomy book, which had a sketch of female and male anatomies. Everyone in the lower years had heard rumours about those chapters, but the reality of the book did not meet our expectations. Our female teacher was so embarrassed by the subject that she only spent a grand total of three minutes on both chapters before moving onto the digestive system. That was all the official sex education I ever had.

I couldn't even go to a gynaecological unit in Ganja. If someone I knew saw me, my very presence there would be interpreted as me being sexually active and might be reported to my family.

It wasn't just the fear of pregnancy that bothered me. It was the realisation that Mahir had never really cared about me. My fantasies of being able to bend him to my will had been just that, the naïve fantasies of the child I no longer was.

★★★

It was back to Baku in June 1994 for my next study session to free me from most physical reminders of the rape, including the presence of Mahir. My mind was clearer in Baku because I could drop the pretence of being friends with him. However, I found there was still rage and bitterness bubbling deep within me. It sometimes made it hard to concentrate. It made me impatient with everyone, including the lecturers. I became almost indifferent to the consequences of not passing the exams, because I had realised that if I failed something I would have an excuse to travel to Baku again, for the resits in September.

I didn't know why, but I didn't tell Lala or Amina about the rape. Part of me didn't see the point in sharing something that couldn't be changed. Instead, I took every opportunity Amina gave me to be involved in her world. We went to the seaside with the girls most weekends. I was happy to go with her to visit her mum in Sumgait. I covered up for her by telling fibs to the young jealous lover she kept 'just for fun'. I accompanied her to more 'meals' with her regular, influential, male friends. I was astounded and delighted when she invited me to her movie premier. I knew she had been having a stab at singing professionally, but I didn't know about the acting.

There were all these wonderful distractions and then there was the retail therapy. I particularly enjoyed our shopping expeditions. Amina liked to go to every sort of shop, from small boutiques to the grandest of department stores. All the staff knew her and treated us like celebrities. We looked at far more than we ever bought, but by the end of my stay I was the proud owner of a whole new wardrobe of clothes to wear only in Baku. These included a brightly coloured yellow, pink and turquoise wrap skirt, a high-neck sleeveless fuchsia shirt, a long stripy silver dress with a black cami top that showed off my cleavage, a beige-patterned playsuit and some bright yellow and black swimwear. I still remember how these new clothes felt to wear, fresh and soft against my skin; a contrast to the handmade clothes I generally wore in Ganja. It might have been wrong to treat myself while Nana struggled frugally at home, but it was mostly my money I spent, though Amina sometimes chipped in. I did not care any more because I felt somehow that I was on borrowed time. I believed that eventually my family would force me into an arranged marriage. Then I would probably have to give up all my freedoms and be a dutiful and useful wife. Until then, I wanted to live every moment of life to the full.

Although I hadn't been that keen on cigarettes before, this time in Baku I smoked throughout my stay. They seemed to take the edge off when I was uptight or upset. Now I was willing to do anything that would numb me and take my mind off my growing desire to punish Mahir. I would fantasise that if I could make enough money, I would hire someone to assault him in exactly the same way as he had assaulted me. An eye for an eye and a tooth for a tooth, that was the saying, wasn't it? It was the least he deserved, I thought.

Unfortunately, I somehow managed to pass all my exams, despite feeling foggy and hardly visiting the library. I was lucky with the lecturers that session. The lecturer in civil law was also from Ganja. As a compatriot, he took me under his wing, insisting on giving me free extra tutorials in preparation for exams. I thought he fancied me, but I was in too much distress to encourage him. The lecturer in criminal justice was impressed that I worked for the Prosecutor's Office. He did make a pass at me during the exam, when he asked whether I was married. When I said 'no', he expressed his disappointment. Would he have propositioned me to sleep with him, if I were someone's wife, I wondered? In the end, he had decided that a connection with someone who worked at the Prosecutor's Office might come in useful one day and awarded me an excellent mark for saying practically nothing about criminal justice. I should have felt happy, but I felt as if someone had poured a bucket of slime over me. The experience somehow solidified my disgust with men. As for logic, the majority of the class paid bribes to the lecturer and he made sure we all passed, so that no one would out him to the dean.

★★★

I met Mama briefly at the end of this stay in Baku. She looked thinner and greyer. I treated her to a meal. Even though she said she was hungry, Mama ate her food slowly and often seemed lost in thought.

'Don't tell Nana,' she said when she had finally emptied

her plate, 'but…' She paused, head down, clenching her fingers.

I expected the worst, remembering a similar occasion, nine years before, when she had told me she was going to marry again. She had sworn me to secrecy then too, which had made my life very difficult for a while.

'I have sold the flat,' she said bleakly.

'You did?' I tensed up inside. 'Where do you live now?' I asked.

'Well, there was a plan to get something better, but…' Her lower lip quivered. Now I was really worried. Her unseeing brown eyes became distant.

'Tell me, Mama, what is it?' I fought an impulse to shake her out of her stupor.

'The money is all gone,' she said. Her voice was hollow. Her pallor was ghostly.

I could not understand exactly what had happened from the garbled explanation that followed. It sounded like her partner wanted to make big money fast, invested the money from the flat into some enterprise that didn't work out and they all ended up on the street. One of Mama's political buddies was now letting them stay in their flat in the Yasamal district of Baku, an even more far-flung area of the capital. They were all squashed together. There were extra travel costs. Neither of them had a steady job. My siblings needed new clothes. At nineteen, I did not know what to say or do to make her feel better. It was with a heavy heart that I said my goodbyes. I had considered finally sharing my troubles with my Mama, but given her more urgent challenges, it felt completely out of the question, yet again.

★★★

I felt physically ill returning to Ganja again. The first shock to my system was seeing Mahir out front, but when I noticed that the Prosecutor was in the car, I was forced to say a polite hello to both of them. The second was finding a new employee sitting in Masha's office.

'I'm Seva, and you must be Gulush,' the tall woman said as she enthusiastically shook my limp hand. Apparently, Masha had a new protégé.

Seva was large in every way. She exuded confidence and sexual allure. Her eyelids above a thick black eyeliner sported several shades of purple eyeshadow meticulously applied: the lightest tone in the middle, getting darker to the edges and with a shimmery highlight tracing her well-plucked eyebrows. When she talked, I was temporarily mesmerised by her lilac glossed lips and pearl-like teeth.

When I got to reception, Arzu was itching to gossip about the new girl. 'She doesn't even bother pretending that she's working half the time. I've heard that she's someone's mistress. He called in a favour with the Prosecutor, who gave her a job. There's not much she can do, so her 'work' is to come to the office at her convenience, then collect her pay every month.' Then, quieter, Arzu said, 'She and Mahir are besties already. He haunts that office. He hardly ever comes in here, these days.'

I felt the sting of her words but kept my face in neutral. I soon found Arzu was not exaggerating. Often, as I passed Seva's open door on my way down the corridor, I was infuriated at the sight of Mahir sitting close to her. One afternoon, when she was alone as I passed, without thinking, I chimed out, in an attempted jokey tone: 'Be careful of that Mahir's charms, Seva. He's not who he pretends to be.'

Seva looked astonished and made no reply, but after that day, Mahir stopped acknowledging me altogether. Seva must have mentioned what I had said. I couldn't understand why I felt so angry about him ignoring me. Arzu's uninformed opinion didn't help. 'Why did you two have to fall out?' She kept pestering me about it. 'We were all having such a good time going out together. Life is so boring now,' she complained.

'I just don't like him any more. He's...' I hesitated for a moment, '... such a brute. Perhaps we could go out with someone else.' *That might make Mahir regret ignoring me*, I thought.

'I've got a friend at the police station who has been asking me out for dinner for ages,' Arzu said. 'He's married, of course,' she shrugged, 'but what harm can a little fun do?'

*A lot*, I thought to myself. I was relieved that this might stop Arzu's interrogation and might bring me some small revenge on Mahir.

'Call your friend, Arzu,' I said. 'Let's do it soon.'

Arzu's friend, Ilgar, turned out to be an investigator. He was lean and smiley. I liked him a lot. I did not like the man chosen to be my companion, his tall friend Musa. Musa had a beer belly that made his body look disproportionately large compared to his head. When he kissed me, without asking, in the back seat of Ilgar's car on our way to the restaurant, I did not like it, but I didn't push him away. I thought this would really annoy Mahir if he ever found out about it.

A few glasses of vodka faded my initial reservations. The two men were quite good company. After several such outings, I convinced myself that it was not so bad. It was better that both men were married. Going out casually with an eligible bachelor was inconceivable in our community. No one would consider marrying you if you were known to have explored a relationship with someone else who was available. The advantage of having fun with married men was that they wanted to keep it all hushed up too.

Our outings with Ilgar and Musa became more reckless than those we had had with Mahir and Farid. On one occasion, they decided to drive us to Mingachevir, which was nearly two hours away.

'We'll be late back,' I complained. 'Nana might call me about something. Is it really worth spending four hours in the car for one meal?'

'Ah, you see, there's a meal, and then there's a meal by the Mingachevir reservoir,' Ilgar said, smacking his lips in anticipation. 'Have you ever been there, Gulush?'

'No.' I pouted.

'Fascinating place,' he said, as he expertly navigated some potholes. 'The reservoir was built on the Kura River in 1953. I suspect even your parents weren't born then. It looks like a sea, seventy kilometres long and eighteen kilometres wide. It's the largest reservoir in the Caucasus. It's also a hydroelectric power station, where one of my friends works.'

'OK, I hear that it's fascinating, but…'

'Stop worrying so much,' Musa interrupted me, 'you'll get frown lines. Look at how chilled Arzu is.'

I sat fuming. It was all very well for Arzu, whose mum was Russian and more relaxed about her daughter's whereabouts. Even Mahir had understood my family situation better than this. I was so irritated when Musa tried to silence me with a wet smacking kiss, something I was growing to hate.

I did not manage to relax fully that day, even after several shots of vodka and sitting with Musa outside after the meal and watching ripples on the surface of the reservoir. Ilgar and Arzu had stayed inside the cabin where we had had our food. When I attempted to go back in, Musa stopped me with a warm embrace. He was wearing a nice cologne, something Mahir rarely did. Musa seemed more sophisticated, but I felt no spark with him.

We got away with being late that day, but soon after, the men arranged another trip to Mingachevir. This time they drove us to a motel after the meal, where they had hired two rooms.

'It's just for an hour,' Ilgar reassured me, 'to let the food settle down.'

'Why do we need two rooms?' I asked.

'I don't know about you two, but I need some private time with my girl.' Ilgar whispered in my ear, 'Have you seen her ass, Gulush? It's magnificent!'

Why did he tell me that? Were he and Arzu doing what Mahir did? Or was he just complimenting her figure? In a daze, I followed Musa to a room with a large bed, covered in musty sheets. I had heard Arzu chuckling to Ilgar that this was where men had sex with prostitutes. In the dim light of the curtained room, I realised Musa was taking his clothes off. I looked away.

'Come here, Gulush. We don't have long,' he said.

'You do realise that I am a virgin, Musa?' I said firmly.

'Of course I do. We're just going to play,' he said, smiling. I realised I wanted him to pleasure me like Mahir used to do; safe and familiar stimulation.

Fully clothed, I joined him on the bed, but within seconds, Musa guided my head down his body.

'Try this,' he coaxed, 'you'll enjoy it.'

I didn't but obviously I had got it right. Musa groaned with pleasure. Then he pushed me down on the bed, pulling my dress up. He tried to help me out of my clothes as I fumbled, my hands shaking. Eventually, he lay on top of me, rubbing himself against me, as I had imagined, except that his belly got in the way and I was crushed by his weight. When he finally came, I got up quickly, then dressed, trying not to look too eager to leave.

'What's the rush?' He went to kiss me, I dodged, picking up my shoes.

'I'm going to be in a lot of trouble if Nana calls work and finds out I'm not there.'

'I'm sure you'll think of an explanation. You're such a clever girl,' he said, dismissing my worries. He took his time to dress.

Never again, I decided as we drove back to Ganja. Never again.

★★★

After that outing, I declined every invitation, despite the fact that Musa rang every day, trying to persuade me. 'My wife is visiting her relatives in Baku again,' he would say, 'so you could all come to mine. We'll order food in. No one knows you round here. The motel was a stupid idea, I get that now. Coming over to mine would be much safer.' He droned on and on.

'You think your neighbours are stupid?' I asked. 'They'll see us going in and out. They're bound to tell your wife.'

Sometimes I would pretend that the line had cut off or that Nana was about to ring, to cut him off mid-proposal. Arzu kept asking me too. I was relieved when an opportunity presented itself to get away from them all for a few days.

My neighbour Aunty Amalia's stepson Vugar was about to marry her niece, Gullu. I arranged with the Prosecutor to take a few days off from work to help out. Gullu had visited Aunty Amalia's house from when I was a child; I had seen her falling in love with blue-eyed smiley Vugar over the course of a few years.

Preparations for the wedding, in early September of 1994, were well underway when I joined the process. My main tasks were helping with the cooking and running errands for anyone that needed me to. This was going to be the most exciting event of the whole year in our neighbourhood. Nana made me a light-pink silky shirt and dark magenta velvet skirt for the wedding itself. I couldn't wait to show it off to the young single men on the big day. Perhaps I would be next, I hoped. Weddings and family gatherings were the primary way in which young people met each other in my community, unless they were lucky to be related like Vugar and Gullu were. I thought it was just a matter of chance and good looks that meant that you could attract a man's attention.

Casual dating was not supposed to happen at all. If a girl showed too keen an interest towards a particular single man, she could lose her good reputation. The presumption being that if you were that forward, you might have shared your affections with someone else before. Any eligible candidates for marriage had to go through official family channels to ask for your hand in marriage.

The wedding was a great success, considering that the food was cooked over open fires in giant pans and the musicians had no amplification. A large military-type marquee was erected on the street, blocking the traffic, in which neighbours and relatives gathered to celebrate the happy couple. Gullu kept beaming at everyone, unlike other brides I had seen. Maybe it was because this was a love match, not an arranged marriage, and since the bride and groom were related, the atmosphere was more relaxed with familiar faces on both sides of the family. I was impatient to dance with the others, in the middle of the tent, but Nana said I needed to be careful to strike the right balance between being visible to potential suitors and not appearing too eager to shine.

The morning after the wedding, I loitered outside the gates in the hope of getting to speak to Gullu about what had happened on the wedding night. Married women did not usually speak to unmarried girls about the mysteries involved until it was their turn, but surely, I thought, Gullu would share her experience with me, since we knew each other so well. Sadly, she had not emerged by the time I had to go to work.

★★★

Mahir was standing outside the building when I arrived. I slowed down, in the hope that he would go in, but to my surprise, he started walking towards me. We had hardly spoken in the past months. Momentarily, I wondered if he was coming to beg me for forgiveness, then I could move on with my life.

'We need to talk,' he said, 'about you. I've been hearing rumours.'

I stopped in my tracks. What did he know? Though I had wanted him to feel anguish, burn with jealousy and lose sleep over me, I was horrified to think someone else might know about my being at the motel. At least Mahir's raping me was a secret. If the "rumours" included the motel I would never live that down.

'It's got to stop!' he roared.

'What are you talking about? And why do you care anyway?' This was his chance to say sorry. Was I willing to forgive him? I did not know, but I knew that deep down a part of me missed him.

'I don't want you to become a hat passed from one head to another,' he said, like a stern father.

My fantasies of reconciliation vanished in an instant. I was enraged by his cheek, telling me off after all that he had done to me!

Before I could find the words to spew out my rage, Mahir turned away and greeted Seva who was coming up the street. They started up the steps together chatting, his hand on her back, leaving me standing there numbly staring after them.

When the nearby clock tower rang nine o'clock, prodding me out of my trance, I made my way to my chair in reception and, without a word to Arzu, I picked up the phone and dialled Musa's number. When he answered, I barked: 'I've changed my mind. The meeting at yours is on. Tomorrow.'

Arzu whooped when I put the receiver down and rushed to give me a hug. I beamed at her, though inside I felt deflated and empty.

★★★

The next day found Arzu and I standing in front of a five-storey building where Ilgar had just dropped us off. I lied to Nana that I was having a meal at Arzu's, so for once, I did not have to be home before dark. Ilgar had told us it was better for us to go up to the flat separately from him. 'Just in case. Second floor, the door on the left. You don't even have to knock. Musa saw us from his balcony.'

Arzu and I rushed into the building, hoping not to bump into any of the neighbours, but we saw no one on our way. Musa opened his door, and we blew in as fast as a blast of wind. I gave him a hug, shaking with relief. He ushered us into a stylish living room perfumed with the smell of kebabs. He switched off the large corner TV and, after fiddling with a remote control, the room filled with slow, ambient music from the stereo.

'What was on the TV? How come you have the voltage for it?' I asked him, shrugging off his attempts to kiss me before I'd got my cardigan off.

'For some reason, the authorities are more generous with the flats here, plus I have a back-up generator. I had the news on. It's a big day today. Didn't you know? Heydar Aliyev is signing the contract of the century.'

134

'What's that?' I was saying, when Ilgar arrived and Arzu flew to his arms as they loudly greeted each other. 'Can you two keep it down?' I snapped. Arzu pulled a face and dragged Ilgar to a sofa by the window to enjoy the view and his embrace.

Musa continued, 'I should have known you'd be interested. You haven't seen the news then? Aliyev is signing a contract with eleven multinational companies, for them to explore our oil reserves. It doesn't get bigger than this, Gulush. It will most likely give our economy a massive boost. Elchibey had started the process, but Surat's coup disrupted the negotiations. Mark my words!' He took a bottle of champagne from the bucket it was chilling in. 'The twentieth of September 1994 will be etched into the history of Azerbaijan. And hopefully,' he said, smiling at me, 'not just because of the contract of the century.' He poured us each a sparkling crystal glass full. 'Let's raise our glasses: to Azerbaijan and to us!'

We sat at the modern, black, smooth-topped table on soft embroidered-cushioned chairs. I vaguely wondered who had decorated them so carefully. An elderly relative, or Musa's own elegant wife, who smiled brightly at us from a wedding photograph on the wall? Musa had been handsome and thinner then. Was this the way all husbands went?

As the champagne tickled its way into my bloodstream, I decided to leave all my anxieties for another day and focus on the positive news. The oil contract had been signed and the ceasefire was holding, most of the time. Although there seemed no hope of resolution and occasional casualties on the borders were the norm, at least the enemy was not advancing on more regions.

I had finished my glass of champagne, even before Musa started serving us kebabs with fresh salad and flat breads, which were still warm. He must have collected the food minutes before we arrived.

'You can't let this style of kebab cool down. It needs to be enjoyed hot to appreciate the full effect of the herbs and spices.' He looked younger and more animated than I had ever seen him in his role as host. He even lit four, gold-dusted, red candles, in fluted silver holders, despite there being a dazzling cut-glass chandelier hanging overhead. I suddenly had an image of Nana, rheumy-eyed, struggling with a book in the dim light of her old lamp. She would never approve of such excess.

'How romantic,' Ilgar smiled, touching Arzu's hand mid-bite.

'It's in case the electricity goes out.' Musa grinned. 'We don't want to find ourselves in a dark room with such ladies. Or do we?' Arzu giggled and I felt the effect of what was clearly a sexual innuendo between my legs.

We ate heartily, finished the champagne and started on the vodka. I think I drank more than I had ever drunk before. My glass was constantly refilled, but my head was strangely clear as I surveyed what I decided, there and then, was my dream flat.

In addition to the large TV and the state-of-the-art sound system, there were many open shelves displaying a range of expensive plates and ornaments. A large sofa made of black leather was set on deep-pile, wall-to-wall carpets. They were probably pure wool. I suspected they must have a cleaner, if the rest of the flat was this tidy. This could be my life, I thought, if I married someone wealthy. Was it fair that some people seemed to have it all, while the rest of us struggled? However, could I see myself with a husband like Musa? How quickly had he lost interest in his wife? Was this lifestyle a good enough compensation for that? His efforts tonight might have charmed me, but I realised I still did not like him.

After our meal, Musa pulled me out of my musings by turning off the big chandelier and encouraging me to slow-dance with him. Arzu and Ilgar were already entwined, swaying gently to the music. I was a lot shorter than Musa. My head pressed into his chest. His bloated stomach thankfully kept me clear of his crotch while we moved to the melancholy harmonies. His hands skilfully caressed my back. After a few minutes, he started to dance me towards the door. I resisted at first, but he murmured, 'Let's give these two special people some privacy, shall we?'

He led me into a bedroom featuring a king-sized bed, covered with a delicate, pearl-coloured throw and matching cushions. The room was in stark contrast to the motel, spacious and light, full of expensive but tasteful furnishings. On an elegant bedside table sat a reminder of who chose the décor – a book with a tasselled bookmark in it, waiting for its mistress to return. I could not see the title, but the front cover sported flowers and a woman. I looked away. It felt so wrong to be in someone else's bedroom. The knowledge that Arzu and Ilgar were next door, already deflowering the family sofa, made the situation seem almost sordid.

'Come join me, Gulush,' Musa spoke softly, as he dimmed the lights with a switch by the bed. He was already lolling, naked on the throw, his stomach mound towering over his erection. 'There's no need to worry,' he added, reassuringly.

Musa didn't realise that my hesitation was more about where we were this time, rather than any fears about my purity, since I had already decided I could trust him. I stripped down slowly, crossed the sea of dark red, deep-pile carpet, crawled up onto the bed and knelt to pleasure him. Just a few minutes later, he gently flipped me onto my back. I gazed at a smaller, ruby-glass chandelier overhead, waiting for him to start rubbing his erection between my thighs, but his stomach got in the way again. He started to lift my legs up. I didn't like that. It made me feel too exposed.

'No, not like that,' I said.

'You need to relax,' he said, 'I know what I'm doing.' I felt something hard pressing on the entrance of my vagina.

I tensed up as I squealed, 'No, no, I don't want this.' I tried to wriggle out from under him, but he was too heavy, holding my thighs firmly, intent on what he was doing.

'It's perfectly all right to go in a little way. Don't worry, I know when to withdraw,' he said, but he wasn't looking at me. The intense concentration on his face was focused on himself and what was in his mind.

'Musa, you're hurting me! Stop, please, stop! I beg you, stop!' Panic choked me, as I was sure there was something trickling out of me.

'Keep still. You're spoiling it for us,' Musa said, groaning with effort.

'But you ARE hurting me!' Tears spilled from my eyes as I scrabbled with my feet on the slippery throw, trying to back away.

'Shush! The others might think something bad has happened.' He somehow loosened his grip and I managed to wriggle out at last.

In irate confusion, I was reaching to snatch up my clothes when I saw it, on the bed next to him – a patch of bright red blood, blooming into the shape of a carnation.

'You said you wouldn't…! I told you to stop! Look what you've done!'

For a split second, his eyes looked like those of a lost and confused child, as he stared at the seeping stain, then the man in him took over. He whipped the crumpled throw off the bed, then the top sheet below.

'It's cold water for blood, isn't it?' he mumbled to himself. 'Then a warm wash. There should be time to do that. But I don't know where the iron is.'

'That's your concern? The bed linen? You just ruined my life and that's what you're worrying about?! What am I going to do? Nana will throttle me!' I sobbed, my body rocking with shock, panic tearing at my lungs. My life was over.

It felt as if a part of me split in that moment, watching my broken, crumpled body on the floor, Musa standing up and dressing quickly to deal with bedding, my clothes in a heap by my side, until Arzu's tinkling laughter broke the spell and it was as if I woke up. No one, absolutely no one could find out about this disaster. I had to gather myself to end the evening as if nothing had happened; otherwise, I was doomed to die.

There I was, taking refuge in a toilet, yet again, having made another mistake that soap and water couldn't erase, my eyelids puffed red with tears. This time I didn't even try to tell myself off. The voices in my head were stunned into silence. After soaking my skin with a cold, wet, perfumed flannel, I repaired my make-up and smoothed down my clothes.

Arzu noticed there was something wrong as soon as I entered the living room, where she, Ilgar and Musa were smoking. My false smile was not bright enough to hide the hurt inside.

'Are you all right?' she said, coming to perch on the chair next to mine.

'It's late, I have to go home,' I said to the room, but whispered to Arzu, 'I've just started my period.' She nodded understandingly.

Musa was refilling our vodka glasses. 'One for the road then?' He was still smiling.

I automatically reached for my glass, hoping it would dull the pain, but my hand shook so much that I had to put it back down after barely a sip. I waited patiently while the others drank theirs, then we all walked to Ilgar's car. Musa, who hadn't yet spoken directly to me, tried to reach my cheek with a kiss goodbye, after I got in the back, but I had jammed myself so far up against the opposite door that he couldn't reach. It was too dark for the other two to notice. They just heard him say, 'We'll speak later, Gulush. It was a lovely evening,' as if everything was fine.

The car journey home was mental and physical torture for me. My body felt every bump in the road and, although I kept trying to say something light or funny to mask the misery I was in, I couldn't think of anything. My fear of the 'happy couple' figuring out what had happened was paralysing.

As I walked up our garden path, having waved the car away, I knew the show wasn't over. Now I had to fool Nana and deal with my bloodied underwear. I snuck into the back garden and rinsed the knickers under a cold tap. As the evidence disappeared into the sewer, the cold reality of the situation stung my heart as well as my sore, chilled hands. It felt like my life was over. I had had one virtue, and I had foolishly lost it to a man I did not even like, a man who, it turned out, had no care for me at all. After drying the knickers past the dripping stage with a rough towel, I crept into the bath house to dry them unseen. When I approached the kitchen door, I heard, with some relief, that Nana had a visitor. Neighbour Amaliya's joyful voice trilled in the living room. I could not help but listen.

'They finally did it,' she announced to Nana, obviously bursting with excitement. 'She's resting now. I made her special *guymag* to help her restore her energy. She's forbidden from doing any housework right now. Girls are so delicate when they've just lost their virginity. The last thing she needs is to be touching cold water.'

'Such an important milestone,' agreed Nana. 'It's always a relief when everything goes well on the wedding night. Little wonder you're so proud. Tomorrow you'll be able to display the bloody sheet for everyone to know that she was pure.'

Every word they said stabbed me to my core. I had failed Nana, who had tried so hard to protect me. I believed I would never get the same gentle care that Gullu was now receiving. The reality of the situation chilled my heart as deeply as the water had numbed my trembling, sore hands.

★★★

I ran into Gullu about a week later, as she was leaving Amaliya's. The late September sun was still warm but without the threat of sunburn. It was the quiet time, around 7.30am, when children left for school and when the few still lucky to be employed in the factories left for work. Gullu's round, dimpled face seemed to be glowing with happiness, as she waved to me.

'Lovely to see you, Gulush,' she said, as I tried to act like my old self and hugged her.

I couldn't stop myself from asking: 'How was it?'

'Oh that,' she laughed, visibly torn between her desire to spill the beans and respecting my virginal status. 'It was great, eventually,' she said, looking down to straighten her brand-new floral dress.

'Do you like it?' I pressed her. She blushed but was obviously pleased to be asked.

'Well, I don't think he's very good at considering me. He gets his pleasure and then leaves me hanging. But I'm not having that,' she said, firmly, 'so we'll be working on it.'

She expected pleasure too? I was amazed. I had worried about Mahir getting an erection without a release, in case it made him impotent, as I had heard it could. Now my concerns for him seemed laughable.

'I had better go now. He'll be wondering what I'm up to if I'm gone too long. You'll be finding out about all this for yourself soon enough, Gulush.' She planted a kiss on my cheek like she was now my aunty or something and scurried off.

# 8.

# A NEW FRIEND

I refused to see Musa after what had happened, but he kept ringing. We had a number of heated discussions. I told him he had ruined my life. He, without caring, complained how hard it was for him. His local laundrette had not managed to remove the bloodstain and his wife had found out that he had had 'some woman' in their marital bed. She was understandably furious. He told me sadly that they were rowing every day. He expected me to feel sorry for him. I wanted him to burn in hell. I was sure in time he would, for he had no remorse about what he had done to me. He said I was making too much of a fuss. He claimed that when the same thing had happened with a girl in Shamakhi, where he used to work, she had told him not to worry, that she'd 'stitch herself up' and would be 'as good as new to marry anyone she wanted'. His last words to me before I slammed the phone down were: 'If you call someone a pig a lot, sooner or later they will start oinking.'

I had no one I could share all this with. I believed I would never be able to marry anyone now, so I needed time to figure out what to do next. I hardly spoke to Arzu. I threw myself into my studies and doubled my productivity at work. When she tried to organise other "outings", I always said no. Consequently, it didn't take long for Arzu, as Mahir had done, to gravitate towards merry Seva. This further alienated me from Arzu. I did not know where her loyalties would lie. We had shared so much, but I never trusted her discretion. I thought she suspected something had happened that night. Who would she share her guesswork with? To control the rumours, I thought it was best for me to concentrate on working hard and not socialising, until all was forgotten. I had no idea what I was going to do after that, especially if my family pressed me to marry. I spent the days that followed in a numb stupor, lacking interest in anything, forcing smiles when visitors arrived and covering Arzu's absences from the reception area with a grey and heavy heart.

The only person who noticed a change in me was the Prosecutor's brother, Dr Adil; a short, balding, benign man. Maybe this was because he was a medical doctor, but every time he visited, he spoke to me and asked me how I was doing. My polite smiles and vague answers did not seem to satisfy him. 'This is my number,' he said one day, when I was feeling particularly depressed. 'Call me if you need to, about anything.'

I thanked him and secreted the piece of paper in my drawer, under a stapler. There was no way I would call him. He was my boss's brother; I couldn't jeopardise my job as well.

As the days passed, my feelings about Arzu's desertion of me grew darker. Being alone in reception, listening to the others laughing down the corridor became harder. While I understood that to Arzu I was no longer the fun, light and cooperative Gulush she had known, I hated the

144

idea that she preferred their company to mine. Then, one day, she betrayed me.

When a colleague's mother died, it was decided that the entire staff would go together to pay our respects to the family. Mahir was assigned to drive the women. I sat quietly beside Arzu, in the back seat, fighting with the memories of my last trip in that car. Mahir seemed unconcerned. He cracked jokes and enjoyed Seva's company in the front. I wondered if he would drop everyone else off first, like he used to. Perhaps if we had a chance to talk, he might finally apologise. Then I might forgive him. However, after an hour at the gathering where all the women dressed in black wailed for the deceased, we trouped back to the car and Mahir announced that he would drop me off first. Clearly, he wanted to get rid of me so he could carry on having fun with Seva and Arzu. I protested. Seva lived on the way to mine. All three of them shrugged off my objections. I hoped that at least Arzu would be on my side, but I sensed that they might have made plans to have fun that did not include me.

After making some acid remark about threesomes, I demanded that Mahir stop the car straight away and I stomped the rest of the way home in a fury.

Now, hearing their laughter brought me visceral pain, aching through every cell of my body. Crouching over my work, I lost my fight against a flood of helpless tears. There was nothing that I could do to hurt Mahir or Musa. They had got away with what they had done and would no doubt move onto someone else. I was sitting, semi-collapsed in my self-pity, when Dr Adil walked in. Caught off guard, I sat up, trying to smile, but it was too late.

'Are you going to tell me what's going on with you? It's most worrying to find you like this.'

'It's nothing, honestly,' I said softly, 'just a headache.'

'No, no, I'm not buying that. I can see that you need to talk to someone. Obviously,' he pointed meaningfully at Arzu's chair, 'your friends are not available.' A burst of laughter floated in from the corridor. 'Give me your phone number and we will speak after work.'

His voice sounded so full of authority and wisdom that, without any further objections, I scribbled down my home phone number and passed it on to him. I was so lonely and wretched I thought I might as well.

From that day on, Dr Adil became my confidant. Of course, I couldn't tell him everything, but at least I got to release some of the pressure I felt from bottling everything up. I talked about Nana's cold house, wearing my coat all the time and having to share her bed for warmth all winter, my study sessions in Baku and my adoration of Amina, without mentioning her profession. I shared my restlessness being in Ganja and my burning desire for a more exciting life. Dr Adil was a good listener, but sometimes he asked questions: 'How come you're not married yet? You are such a beautiful woman.'

'I'll never marry,' I replied with a sigh.

'Of course you will. You just haven't met the right man yet.'

I let him think he'd convinced me, but inside he never did. Marriage was a door forever closed to me, I believed. Some women might have the resources to 'restore' their virginity, surgically, or by spilling a hidden vial of blood on their wedding bed, but I knew I wouldn't be able to stand

146

the pressure of such lies. Telling the truth was not an option either, in case my partner either rejected and exposed me, or accepted my fault initially, then used it against me for the rest of my life.

★★★

The Prosecutor's wife was refusing to move to Ganja from Baku, so he divided his time between the cities, taking Mahir with him for many days at a time. It felt calmer without them around, even though Arzu and I were no longer allies. Some errands still needed to be run in Mahir's absence, so the Prosecutor hired Vafadar as a second driver for the office. Vafadar was in his late twenties, shy and skinny with curly light-brown hair. He preferred to spend most of his time waiting by the car, ready to whizz off on any errand requested. He had some problem with his teeth, two of his front ones were missing. This probably accounted for his shyness, and why he seldom smiled. To escape the awkward silences in reception, I asked him if he would give me some driving lessons during the lunch breaks. I was delighted when he agreed with the same enthusiasm as he showed to any request. He took me out for a blissful hour of driving instruction, in the less busy neighbourhoods, every day the Prosecutor was in Baku.

'You must learn to trust your own judgement,' he said when I asked whether I should pull out on the junction. 'Can you exit fast enough, before the oncoming vehicle reaches us?'

I did not always judge things exactly right, but my confidence grew every day, especially when I was on deserted roads. Then I could drive fast. I loved the sensation. It felt like all my worries were blown away. Vafadar would sit calmly in the passenger seat and even smiled when I revved the car and revelled in getting it up to 110km an hour.

My friendship with him was soon noticed by my colleagues, especially because I would ask Vafadar for a lift home, while the other girls were happy to pile into Mahir's car. Vafadar was always respectful towards me. He did not attempt to cross any boundaries. I felt safer with him than anyone else in the office. Since I had never warmed to the new investigation staff, who had replaced my original colleagues, or even Farid *muellim*, apart from Vafadar, I was now a loner at work, as well as at home. I eagerly counted down the days to my next study sessions when I could be reunited with Amina and the fun of being around her. In the meantime, the loneliness was utterly unbearable, and I started to rebel against it.

One day, as I was getting ready to leave for home, I heard male and female voices coming from a ground floor office. It sounded like they were having a good time. My curiosity drew me down the stairs to Nazim's office, where I found seven investigators, along with Mahir, Seva and Arzu, having shots of vodka.

'What's happening?' I said cheerfully from the open door. I wasn't going to let on that I was hurt that no one had bothered to invite me.

'I thought you would have heard the news?' said Nazim, smiling. 'I've just been promoted. I'm going to be a senior investigator in Baku.'

'I haven't heard the news, probably because unfortunately everyone upstairs forgot to tell me,' I said sarcastically. I beamed a warm smile at Nazim as he passed me a shot of vodka. 'Congratulations, Nazim *muellim*! You'll find Baku a far better place to be,' I said, knocking the shot back in one. Mahir had warned me only to drink alcohol after food to avoid getting drunk, but that day I decided I wanted to. I stalked into the room and sat right next to Nazim; although I liked him the least, he had the bottle. Though tall, he was wiry, with thin features and had always seemed too meticulous to me, both in his appearance and his work, in a way that felt rigid and tight. He was the person who requested the most retyping.

After we'd all had three shots of vodka, Mahir got up to leave and came to shake Nazim's hand. As the others cheered Nazim opening another bottle, Mahir whispered to me, 'I need to have a word with you.'

Was he going to apologise? Reluctantly, I followed him to the doorway.

'You've had enough. Let me take you home.'

'What do you care?' I hissed. 'It's none of your business. And...' I'd caught sight of Vafadar in the lobby, 'I have a lift home anyway.' I strolled towards Vafadar, taking care to walk straight. I asked him to take me home after the party and he agreed with his usual enthusiasm. I returned to Nazim's office in time to see Arzu and Seva make their exits. Doubtless Mahir was to be their chauffeur. That thought infuriated me so much that I washed it away with another vodka. One by one, those remaining left too, but I didn't notice. I sat at the table trying to silence my inner demons by refilling my empty glass. How dare Mahir pretend he cared about me after all he had done? I was so incensed I did not realise that Nazim and I were alone, until I heard the clunk as he closed his door.

'I have always fancied you,' he said. I stood up, but not fast enough. He grasped my hips with his bony hands. 'Beautiful Gulush,' he murmured. My brain was too soused to move my body. Nazim pushed me back onto his desk amongst the case files. The alcohol had temporarily loosened my usual inhibitions. As he deftly snaked his hands under my shirt, I felt myself starting to respond to his touch. Then he pushed up the silky fabric and my bra, baring my breasts. He gripped them with his long fingers and slurred, 'I love your titties.'

That word, "titties", shot through my head with sobering disgust. I pushed him away and sprang to my feet, grabbed my handbag and fled to the door with a backwards: 'I have to go now.' He was obviously in no state to stop me.

As I picked my way carefully through the dusky building to the car park, I hated the realisation that Mahir had been right, this time. If I had left when he'd suggested, I would have escaped the indignity of being groped again. The idea that Nazim might boast to our colleagues worried me; every incident like this was seen as a gold star on a man's track record, and a black mark on a woman's.

'Are you OK?' Vafadar asked from the shadows by the car, making me jump.

'No,' I answered, without elaborating.

As I went to get in the passenger side, he said, 'Want to do some night driving? It might cheer you up.'

I hesitated, listening to the debate in my head. The sensible thing would be to admit I was drunk and get Vafadar to drive me home. I was too angry, though, and craved distraction. The speed would probably sober me up as well as liberate me from all my cares.

'Great idea,' I said and glided behind the steering wheel, eager to start. I let Vafadar run through the key points about night driving, although his calm tones drifted into my ears without connecting with my brain. Then I manoeuvred perfectly out of the car park, which boosted my confidence. We headed into the countryside, once I had mastered the headlights.

The drive was exhilarating. All my senses seemed heightened. I felt truly alive for the first time since everything went so terribly wrong with Mahir and Musa. I laughed joyfully, letting the speed creep up to 110km an hour. We swept past the silhouettes of trees, barns and beasts in the fields. Where to? I didn't mind – until Vafadar said, 'You're doing so well, Gulush,' and stroked the back of my head.

I stiffened. *Not you too*. What was the matter with men? Or was there something about me? I shuddered, my hands momentarily slackening on the wheel. Vafadar shouted something. He reached for the wheel then…

Crash. Black. Silence.

The next thing I heard was a distant voice asking me if I was all right. My head was ringing, I tasted blood in my mouth. I had smashed my face on the steering wheel. My height had saved me from worse. We had no seat belts in the cars. My chest felt sore and my right foot was jammed under one of the pedals. Vafadar was groaning next to me and, when I managed to look at him properly, there was blood on his forehead.

'Let's get you out of here,' Vafadar croaked.

I realised in horror that the front of the car was buckled in. We had hit a large tree. I dragged myself out of the car, crying with panic and remorse. Two of my front teeth were broken and my ankle felt painfully swollen.

I gasped as Vafadar hobbled towards me, blood all down his work suit.

'I'm so sorry,' I said. I started to shake with shock as well as the cold. I could have killed him, killed us. What would Nana have thought of me being found dead, drunk, on a deserted road with a male stranger? It would have disgraced the whole family, and if there was a post-mortem, everyone would have known that...

'You have not been here, Gulush,' said Vafadar gently. 'I'll take care of this. We must get you back home.'

We stood by the side of the road until a lone car approached and kindly stopped to give me a lift to Nana's.

Once home, despite being sore and still woozy, I played my part well, and convinced Nana that a tragic accident had been averted when a child had run into the road and Vafadar had had to choose between hitting the child or a tree. Luckily, I was able to include Arzu and Seva in my version of events because Nana didn't know any of their families or anyone in their neighbourhoods. However, she insisted on calling an ambulance and getting dressed to go with me to the hospital. 'You are covered in blood, Gulush. Your teeth are broken. Your ankle may be too and who knows what else?'

As she fussed about, I reached out to the only person I thought could help with the situation. I dialled and prayed no one else would answer. 'Dr Adil, it's me, Gulush. I crashed Vafadar's car, he's been teaching me to drive. He's going to need help. Please can you make sure he doesn't get into trouble? I'm not sure he has enough money to get it repaired. It was all my fault.' I spoke urgently.

'Don't worry. I'll speak to Vafadar about the car. But tell me now, are you all right?'

'I hurt all over. I'm waiting at Nana's for the ambulance, for Central Hospital.'

'I'll see you there. I won't approach you openly, but I'll make sure that you're taken care of.'

I put the phone down just in time, as both Nana's bedroom door and the entrance door to the house were flung open simultaneously. Trembling all over, a blanket draped over me, I was guided into the ambulance with Nana at my side.

My ankle hurt so badly when I got to the hospital that I couldn't put my weight on it and I had to be half carried by the ambulance crew into an examination cubicle. I had glimpsed Dr Adil's worried face as he shadowed our progress. As good as his word, he had obviously pulled some strings for me. I didn't have to wait and was taken for several X-rays. There was extensive painful bruising on my neck, torso and spine. My ankle was fractured. They told me that though it would hurt as it mended, it shouldn't result in any lasting weakness. I was so relieved there was no sign of a head injury or anything else life threatening, but, as a nineteen-year-old, I was devastated when the dental specialist said I would need false front teeth. I was discharged after they had plastered my ankle and given me strict instructions to rest, but no pain relief. I was in as much pain when I left as when I arrived.

The next days were a mixture of bliss and agony. On

the bliss side, I had a legitimate excuse not to go to work, so had a rest from all those hateful faces; Nana was wonderful, treating me to clotted cream and honey, and I could stay in bed, chatting to Dr Adil on the phone when Nana was out. On the agony side, I was in constant pain while my body healed, especially at night, which made sleep almost impossible. I couldn't even groan or easily change positions but had to stay still and quiet so as not to wake up Nana who was still sleeping next to me.

As soon as I was able to walk again, I went to see a dentist, who understood my needs. He managed to fit perfect caps onto the remains of my front teeth, so I didn't have to have a set of false teeth after all. I felt much better now that my looks were restored.

Dr Adil suggested I might like a day in the countryside in the fresh air. He collected me one morning after I made a pretence to Nana that I was going back to work. Dr Adil drove me to see a farm that he owned. It was larger and quieter than I had expected. He explained that over the winter most activities took place inside the many out-buildings, not in the fields, so we would be able to stroll in the fresh air, across the land, quite privately. As we did so, I noticed how calming his gentle presence was to me, even when we talked about the car accident.

'Vafadar is recovering well, he sends his regards,' he said. 'His car was given a complete overhaul and my dear brother is none the wiser. I took care of it all.' My heart swelled with gratitude. I felt so lucky to know such a kind person. We stopped, so I could rest my leg. 'Now you can tell me the truth,' he continued. 'What really happened that night?'

I winced at the question. Then I sighed. 'I was drunk,'

I confessed, hanging my head.

'You were what?' He looked genuinely alarmed. 'Do you realise how lucky you were? You could have died. I can't believe…'

'I know, I know,' I interrupted him, 'I wasn't thinking straight. Perhaps… at the time… a part of me… wanted to die.'

'What do you mean?' He stared at me, like he was trying to read my thoughts. 'What has happened to you to make you like this? I remember how you were not so long ago. You've lost that sparkle, your eyes look so sad sometimes, almost haunted. You must tell me why!'

I could not lie any more. The dam I had created to hold in my sorrows cracked open and everything flooded out as I sobbed my story into his arms.

'My life is over. It's all over. I made such mistakes. I lost my virginity. I can never have a future. Not one like other girls can!'

He said nothing for a while, as if considering what to say. I watched a flock of birds wheeling over the fields, swooping in patterns across the sky. Then he took my hands in his. 'What a silly girl you have been. Is that all that is worrying you?' He laughed softly. 'I think if a man truly loves you, that sort of thing would never be a barrier.'

'That's what you say, because you're not looking to marry me. That's not what young men and their families would say.'

He reached out his hands to my face and kissed me on my flaming cheeks. His kisses landed soft as butterfly wings on my skin and melted away all my defences.

'Let's go somewhere private. We won't be doing

anything you don't want to, and I won't be boasting of any conquest to anyone. We'll just talk and enjoy each other's company. My dad has a beautiful flat. He's been using it to see his mistress for years,' he said, 'and I've got the keys. They're both out of town right now, so… Come on, you know you're safe with me.'

He looked so sincere in that moment. I was aware that he might just be taking advantage of my vulnerability. He was nearly forty, like my mum, twice my age, but I didn't care as I craved comfort and more beautiful days, to keep my mind free of the past. Besides which, I still felt I had nothing more to lose.

★★★

Physically, Dr Adil was a gentle man. With him, I taught myself to be a woman. I learnt different sexual positions, and the art of faking an orgasm. To start with, I had no clue what I was doing or how to fully relax, but he never seemed to mind, he enjoyed being with me. Our secret affair continued through early 1995. I did not like all the sneaking around, but there was no other way. Afterwards, as we sipped cheap champagne and munched Ferrero Raffaello coconut and almond pralines, I would sometimes smile inside and admit to myself that I too enjoyed our encounters. We even dined out together in Baku. He took me to an upmarket café near the university that served extravagant dishes like julienne de champignons, a French-Russian dish of mushrooms, cream and Comté cheese in a dill and garlic-infused béchamel sauce. As well as buying me meals, he would take me to his brother's summer house with sauna and swimming pool. When he first offered me money, two hundred US dollars, to spend on whatever I wanted, I refused it, but he didn't take my 'no' for an answer. Reluctantly, I accepted his money and squirrelled it away for a rainy day.

My relationship with him was the only thing that kept me going during the long days at work. I knew I could not quit my job without raising Nana's suspicions that something was wrong. As the main breadwinner in the family, I could not afford to be that irresponsible and my job served as a cover for my liaisons with Dr Adil. Without it, I would have had to stay at home. I became an efficient, empty shell at work and saved my vitality for the privacy of our borrowed love nest. As the ceasefire with Armenia had stabilised our country, my relationship with Dr Adil stabilised me; but both were temporary. There was no long-term future for us. I did not want to end my days with being a mistress as my greatest achievement.

9.

# DELUSIONS

My recklessly regular "appointments" with the doctor broke up the monotony of my existence in Ganja, but deep down, I wanted so much more from life, even though I did not really know what that was or how I was going to get it. I hated feeling like I was damaged goods, worthless and unlovable, with little to look forward to. I ached to cast off my community's straitjacket of expectations about being a "good girl". I wanted to explore all possibilities; to have a profession and my own house, to travel and to have fun. But a crippling terror lurked in my mind, telling me that it was only a matter of time before I was pushed into an arranged marriage. What would happen to my dreams then? I did not know.

I carried my woes to work every day, like a farm labourer lugging an oversized sack of potatoes to market. The effort left me bitter and withdrawn, with hardly a good word for anyone. At home, the mask of dutiful, smiling child got harder to wear. I think Nana noticed and wasn't convinced by any of my cover stories – study headaches, my period, too much typing, having insomnia – but she lacked the energy to keep quizzing me, having endured another winter of power cuts and meagre meals. Some days, it was as if we were two befuddled bears forced to hibernate together.

By the time I reached my twentieth birthday in March 1995, I had really started to appreciate the sweetness of having a "sugar daddy". Although Dr Adil's gifts were limited to special occasions and not what I considered transactional, I began to understand Amina's choices in life, albeit on a much smaller scale.

Seeing my distress, Nana decided to throw me a birthday party that year. When I tried to object, she brushed off my reservations. 'You haven't had a birthday celebration since you were five! Twenty is a big milestone.'

'But Nana,' I argued, 'there's no one I want to invite. I don't know where any of my school friends have got to and it's too far for the students to come,' I lied. 'And you know I prefer to keep work and home life separate.'

She invited the entire staff of the Prosecutor's Office by calling Arzu personally on the reception number and asking her to pass the message on. My birthday fell on Sunday and the guests were requested to arrive at 6pm.

It took days to get everything ready. I had to clean the entire main house as Nana had decided to host it in the drawing room. I cursed the day I was born as I watched her struggling to cook my favourite dishes on a combination of open fires and electric hot plates. She spent two days on preliminary preparations. It took hours to boil vegetables for a Russian-style salad, which I chopped into pea-sized chunks. I minced fresh locally sourced lamb and onions, which she seasoned with salt, pepper, crushed mint and basil for me to wrap in individual pickled vine leave parcels. She insisted I bought sweets and cakes from a newly opened shop that stocked imported Turkish and Iranian produce. There was also to be alcoholic beverages, for the men.

On the day, Nana made *pilav* with caramelised onions, lamb and all the other trimmings. By the time guests started to arrive, we were both worn out. I plastered a smile on my face and led guests into the drawing room. The atmosphere there was chilly, partly because it was difficult to heat and partly because of the social tensions. However, my colleagues ate all the food with enthusiasm and, each time Nana brought in another dish, they thanked her profusely for being such a splendid cook. She beamed with delight.

Then they took it in turns to make pompous speeches about my virtues, which made me squirm with embarrassment. Their largely empty words reminded me of when the men had raised toasts to women at the International Women's Day celebration. That was the day it had all started with Mahir. I felt suddenly angry. How dare he show up to this party? He should have had the decency to make his excuses. I glared in his direction, but he was clearly intent on eating and drinking.

Nana was oblivious to all this. 'I liked your colleagues,' she said afterwards, 'they are so serious.' She hated people who were giggly and immature. 'I'm so happy you work in such a mature environment. It's shaping you into someone responsible.'

It was almost funny. As I hugged Nana and thanked her for all her efforts, it was hard to hide my tears.

★★★

The twentieth year of my life, which seemed to have started on the wrong foot, fell further downhill after the party. Nana became ill and, no matter how many doctors we visited and how many appointments we paid for, no one could confidently diagnose her condition. She was in agonising pain much of the time, describing it as being like someone was chopping up her innards. I felt helpless and scared, remembering Baba's final years when I had had to become his carer aged thirteen. What if Nana required the same level of care? How would I ever graduate from university? Who would pay our extra bills?

The atmosphere was heavy at home and unbearable at work. I felt so guilty for ruining Vafadar's car that I withdrew even further into my shell. Every day, I couldn't wait for the workday to be over, but didn't want to rush home either. To prolong the inevitable return to where Nana groaned with pain and I felt helpless, I started walking home after work. The spring evenings felt gentle, and I started wearing the clothes I'd bought in Baku; the bright wrap skirt with splashes of yellow, turquoise and pink, which was well matched with my tight turquoise or fuchsia tops. It was hard to walk fast in my high heels, so I often took my time getting home.

One evening, as the warm wind ruffled my short hair and tried to blow my wrap skirt open, a car slowed down next to me. At first, I thought it was one of my colleagues who wanted to give me a lift, but I soon realised that I didn't know the handsome young man behind the wheel, so I turned away and refused to acknowledge him. I was somewhat annoyed and yet also intrigued that he drove slowly besides me for the next ten minutes. Luckily, I managed to turn into a side street and lose him. The next day, he was in a similar location, intent on getting my attention. I looked for opportunities to change my familiar route, again both irritated but curious about his advances. I stayed strong in my reluctance to engage with him. Hadn't I got enough problems in my life without getting involved with a complete stranger? To be on the safe side, I took the bus for a couple of days in the hope that he would give up stalking me.

When I ventured walking home again a few days later, there he was at the regular spot at the usual time.

'Please, please, just get in the car. I swear to Allah, I just want to speak to you and you're attracting far too much attention to yourself this way.'

As if on cue, a driver in a passing car leant on his horn and leered at us unhelpfully. Against all my better judgement, I opened the back door of his car and climbed in.

'Finally,' he sighed with relief. 'You're certainly tough work to get to know. I'm Tamerlan by the way. It's nice to meet you. And you are?' He paused meaningfully, his deep dark eyes peering intently at me through the rearview mirror.

'What do you want?' I had no intention of disclosing any details to him at this stage of our conversation.

'Nothing!' He beamed, turning towards me with an open, friendly face while skilfully navigating the busy road. He was a good-looking young man with a shock of dark hair, a big smile and was probably not that much older than me. 'I just want to get to know you.'

'Why?' I demanded.

'Is that a crime?' He laughed heartily. 'Listen, I know it's not a thing in Ganja, but I have spent the last few years working in Turkey where people don't hold back from getting to know each other. You seem different, not like the other girls in Ganja. I'm genuinely curious.'

Something in his mannerisms had a relaxing effect on me. He seemed like a sweet guy who wanted connection. In truth, so did I.

'Do you mind if I drive around for a bit for us to chat?' he asked. 'I promise I'll drop you off wherever you wish at whatever hour that's convenient for you.'

'My grandmother is ill, so I can't linger long, but...' I checked my wristwatch. 'I can spare fifteen minutes and I want you to drop me off near the textile factory.'

'Consider it done!' He saluted to me as if I was a military officer and I couldn't help but laugh.

Tamerlan was like a breath of fresh air. He spoke without holding back and, within ten minutes, I found out that we went to the same school, he was nine years older than me, his family arranged a marriage that he was forced to accept, he had a shop not far from my house, and he regularly travelled to Turkey to buy provisions for it.

By the time he was dropping me off, I felt at ease with him, so when he invited me to have a meal out with him, without giving it a second thought, I said yes. What did I have to lose, after all?

We agreed to meet two days later. I managed to make excuses at work and left earlier than usual. I didn't give him my work address but met him at a bus stop.

Tamerlan was easy company. He made me laugh a lot, recounting anecdotes from our school years.

'When I was in my final year, the school director asked me to decorate the school hall. Do you remember anything unusual about the balloons in your first year?' he asked.

'Not really,' I shrugged. 'What about them?'

'Well, the school director gave me money to buy some balloons but some guys and I went out and bought a bottle of champagne instead. There wasn't enough money for balloons, but I managed to persuade a blushing young pharmacist to sell me ten packs of outdated condoms, which we inflated to decorate the school hall. No one said a word, but those who were in on the joke giggled the whole evening.'

We laughed, imagining the reaction of the adults who may have realised why all the balloons were mono-coloured.

'You know, I've never seen a condom,' I confided in him.

'I know, men here think it somehow reduces their sensitivity, but frankly it's stupid. When I'm in Turkey, I'm not prepared to take any risks. Besides, poor women here have to use abortion as the only means of contraception. It's so wrong! It's bad for their health, emotionally too.'

I didn't even notice how we made it to a restaurant, similar to the one I'd been to with Mahir, Arzu and Farid *muellim* in Hajikand all those moons ago when life was so normal – when I was so normal.

Tamerlan clocked my temporary collapse.

'You OK to come in? I can drive us back if you don't like this.' He spoke with such genuine concern.

'No, no, I'm OK to come in.'

The meal was nice, but talking was even better. It

seemed that no topic was off-limits and Tamerlan appeared to be brutally honest. Yes, he slept around when he was in Turkey. He cared about his wife, but he wasn't in love with her. He told me about his first sexual experiences, shockingly with one of our schoolteachers who seduced him. I watched his animated gestures, the way his lean, muscular body moved in his black shirt and tight jeans, and the sparkle in his eyes, and realised that I was smitten.

From that day on, we met as regularly as we could, walking in parks, driving aimlessly in the countryside and going for meals, talking incessantly about anything and everything. I felt no pressure from him to have sex. Tamerlan seemed genuinely caring, and this was the closest to feeling in love I had ever felt.

'Would you let me love you up?' he asked one day, after we had a meal out. It was getting dark, but he let me drive his car on the winding country roads, speeding up into the starry evening. 'My friend is away at the moment and we could go to his flat.'

I said yes. I didn't feel judged by Tamerlan, nor did I feel any need to explain what had happened. It was my first experience of making love, even though I knew I shouldn't love someone else's husband.

When Dr Adil came back from his family holiday, I decided it was too risky to break up with him in case he started asking too many questions. I blamed my lack of availability on Nana's health and saw him on rare occasions when Tamerlan was in Turkey.

***

Much to everyone's relief, including mine, by the time the summer exam session of 1995 arrived, Nana was no worse. Suju, one of Mama's cousins, who had been popping in to check on Nana when I was at work, agreed to stay there full time for a while. I headed for Baku, along with another gift from Dr Adil. This time, I decided to take it easy and just bribe my way through the exams like Amina did. All that stress and effort was really not worth it, I thought. I still attended classes but didn't visit the library once. Instead, I spent most afternoons with Amina and her cousins on the shores of the Caspian Sea. We went to private beaches, not the public ones I used to go to with my family. There were white plastic recliners to rest on, changing rooms and even showers. The heat was scorching and I tanned quickly to a deep brown. Amina used sunscreen, something I had never seen before. As a child, I had been expected to burn until I blistered and could then peel my skin off.

Splashing in warm water with the girls reminded me of playing there with Mama when I was little, but I tried to push the memory away, since it only led me to worrying about her financial situation. I even felt guilty when Amina took us to expensive restaurants, thinking of my siblings perhaps hungry, while I was being treated to starters and kebabs; although the reality was that I couldn't do anything about that.

I knew I needed to let go of my worries and enjoy my freedom while it lasted, though ghostly images of what had happened in Ganja and Nana's continued ill health haunted me in every quiet moment. If Nana became terminally ill, she could insist I marry so that I would not be left alone. Moving in with Mama in her borrowed flat was not an option, physically or financially. Each time I looked at myself in a restroom mirror as I reapplied my make-up, in my stylish and glamorous clothes, I was ever more determined to enjoy what there was to enjoy and leave the suffering for later. I was Amina's shadow, though I could not for the life of me fathom why she invited me out all the time. I was deeply grateful for the experiences she had given me, which I was not likely to have otherwise. In the background, as each exam slid by effortlessly, thanks to my dollar bills, my dread of returning to Ganja grew stronger and stronger. Even Tamerlan's presence there didn't make it appealing enough.

★★★

When I arrived back, I found that Nana was now seriously ill. She had forbidden Suju to try to contact me. I turned again to Dr Adil, who sent specialist after specialist, but they all failed to relieve Nana's growing discomfort. As the autumn deepened, the situation was becoming hopeless. As much as I hated going to work, I now also struggled to cope at home. Helplessly listening to Nana's never-ending groans of pain at night robbed me of most of my sleep and, despite Suju's help, the endless parade of concerned visitors and medics left me even less time to study, rest or even speak with Tamerlan.

A solution came miraculously, when Uncle Salman, who lived in Moscow, unexpectedly contacted us saying he had found a specialist who would be willing to treat Nana. He insisted she should fly out to Russia immediately, so Suju and I packed her some winter clothes and I bought her a flight to Moscow.

'You realise that I may not return, Gulush?' she said, embracing me, as I tried not to cry.

'Don't say that, Nana. Please get better soon and come home.'

Nana tried to press some money into my hand, but I refused it. 'I'll be paid soon, Nana. You need this more than me.'

We were parted abruptly by the taxi arriving to take her to the airport. I waved her away, trying to look as cheerful as I could, for the watching neighbours, but I spent that first evening alone stirring restlessly through my past. It seemed that everyone left me behind sooner or later. My parents had separated when I was three weeks old because my dad's extreme jealousy made him violent and unpredictable. My Mama, when she remarried, had left me behind with Baba and Nana. My uncles, who now lived in Moscow, didn't show any concern for me either. People like Dr Adil and Tamerlan were nice but if they had to choose between me and their family, I'd never be a priority.

Alone in the deserted house, my mind ran back again to the days when our household had been a bustling fifteen souls strong. I smiled at the images of hot meals enthusiastically shared with family and neighbours alike, of the stairs stacked with all manner of visitors' shoes, of me and my young cousins running in and out of the garden, being alternately scolded, or rewarded with treats. I wept at the visions of Baba dying, the rooms crowded with mourners, the women wailing and me, kneeling beside them, trying to imitate them but not really knowing how. Now they were all gone, and it was just me, empty rooms and the cold November of 1995.

I stood up and started to pace the room, my breath hanging like clouds in the dying daylight. There were positives to this situation, I reminded myself. Now that Nana was away, I didn't have to justify leaving my job. I decided I would quit in the morning, ending my torment. I'd never have to see Mahir, Arzu or the rest of them ever again, I thought. What would I do instead? I was scared of the unknown, but a feeling of urgency surged up inside me and I knew I could not spend another day shutting myself down because of my phoney friends and my secret rapist.

After what felt like the longest night of my life, during which I had alternately dozed and tidied, I gathered my sparse belongings into Mama's discarded maroon glide-along suitcase, dressed warmly and smartly and slipped out of the house, locking all the doors. I put the bunch of well-worn keys into an envelope, with a few dollars for Suju, together with a note saying I was going to my study session in Baku, asking her to take care of the house for a while and promising I would be in touch soon. I posted it carefully through her brass letterbox, taking care not to let it snap shut. Then I headed to the nearest ticket office, waited impatiently for it to open, lest I'd be spotted by a neighbour, and treated myself to a single plane ticket to Baku.

I didn't phone anyone from work, Dr Adil or Tamerlan. I feared that Dr Adil would have felt duty bound to tell his brother. And Tamerlan? He was a part of my life in Ganja. I was leaving all that behind me. I smiled as I boarded the plane, as hope and anticipation, long dormant emotions, rose up from deep within as I flew high over the clouds, in clear blue skies, towards Baku.

As the plane touched down, I decided to head straight for Amina's flat. She was surprised to see me but welcomed me warmly. I think one look at my pale face and tired eyes told her all she needed to know at that moment. She chivvied me into the kitchen, asked her cousins to prepare a delicious cold chicken salad with warmed flat breads, while we sipped on a cup of tea. I told her about Nana's illness and that I had decided it was time to leave Ganja and my job. Then I nervously broached the subject of why. I hadn't planned to tell her straight away, but I felt I had no other option.

'I need to tell you something else,' I said, after taking a larger than usual gulp of tea.

'You sound so serious, Gulush. Nothing can be that bad.'

'I'm not a virgin any more,' I declared, cutting through her smile.

'What? When did it happen?'

'Last year,' I said blankly. 'It wasn't my choice.'

'Right,' she touched my hand, 'I understand. But you didn't tell me? Why not? You don't look so well. You're not pregnant, are you?'

'No, no, nothing like that. I just needed to get some space between me and…'

'I wish you'd told me sooner.' She stretched out on the sofa. 'We've had such an amazingly busy time this year. Men were paying a lot of money for just going out for a meal. I don't know whether it's the ceasefire that's finally made them want to relax a bit, or whether it's the oil money flowing into the country, but they have been so generous.' She paused. I thought I saw an idea flicker across her face.

'Well, I'm so glad that you've felt able to tell me now.' She reached for a pack of Parliament cigarettes and offered me one. 'What made you come to Baku?'

'Nana has gone to Russia for treatment. I don't know if she'll come back.' I choked on my tears and my cigarette. Amina patted me on my back as I sobbed it all out. 'I thought this was my one chance to… to do something different with my life. But I haven't told anyone officially because… I'm not even sure if I can quit or not… or keep studying.'

'Do you want my… help?' Amina's caramel eyes were suddenly intensely focused on mine.

It was like she had read my mind, but I still hesitated. I knew I wanted her lifestyle, but could I see myself as an escort, a prostitute? Then her phone rang.

'I won't be a moment,' she said, taking her cup with her to her bedroom. I could hear her laughing at whatever the caller was saying. Probably a client. It gave me time to think.

My lost virginity was irredeemable, but perhaps Dr Adil had had a point, when he said, if I met the right kind of man they might understand. Someone like Tamerlan. I wondered if Tamerlan were single would we have a chance together. I'd never know. Having an affair didn't seem so outrageous any more, if it was discreet; but prostitution, I had heard people say, was an entirely different level of sin, one of those no-return tickets to hell. Would I be closing the door on any chance of leading an honest life, one day? Would my best hope be to become someone's mistress?

Amina returned, humming Aygün Kazimova's current pop hit. She sashayed to the kitchen to check on the progress of the meal.

'Food is ready,' she smiled, 'and here's food for your thoughts. I know it's a big decision. It always is. But it has to be your choice. For what it's worth, I think you'll do just fine,' she said as we settled around the table.

'I can't see any other way,' I croaked through my tears.

'Just leave it to me. I'll make sure you have a good start. And you're staying with us, until we figure something else out. All right? Eat your food. We'll watch a movie and then we'll get you to bed. We both need our beauty sleep. Our faces are our fortunes.' She laughed.

I sighed with relief at a decision made and braced myself for the next phase of my new life.

★★★

I had half expected that Amina would talk me through the "rules" of my new profession, but she was so busy for the next few days, fluttering from one appointment to another, that I decided to do my own homework. While Amina's cousins were at secondary school, I had rummaged through Amina's video cassette collection and found some saucy movies hidden behind the others. I imagined I would have to be ready to have sex at the drop of a hat, so I watched them attentively and practised arousing myself. Luckily, nothing was arranged for me for several days. It almost felt like my usual study session in Baku was about to start.

I had still not called work, Tamerlan or Dr Adil, though Amina had told me I was free to use the phone any time I needed it. Again, the debates raged in my head. Should I go back and wait for Nana to return? It wasn't too late, yet, no one knew my plans. What had happened with Dr Adil,

Tamerlan and even Mahir was different from sleeping with strangers. I knew them as friends first. I had had cause to trust them. My mind walked me repeatedly through all the implications. But how could I turn around now that my friend Amina was looking for suitable customers for me? We had talked it through. I had decided. How could I go back on my word?

A few days later, Amina announced that she wanted me to dress up and come out for a meal. She told me she had a long-standing client whose friend was looking for a new girl companion. If we clicked, he was willing to rent me a flat for four months, initially. I couldn't believe it. Could I click with this man enough to convince him to invest in me?

'Just relax,' Amina reassured me. 'He was seeing one of my friends for a while. She said he lasts five minutes tops. In and out and it's all done. Plus, he only came to see her every couple of weeks, so she had plenty of time to herself. He's a good catch. Just smile and nod, while I do the talking.'

The men met us at the entrance to an expensive restaurant. My "date", Yusif, was pleasant to look at, being tall, dark and not too old, or podgy. I noticed that both the men and Amina had the same digits in their car number plates. It probably meant that this was not just a casual encounter for her. I found that reassuring. We were ushered into a familiarly spacious private room containing an octagonal, smoky glass-topped chrome table with matching leather chairs and two long sofas. The table's surface was quickly crowded with the usual delicacies in gleaming steel bowls. The top-class caviar smelt amazing, the variety of kebabs was almost overwhelming and the others tucked in heartily, as the first bottle of vodka was poured for the men and champagne for the women by the smartest waiter I had ever seen. I was not interested in the food. I nibbled a flat bread, as my attention drifted to two closed doors in the far wall. Were they bedrooms?

While I mused about the practicalities of getting to know Yusif, Amina chirped away charmingly, keeping both men fully engaged. Her "lover", Saleh, seemed to be entranced by her looks, the sound of her voice and her sense of humour. His face carried the laughter lines of a happy, confident man. Yusif, by contrast, turned out to be even shyer than I was. It was me who was left to open him up. I thought I would ask him about his life, so, intending not to make my questions too personal, I started with the obvious. 'Where are you from?' I said, tilting my head, trying to look interested.

'Agdam,' he answered. 'Saleh and I had to flee from our homes as the Armenians invaded. We left everything behind and have had to start from scratch here.'

I certainly had not expected that answer. I wanted to ask what kind of business they were in that they could build themselves back up so quickly, but I did not dare, so our conversation dried up. I pretended to be listening to Amina's chatter, as I desperately trawled my mind for another subject, but the more I tried, the harder it got. After my glass of champagne was topped up, I felt a little more sparkly. Looking up, I caught Yusif's eye and we shared a smile. I don't know what it meant to either of us, but it helped my stomach, which was tight with anticipation, to relax, but not enough to eat.

As soon as the table was cleared, Amina and Saleh got up, smiled encouragingly at us and then exited through one of the two doors. I sat awkwardly waiting for Yusif to say or do something, eyes on my new black shoes. He got up and tentatively put his hand on my back. 'Shall we?' he said softly and led me to the other bedroom; a pristine palace of white linen and lace, with a big bed and net-shrouded windows, which looked out on a courtyard garden. Yusif undressed quickly. I followed his example, trying to remember to be graceful, and joined him under the covers.

Amina was right: after a few caresses and kisses that made me wince as I didn't like his smell, Yusif lay on top of me and quickly became hard and excited. The act itself was over in minutes. He panted his thanks, slid off and reached for his cigarettes. I had mostly lain still, unsure what to do, especially after he had emptied himself inside me. Dr Adil had always been careful about contraception, Tamerlan was equally thoughtful, but until that moment I had not thought about the means of protecting myself. It hadn't featured in any of the videos and Amina hadn't mentioned it either. I had heard Nana chatting matter-of-factly to neighbours about terminations. They seemed to view them as just another part of a woman's life. Although I hadn't betrayed any of this worry physically to Yusif, it had taken me, temporarily, away from what was happening. I felt like I was submerged under water and all the sounds and sensations were coming from far away. I dressed as quickly as my shell-shocked brain would allow. Then I took time, as Amina had suggested, to visit the en suite, sitting at the ornate dressing table to reapply my subtle make-up and brush my hair. Only then did I open the door and join

175

Yusif and Saleh back at the dining table for another drink. I was pleased when Yusif greeted me with a smile and rose to pull out my chair for me.

Amina emerged shortly after from the other room, looking as impeccably turned out as ever, her hair neat and her make-up perfect. She gave me an approving glance. 'I've got to collect the girls from school, Saleh, thank you, my love. We had better go, Gulya,' she said cheerfully. 'It's been a pleasure in every way.' She kissed Saleh on the lips.

I wondered if I was supposed to do something similar to Yusif, but before I mustered the courage, he pecked me on the cheek. I stood up.

'I'll be in touch,' Amina said, pausing in the doorway while I said goodbye to Saleh and gave Yusif a shy wave.

'He definitely liked you,' Amina said as soon as she started the car.

'How do you know?'

'I know these things, remember, I'm a professional.' She laughed at her own joke.

I still did not know whether I wanted Yusif to like me or not. His verdict came as we drove off. Saleh texted Amina to say that Yusif was smitten with me. He was already looking for a nice flat for me, near the university.

'It feels so strange, Amina, so sudden,' I said. 'It'll be wonderful to have somewhere to stay for a few months, but...'

'I know, you'll get used to it. The next thing I need to do is to introduce you to a couple of women who supply escorts to important officials.'

'I thought I'd be with Yusif?' Amina had surprised me again.

176

'Not exclusively, silly. You're not marrying the guy! He's not paying all your bills. And another thing, I have a favour to ask you now. I was thinking, could you have the girls with you in your new flat, just for a while? I'm buying a new flat but moving home can be so hectic and I don't want their lives disrupted too much. What do you think?'

'I'd love that. I have never actually lived on my own before.'

'Exactly what I thought. You have us now, Gulya. You'll never be alone again. I'll help with the shopping and everything else that may need doing. Relax, all will be well,' Amina said, putting her foot down on the accelerator with a grin.

★★★

Despite my new job getting off to such a good and busy start, I never really got the hang of being relaxed. I felt nervous before every outing. My initial delusion, that I was expected to be sexually aroused every time, quickly faded. It wasn't ever about me, it was always about them, the clients. Some encounters were pleasant, when I felt connected with the man and therefore more at ease, but for the most part, I remained tense and sometimes as tight physically as I was mentally. I felt anxious about my ability to make intelligent or scintillating conversation. I had to crush all my learnt self-consciousness around nudity. Above all, I continued to dread penetration, a lack of contraception and even STDs.

Neither Amina nor any other working girls I met during my outings talked about the rules of the profession, although I did pick up a few cues from some of the

FRAGILE FREEDOM

disparaging remarks Amina made about others in the trade, including: never kiss a client on the lips, unless he initiates it, as for the most part, they assume that you gave someone a blow job just before seeing them; and don't give anyone a blow job, unless they ask for it, otherwise you'll make yourself look cheap and they won't see you as special or worthy of their money.

In my encounters with clients, I used what I had learnt in my liaisons with Dr Adil – the things he enjoyed and appreciated the most. I also aped the moves of the women I had seen in erotic movies, but I didn't always get it right. I got into the habit of moaning and groaning a lot to convince a client I was aroused and enjoying it. That backfired one night when Amina's friend Aida barged into my bedroom, and angrily accused 'the bastard', my client, of hurting me. I had to convince her I was all right before she'd leave. The "bastard", a mild-mannered Turkish businessman, was so spooked that he insisted we 'call it a night', although he still paid me for my time. The experience taught me to be more subtle in future.

I was soon swept up in the whirlwind of appointments, with some repeat clients and many new ones too. Sleep was hard to come by as I had to stay up at times when others slept and try to sleep when the rest of the world was up. The constant pressure to perform and keep smiling, even when I wanted to rage or scream, left me exhausted. When I was not "on duty", I would simply collapse. The initial adrenalin rush of being so popular and being so wanted, and my curiosity about what might happen during my outings, started to wane. I gradually became cynical about the set-up I was involved in. I felt increasingly bitter towards both the "madams" who supplied girls like me to men, as well as the men who used our services.

\*\*\*

In early December 1995, Amina announced she was going to introduce me to a new madam, a well-known gynaecologist, who had access to the best clients in the country.

'Today's outing is very important,' Amina said as she talked me through the details on the phone. 'Choose something from my wardrobe if you like.' She mentioned a top civil servant, amongst others. 'You know all the girls who are coming along. Relax,' she said as she always did, 'let the lady do all the talking.'

I caught a taxi to the arranged restaurant. Standing outside, waiting for this new madam to take me in, I kept nervously straightening the elegant, black skirt suit I had borrowed from Amina. The restaurant's mirrored glass window showed how good I looked in it. I was ushered inside with several other girls. The men were already at the table when we arrived, to be distributed amongst them. I perched on my satin chair after we had greeted them. On first sight, I did not like any of them. As the dinner 'ritual' progressed, I wondered who my customer was going to be.

I recognised the top civil servant Amina described, but had never seen the other men. One of them seemed particularly obnoxious. He kept speaking loudly, even when his mouth was full. 'Oh, Nazila, you've offended me.' He pouted at the madam.

'What have I done?!' she said calmly. She was a stylish woman of about forty, whose beauty had survived well but hardened around the edges. I would not have dared speak to her like that. 'Let me know, because I'd love to remedy that, straight away.'

'Tell me, how many days there are in a year?' he drawled, wiping his greasy lips with a napkin.

'Three hundred and sixty-five,' she said patiently. 'Three hundred and sixty-six in a leap year.'

'Well, that's how many virgins I want each year. One for each day. This lot doesn't seem to fit the bill. What does it cost these days? Two thousand dollars? I can pay you right now! I tell you, I want a fresh one, every time I fuck!'

I fought to hide the hatred rising in my chest. I wanted to scream and rage at him: 'Every time you take someone's virginity, you ruin their life, you bastard!' Just two thousand dollars to take their futures? How could this madam do this to young women? Where was she going to get them all from, anyway?

'I can do that, no problem,' she replied calmly.

The man laughed, satisfied with her answer. My fellow women sat with doll-like smiles etched on their faces, betraying no internal emotions. I prayed with vehemence that I did not end up with this man, who, at that moment, I despised with every fibre of my being. Thankfully, the top civil servant chose me. Taking me by the arm, he led me to a bedroom.

My performance anxiety returned in full force. I felt under pressure to satisfy this well-known elder. I undressed clumsily. My usual faked enthusiasm had the opposite effect from what was intended. The man actually lost his erection. I had not encountered such a problem before and didn't know what I was supposed to do to revive him. I tried to excite him with oral sex but that failed. I was astonished when he started to cry. 'I'm still so young,' he lamented. 'Fifty-six is no age for a man. I don't know what's happening to me.'

I lay still, holding my breath, not sure what to say.

'It must be all the hardship and stress catching up with me,' he continued, as he sat up, sniffing and lighting a cigarette. 'When I was growing up, there were eight of us children in the family. A lot of mouths to feed. When one of us went in to the kitchen to fetch something, they had to keep talking, so that the rest of us knew that they weren't scoffing any food.'

I was amazed to find myself feeling sorry for him because my childhood had been similar. I wasn't allowed to help myself to the smallest piece of bread without permission. I assumed he wasn't interested in my life, though, so I just sat and listened, accepting a cigarette when it was offered. I was sure he wouldn't want to come out of our bedroom too early, in case someone suspected he could not perform. I still wondered, was it something I'd done wrong, due to my inexperience? Maybe he too liked a virgin-type, who did not have a clue what to do. It was clear he liked me enough to talk to me and was going to stay for as long as he wanted. He didn't even mind when I slipped my clothes back on, while he spoke. I continued to nod and fake a different kind of appreciative noise. He was my first talker, and he wasn't to be my last. At one point, I had to stifle a giggle when a funny story Lala had told me popped into my head. I could hear her reciting it: 'Three men are discussing what kind of women they like. The first one says, "I love virgins, they know nothing and are so pure."

The second man says, "Well, I like seasoned women, those who know what they are doing." The third man thinks a little bit and says: "Personally, I prefer pensioners because they think it might be the last time they will ever have sex, so they do unspeakable things!'"

The thought that the client would be happier with a pensioner made me feel better about the experience. He paid me five hundred US dollars for my company, and I decided to put the experience behind me.

★★★

I could not believe how I had changed, two months after my "escape" to Baku. Things I had craved in Ganja, like going to a restaurant, no longer excited me. Although I had all the creature comforts in the world – a warm, well-furnished flat in a great area with an indoor shower and toilet, an abundance of food paid for by Amina and expertly cooked by Irada and more money than I had ever imagined was possible – I found myself growing strangely numb and dead on the inside. Even in Ganja, I thought, there had been unexpected glimmers of fun and Nana's constant and protective love balancing the bad times. Now my life felt almost dull, without the highs and lows, the joys and the passions of before. By repetition, my mind had become as desensitised to sex and other physical pleasures, as it had to the daily details of murder and rape cases during my first few weeks at the Prosecutor's Office: the extraordinary had become normal. The difference was that my new life in Baku, with its irregular hours, repressions and excesses, was also sapping my energy and my interest in life itself.

My unhappiness translated into chain smoking and drinking too much to numb my experience. During sex, I escaped from what was inflicted on my body in the present moment by imagining myself in a different time and place. The levels of hatred and disgust I felt towards my body and my clients' bodies became so heightened that I courted self-destruction.

New Year 1996 found me swept up into the most lavish celebration I had ever experienced. On New Year's Eve, Amina insisted on taking me and the girls to an expensive restaurant, where our lovely meal cost one hundred US dollars a head. We were entertained by the most popular singers of the day: Aygün Kazimova, Zulfiya Khanbabayeva and Fuad Agayev. The music was vibrant, almost deafening, the atmosphere electric with people singing and dancing along, all smiles and euphoria. But, deep inside me, it was as sad and silent as a tomb. I was at my loneliest ever, in the midst of the surging crowd of revellers, because the people I loved weren't with me.

Nana was still in Moscow recovering from her recent surgery. I had begun to miss her so much. The Russian doctors had discovered the cause of her illness: she had had a severe stomach ulcer. She would not be back in Ganja for at least another three months. I had only managed to speak to her once on the phone but hadn't had the courage to tell her I had moved to Baku. Suju was still taking care of the house, but I didn't want Nana to have any need to worry, or to have the chance to question me. Nana was always very perceptive once she knew where to focus her attention.

Mama, though just the other side of the city, might as well have been on the moon. I hadn't told her what I was doing either, and she hadn't asked. She was still struggling; even though I had been able to help her a bit financially, it wasn't enough to resolve her family's housing situation. We had met in December. I had treated them to a meal and some gifts – my siblings had been delighted with theirs – but it hadn't been the time or place to talk, mother to daughter.

Then there was sweet Tamerlan. I couldn't risk him finding out what I was up to. He was so sensitive and would no doubt feel the change in me. I couldn't tell him my deepest secrets any more because I thought the truth would repulse him. It was better if we had no contact.

As for Dr Adil... After mournfully reviewing the past year, I had felt compelled to call him for the first time since I'd left Ganja. At first, he had been understandably furious with me. 'Do you have any idea what you've put me through? I've been worried sick about you! And you haven't even contacted your work. Do you know that they held your space for a while because they thought you had a study session? But not any more. It's been two months now. What happened? Of course I want to see you. But why are you phoning now? Are you in trouble?' He was almost shouting down the phone.

'I just rang because I needed to hear a friendly voice,' I said weakly, trying to suppress the chesty cough I had been struggling to shake off for ages.

Despite his stern tone, part of me felt loved by him. I knew it could never be a real, lifelong, romantic love, but I thought it was as close to that as I would ever get. Once he had calmed down, we talked for a while, about our past times together, but the contrast between those almost innocent days and my present life circumstances seemed huge. Fighting hard to hide my emotions, I promised I would be in touch again soon, that we would meet up and I would ring the office after the holiday period. I put the phone down before he could hear my tears.

As the chimes of the New Year rang out in the restaurant that night, I stood, poised and beautifully dressed, looking like I was truly part of "the best crowd"; but inside, I knew the bitter reality. It didn't matter how much I could earn. That was irrelevant now because of something I had discovered a few hours before, something that had set my mind thinking of Nana, of Mama, of Tamerlan, of Dr Adil, of my whole life: I was pregnant.

## 10.

## BRUISED

'Hi, Lala, how are you? It's been ages since we spoke,' I said, trying to keep my tone light and carefree. 'Yes, I'm looking forward to seeing you at the study session too, but listen, I have a favour to ask of you.' I was alone in my flat, clutching the landline phone like it was a lifeline at sea.

I felt sure that Lala was the only person who would understand my predicament; besides which, she owed me. I had paid for her to have a termination and I had been there to hold her hand.

'I'm in Baku,' I continued, 'and I have the same problem you had not long ago. Don't say it, I'm sure you've guessed right. Listen, I don't want to go to the appointment alone. I really need you to come with me.'

'Oh,' she said. Then nothing.

'Lala, are you still there?' I asked, thinking the line had cut off.

'I'm here,' she said quietly.

'I've got the money,' I said hastily, in case she thought I wanted compensating, 'I just... you know... want the company. You know how it is.'

'I can't,' she replied.

'What?' I was stunned. My fingers gripped the receiver hard.

'It's just... He won't like it,' Lala said lamely.

My initial impulse was to rage at her, but I felt my whole being collapse inside. Without another word, I put the receiver down. He wouldn't like it? So what? Wasn't he the same bastard who had impregnated her and refused to pay for the procedure? Why was she choosing him over our friendship? Shaking with the betrayal, I paced around the two-bedroom flat. I didn't need her money. I could take it out of the six thousand dollars I had already saved towards a payment on a flat. I had just needed her as a friend. I couldn't ask Amina. Not only was she busy with moving house, but she was desperately trying to get pregnant herself. It would be insensitive to tell her about it. Her cousins were too young to be involved. That left... no one.

At least, thanks to my experience with Lala, I knew what to do. I arranged an appointment at the same centre and I gave a false name. The doctor who examined me seemed kind and accepted my reasons for needing the procedure.

'Since you're still in the early stage of pregnancy, we can use the suction method. It's less likely to cause any long-term damage,' she said. 'We can do it right now. Do you want that?' I nodded. My neck was painfully tense.

In the operating theatre, next door, several nurses were getting ready for the procedure. They did not give me any privacy, just a gown, so I quickly removed my lower garments and climbed unaided onto the operation couch. There I laid, with my legs splayed wide, swallowing back my fears while scolding myself inside. This is the price you have to pay for your choices. Did you think that you could get away with it, without any trouble? Foolish girl!

The doctor and the three nurses all seemed to be staring at my exposed vagina, as the doctor stretched it wider with a freezing steel speculum, which looked like a large pair of waffle tongs.

'Relax and breathe,' they all kept saying, but I was given no pain relief. My body tried to wriggle away from the cold metal. I could feel everything as the doctor manoeuvred the suction device into position. It was so hard not to yelp and whimper like an injured dog, for the pain was excruciating. The doctor attempted to reassure me by continually using my fake name, Parvana, as she explained what she was doing. I lost all sense of time and almost consciousness. The ordeal seemed endless. Finally, the doctor announced they had finished. I struggled off the couch, every nerve trembling. The nurses had already started cleaning up ready for the next patient.

'We need to do an ultrasound scan to be sure we got everything, Parvana,' the doctor said, and I waddled, a bloodied pad between my legs, clutching my gown around me, to another room.

I lay on the couch, my gown pulled right up, as the scan operator put clear, cold gel on my belly. The doctor peered at the image on the screen, which was turned away from me. She requested a second opinion from a colleague. They discussed what they were looking at in whispers in the corridor. Something wasn't right.

'I am so sorry, Parvana,' the doctor said. She seemed to be embarrassed and flustered. 'It looks like you were carrying twins. We'll have to perform the procedure again.

Are you sure there is no one you would like us to call to be with you?'

I shook my head miserably. I couldn't believe it. I had always dreamt of having twins, but not like this, when I didn't even know who the father was. They executed the procedure for a second time, while I tried to push my guilt away. I had to clench my jaw to suppress the howl of anguish I was aching to release.

This time the scan was satisfactory. I sighed with relief. As I dressed slowly and painfully, I felt empty and bruised on the inside, while on the outside, my skin was pale and I shivered uncontrollably.

'Parvana, where is your friend waiting for you?' The doctor had to repeat the question, because I was in no state to remember I had given a false name. 'Remember, you have just had surgery and it's best if someone picks you up.'

The girl in me wanted to cry out that I did not have anyone, but the adult in me didn't want to let strangers see my pain, so I forced a smile and lied: 'It's all right, my friend is waiting outside.'

Out on the street, the skies were as dark as my thoughts. The famous Baku wind nearly swept me off my feet. I had not eaten all day, because of nerves, so my head spun like the dead leaves in the gutter. Even raising my arm to hail a taxi felt like too much effort, but I managed to flag one down. I winced as I climbed carefully into the back seat and sat down. I felt like I might vomit but knew there was nothing there. Silent tears soaked into my brand-new purple silk scarf, but they could not wash away my grief.

Back at the flat, Irada and Nargiz knew there was something wrong, but were too wise to ask what. They gave me some fresh tea and sympathetic hugs. We were about to eat the dinner they had both prepared when the doorbell chimed.

'I bet that's Amina,' Nargiz chirped, rising to answer the door, 'she has a sixth sense when it comes to food.' It wasn't Amina. The caller sounded like a man. Nargiz returned. 'It's Yusif,' she whispered. 'Shall I tell him to go away?'

It was too late. Yusif had followed her into the kitchen, all smiles. I couldn't tell him what I had done, the shame I felt about the whole experience. There was only one thing for it.

I got up, arranging my face in some semblance of a smile and took Yusif by the hand and led him into the bedroom. There was no way I could let him go anywhere near my vagina today, so again I lied and told him I had an unexpected period. Yusif, unlike some men, had always respected that time, even though the rumours were that you couldn't conceive then. He was, as usual, sympathetic, and after I had used other ways to pleasure him, he said goodbye and left. Exhausted from the effort and the events of the day, I stayed collapsed on the bed until I passed out.

★★★

My fears of getting pregnant again dominated my thoughts. I actively avoided outings whenever I could. My body found its own way of protecting me for a couple of weeks. I developed a nasty vaginal discharge and I had to go to see Amina's gynaecologist friend. Two weeks of pills, pessaries and sexual abstinence were prescribed to clear it up, which gave me a much-needed breather. When I was finally coaxed into going out again, I tried to deflect my clients from penetrative sex, which was only partially successful.

While at home, I spent more time with the girls. I liked Irada the best, as she was light-hearted and caring. We spent hours lounging on my bed, watching TV and talking about anything that came to mind. It was on one of those lazy afternoons that she confided in me. 'You know that guy Amina was seeing, the jealous, young one, Rashad? He used to come with his best friend Elshan, sometimes. Well, when Amina and Rashad were "busy", I got to know Elshan, quite… a little bit.' I felt something ominous coming, but tried not to show it, as she continued. 'Elshan, he was charming and sweet to me, so when Amina was in France and Nargiz had a sleepover, I… I invited him over.' Irada suddenly looked teary.

I put my arm around her. 'Don't worry. You can tell me. Did he hurt you?' I was very concerned.

'No, no, he didn't, the opposite. It was all so nice that I just… we just… couldn't help it. I didn't want to stop. We lost control. It was only once but now… I'll have to tell Amina. I think she'll kill me!' She started to cry.

'Oh, Irada,' I said. 'Don't worry, she won't do that. Amina will understand.' I felt very protective of Irada. She was only seventeen and I knew only too well that stupid things happened in life. Surely Amina wouldn't punish her, when it was partly her fault, for leaving her alone with Elshan so many times.

For the next few days, I kept trying to reassure Irada that it would all work out somehow; she was young and beautiful, I said. Perhaps Elshan's family would honour his actions? Then she told me they had rejected the idea and were arranging a suitable marriage for him.

I was also very wrong about Amina's reaction. To start with, she raged as my Nana would have done. How had she, Amina, managed to miss something as important as this? How could Irada have gone behind her back? I couldn't believe what she did next.

Within two days of Irada's confession to her, she was taken to a gynaecologist, stitched up and sold as a virgin to the man who had wanted to have a virgin for every day of the year. Then Irada was stitched up again and sold to the top civil servant, for the same price, two thousand US dollars. It turned out that he preferred virgins to pensioners and was able to perform with her.

In a week, Irada had earnt more money than I had in three months. From then on, she was sent on outings with me several times a week. I still felt protective of her and made sure I not only negotiated a fair price for the night, but tried to avoid her going with someone, if she did not want to. Amina's spell over me was fading fast. How could she treat her own young cousin this way? I made excuses to avoid any contact with her, even our once famous shopping sprees.

When she called me late one cold February evening telling me I needed to get ready to entertain an important client, I found it hard to hide my reluctance.

'He pays a lot, like a lot, Gulya,' she said adamantly, oblivious to my objections. 'Bills on a flat like yours don't pay themselves, do they? Exactly. So, make sure you are both at your best. I will be with you in thirty minutes.' The phone clicked off before I could say any more, leaving Irada and I to rush around frantically getting ready.

The restaurant we were taken to by Amina indeed had amazing facilities. Each unit, comprising the usual dining room and bedrooms, also had a sauna and a small private pool. Our host, a fat old man with a big grin and smoky eyes, was sitting at the table waiting for us. He greeted Amina warmly, with a kiss on both cheeks. I assumed the man was another former regular of hers. Amina first introduced Irada to him and got her to sit between them. The waiters brought out the food, but I still had no idea what the purpose of my presence there was. Not a threesome, I prayed. Not with Irada. I couldn't stomach that.

'I have a special friend coming soon,' the man smiled at me. We dined lavishly on dishes of Ossetra caviar, a whole roasted salmon, a lamb shank and pan-fried whole chicken, as well as the usual accompaniments. The host paid compliments to Irada and charmed Amina, leaving me to gorge myself hopefully to oblivion.

When my intended companion arrived, Amina collected her hefty payment for delivering us and fluttered away. I missed hearing the friend's name and did not dare to ask. He was tall, dark and watchful, preferring to blend into the background, letting his friend run the show. When our host took Irada next door, Mr Tall and I sat awkwardly for a while, not speaking, until he took my hand and silently led me through the door of an adjacent room.

It wasn't the bedroom I had been expecting, but a large washroom with fancy tiles that led to the sauna and the swimming pool. I was confused. Did he want to have sex in here, presumably standing up? I had always hated being taken from behind since Mahir had raped me. That was not going to happen. Since he was already taking off his trousers, I decided to take charge of the situation. I stripped off my sheath dress and dropped down onto my knees in my underwear and started pleasuring him. He stood ramrod straight for a moment. Had I misjudged the situation? Then, his body started to respond to my stimulations. As he stood towering over me, getting more and more excited, I had hopes that it would all be over quickly and painlessly. I was wrong.

He grabbed my hair roughly, tilting my head back, looking straight into my eyes, then he leant down, ripped off my bra and grasped both of my breasts in his large strong hands. As I continued to pleasure him, desperately hoping he would reach his climax, he started to squeeze my breasts harder and harder. His thrusts grew faster and more frantic as his grip tightened in excruciating agony. Why was he hurting me? I couldn't think for the pain. I was paralysed with fear and loathing, then suddenly, at last, he came in a shuddering release still clasping vice-like onto my bruised and battered breasts, staring hawkishly into my tear-spilling, pleading eyes.

I fell back onto the tiles, gagging and struggling not to retch, overwhelmed by shock and pain, as he calmly dressed, without a glance or a word in my direction. The door clicked behind him as he left. I heard his feet pacing across the dining room and away. I lay there, in a foetal position, for a few minutes, terrified he might return, the chill of the tiles soothing my aching breasts. Soon, reason told me I didn't want anyone to find me like this, so I forced myself to stand. In the washroom's full-length mirrors, I could clearly see the imprints of his fingers, red and raw, on my pale skin. I carefully pulled my dress back on, repaired my make-up, returned to the dining room and covered my upper body with my glittery, black pashmina. Surely, he would not return? I rang the service bell, ordered lemon water with ice, and as soon as the waiter had left, I started applying the cubes, one by one, to my battered breasts, hoping to lessen the bruising. As the ice melted on my burning flesh, the water ran down inside the dress, but I did not care any more. It just made the fabric as shiny on the inside as it was on the outside. What the staff would make of a sodden chair wasn't my problem.

Our host reappeared with Irada. He was smiling and still talking away. She was her usual gentle, silent self. Irada had never complained about her recent experiences, but she no longer chattered as she used to do. Her silence was taken as innocence by some and elegant poise by others. He had been happy with her, I thought bitterly. Did he know of his friend's sadistic desires? Inside, I was still a pressure cooker of emotions threatening to explode.

'What's happened here? What have you done to my friend?' he said jovially.

His words jarred. He should be asking what his friend had done to me! He eyed me expectantly, but my tight set mouth refused to obey his need to see at least a polite smile.

'Hmmm, we'd better cheer you up,' he said, sinking onto a chair. He poured us all a glass of pink champagne from the bottle a waiter had just whisked in. I did not drink mine. Before downing his, the man pulled out a shiny, black business card and placed it on the table in front of me.

'It's one of my shops. A neck as beautiful as yours demands to be adorned as well as adored. Go there tomorrow and choose any necklace or choker or pendant your heart desires.' I squeezed out a thank you through my pursed lips.

He turned back to Irada, who seemed remarkably at ease with him. Perhaps she had met him before, or perhaps going out with Amina and her men for meals all those years had taught her how to handle these situations.

I think my lack of responsiveness was still bothering him, though, because after his third glass of champagne, he reached out and retrieved the card. I looked up for the first time, searching his face for a reason. Was this a penalty for not continuing to sparkle? Had I not been punished enough for one evening? His eyes showed only discomfort, not malice.

'Why delay till tomorrow what you could do today?' he said grandly. He produced a roll of dollar bills from deep in his velvet jacket and counted out a thousand dollars, with a flourish. 'This is just for you. You can buy gold, diamonds, clothes – whatever makes you happy.'

I had ceased to blame him, my anger abated, for he had looked genuinely concerned. I took the money, gave him my most dazzling fake smile and muttered something about a headache as I stuffed it into my tiny clutch purse. Did I even know what would make me happy? Maybe I was beginning to, but right then, leaving the restaurant seemed a good way to start looking.

'Let's call it a day, then,' he said, sounding relieved. He counted out one thousand dollars for Irada and he pulled her in for a kiss on the mouth. 'I'll be seeing you soon, baby.'

Baby is the right word, I thought grimly, as we were escorted to a flashy car to be taken back to my flat by the man's chauffeur. Irada could have been his granddaughter. In the cosy darkness of the car, Irada tried to start a conversation with me, but I easily feigned tiredness. In truth, I could not have taken a single word in. We sat motionless, like monarchs on their state thrones, as the lights of Baku flashed by.

Once home, I gave Irada a soft hug goodnight and I went to get ready for bed. I was half undressed when she entered without knocking. Perhaps I needed to say something more, so that she did not worry about me?

'Listen,' Irada spoke tentatively, but not in her usual tone, 'that money Mr B gave you... you should share it with Amina. After all, she took us to the clients.'

Her words hit hard, coming from a seventeen-year-old girl that I thought I'd been protecting. I had even gone with someone I did not like to shield her from the experience, which ended badly for me. This "child", who had been terrified of the implications of losing her virginity, had clearly now been instructed to keep me in order. The rage I hadn't been able to express towards the men who'd hurt me, the frustrations of the past months, my disappointments and suppressed griefs, came pouring out as angry tears. 'You think I should pay Amina?' I exclaimed. 'Did she go through this with me?' I tore off my bra, exposing my breasts, now defaced with darkening livid bruises.

Irada gasped, backing away from me, but shook her head. 'It's just...' she bit her lip, the way I used to do when I was young. 'This is how things are done,' she said robotically. 'You should... consider... giving Amina, say four hundred dollars? She doesn't want half as much as some do. She's been so generous to us.'

I turned away from her in disgust. Her seeming transformation appalled me. There was not a single innocent bone left in her body. Perhaps she had always known more than she had appeared to. Perhaps the loss of her virginity was the catalyst not the cause of her metamorphosis. Perhaps it had only been a matter of time, her "coming of age", before she joined the family profession.

Tentacles of hatred reached out in my head towards Amina and her girls, towards the men who had used and discarded me and even towards my own body for what it had done. I had gone against the moral code I had been taught from birth. I could not reconcile my current identity with that of the good home-grown girl I had been, destined for marriage and a life of service to her family. Now I knew for certain that all the glitz and glamour of Amina's life, which I had craved, was fake. There was nothing glamorous at all about being used for sex by strangers, no matter how much they paid. Nothing about it brought me any lasting joy or self-respect and my mental health had hit rock bottom. Added to that, my period was late again.

I paced the bedroom, crashing about, opening and closing cupboards and drawers, flinging my new possessions round the room. They meant nothing to me any more. I wanted out. How had Amina managed to live like this for so many years and still enjoy her life? There was an alien all-consuming darkness building inside me. It was so strong that I imagined hurting someone to get the poison out of my system: Amina, that sick bastard of a client, anyone who tried to hurt me, or tell me what to do. I collapsed, defeated and sobbing onto the bed amongst the starched clean bedsheets. Irada and Nargiz did not come to comfort me this time.

\*\*\*

I woke to the clatter of breakfast cooking in the kitchen. The radio was on and I could hear the girls loudly singing along with one of their favourite songs. I imagined them bopping around in their cartoon aprons, laughing, while I was cold, empty and alone in the ruins of my room. Something was sticking in my back. I groaned, rolling to one side to pull it from under me. It was my battered old address book, the page open at "A". Pulling a black T-shirt on, from under my feet, I dialled the number and prayed he would answer.

'It's me, Gulush.' My voice was husky with cigarettes and tears.

'It's you! At last! Have you been crying?' Dr Adil's voice was full of concern. I had not heard that in anyone's voice for a long time.

'Yes, it's just... I feel a bit lonely here and I thought... Nana is still in Moscow and I miss her.' I momentarily lost control. I couldn't stop crying.

'You sound awful, Gulush. It must be more than that. Listen, I'm going to leave right now, OK? Tell me your address and I'll be with you in five hours at most.'

I hadn't expected him to say that.

'Oh no, not today... it's not a good day for me,' I said. How would I explain the bruises?

'Nonsense, you rang me because you needed me, so I'm coming.'

I frantically searched my mind for an excuse. This was usually Irada's department, she was good at concocting stories, but of course I couldn't ask her any more.

'I'm on my period,' I blurted out.

'We'll just have a meal together and catch up. Is there another reason? Are you seeing someone else? Be honest with me.'

'Of course not,' I replied, but for a minute, I felt loved – he was willing to drive five hours just to talk to me. So, I relented and told him my address.

'I'm too tired today, but tomorrow would be perfect,' I insisted.

★★★

I was genuinely happy to see Dr Adil and his little black car the next day. He held me and I felt my body relax for the first time in weeks. I sobbed on his shoulder out of sheer familiarity with his scent and his warm arms.

'I missed you too,' he said.

I couldn't bear to tell him the real cause of my sadness. My affair with him felt so innocent in comparison to the horror of my current experience. I was a mismatch inside, simultaneously young and mature, tainted and vulnerable. I got in the front passenger seat next to him and he swiftly navigated through the heavy, Baku lunchtime traffic, towards the suburbs and then beyond.

'Where are we going?' I asked, puzzled.

'The summer house,' he replied, smiling.

Any other day, I would have loved to experience the peace and luxury of his brother's summer house again, with its pool and gardens; but today I could not let him see me naked.

'I told you I have my period. I'm really tired, too,' I said, feeling helpless.

'You know it doesn't bother me. I like you as you are, whatever,' he said, placing his hand on my knee.

'I really can't,' I insisted, failing to hide the edge in my voice.

'You are hiding something from me,' he said. I could see his eyebrows arch.

'There's nothing,' I said, trying to think of a way out of this. I had just wanted some comfort and someone to care, not to have my lifestyle revealed with a glance. As Nana would say: 'You knocked out an eye, trying to fix a brow.' I kept quiet for the rest of the journey, hoping to hit on a solution, but still hadn't found one by the time we drew into the front drive of the fashionably designed house. I knew there were beautiful views from the second-floor bedroom balcony. A salt-scented sea breeze ruffled my short hair.

'Come in, it's cold today. You had such a nasty cough when you called me on New Year's Eve.'

It was sweet, that he had noticed and remembered.

'Yes, it's lasted for ages. I still haven't completely lost it,' I said.

We were taking off our shoes and donning warm slippers when I caught the unmistakable smell of kebabs wafting down the heated hallway. Dr Adil smiled as I wrinkled my nose.

'I asked my cousin to take care of it all. Lunch is served,' he said, and led me into the kitchen-diner where a large wooden table was covered in simple fragrant food. Once this would have delighted me; nowadays, my appetite for it was hard to find.

'Let's eat while it's all warm.' Dr Adil fussed with my chair.

Suddenly I felt so weary, knowing that he was going to quiz me about the past few months. He filled my plate. I picked at a rough-cut lamb rib while he enthused about all things relating to Ganja. All the worst memories of my former work and home life clattered into my head, with their shames and blames. I could not take in a word that Dr Adil was saying. I wished he had known why I left, but I knew I could never tell him.

'You've hardly eaten,' he said, finally noticing my still full plate.

'I've an awful headache,' I said, scrunching up my face.

'Nothing that the sea air and a stiff vodka can't cure,' he said, but I covered the crystal glass with my right palm. 'What, you don't drink any more? How come?'

I wanted to say my repeated bouts of thrush, due to sleeping with strangers, required me to take antibiotics, which didn't work if you drank alcohol – but I couldn't.

'I need to keep a clear head for my studies,' I said. That was one of my regular excuses. I had increasingly found that alcohol left me even more depressed the morning after. What was the point of it? I had learnt several tricks to vanish it, including fake sipping or emptying it into a glass with juice.

'I thought your study sessions were over by now.' Dr Adil frowned but put the bottle down. 'Wasn't it in January?'

'Yes, but I like to keep up… with new developments.'

'Have you failed something? Don't blow your opportunities, Gulush. I could pay, if necessary, for you to get through.'

'Thank you. There's no need. I have passed everything so far.' He didn't need to know I had handled my own bribes.

'You seem different,' Dr Adil said, after a few conversations had died back quickly, once I'd realised I was about to let out more than it was safe to share.

'I'm just soooo tired. Someone is on night shift in our building. He's back at all hours. I think I want to go home now,' I said with a real yawn.

'You're not going to leave without a little bit of fun,' he said, edging closer, obviously about to kiss me.

'It's that time of the month,' I said, making to get up, 'I told you. In a few days' time.'

'That won't be a problem in the steam room,' he said, kissing my neck. 'It's wipe clean and lovely and hot. As a doctor, I particularly recommend saunas to ease cramps, along with a massage,' he said playfully. I tried not to panic as he led me to the basement like I was a puppy on a leash.

'I need a shower first,' he said happily, 'it's been a very busy week.' He hung his clothes on a peg and sauntered into the cubicle, his eagerness on full display.

Why had I come? Desperate for any affection? There would be no more once he saw... Then I noticed the steam room was not only steamy, but dimly lit. If I let him come behind me? Though I shivered at the prospect, I knew it was my only chance. I undressed quickly and wrapped myself in the largest, darkest towel I could find. I positioned myself nervously on the wet heated tiled bench to wait. Afterwards, I would dress quickly when he went to clean himself.

As soon as he started to caress me, I knew that the magic feeling between us was gone for me. My numb body, now used to unwanted invasions, went through the motions, as any other day. He soon climaxed, but instead of leaving, he sat by me doggedly attempting to massage my shoulders. Clasping the towel round me, I was getting hotter, craving a cool shower myself. Panting, I got up.

'I need to wash,' I said, pushing the heavy door open to leave, but he followed me out.

A wave of nausea hit me, and my hand slipped momentarily off the towel.

'What's that on your breast?' he said, spotting one of the bruises.

I hastily covered myself up.

'It's nothing... I fell,' I lied.

'Sit down and let me examine you,' he said, suddenly the doctor again, as he wrestled the damp towel from my weak hands. 'Oh my God, Gulush, these are finger marks. Who has done this to you?'

Though I started with a lie – that I had been forced into prostitution because of a debt I couldn't pay to a moneylender – all my grief and shame bubbled out and I told Dr Adil the truth about my last client. His reaction was not at all what I had expected. He was initially angry with 'the brute' and held me as I cried, telling me it 'didn't matter' to him what I had done; but then he seemed almost proud to have a lover who got paid 'one thousand dollars' for a few hours' work.

***

'I don't want to do it any more.' I told him, when I was all cried out. We were back in the kitchen, sipping hot tea, having showered and dressed.

'I understand,' he said.

'I have enough money for my own flat now. Would you help me find somewhere? I'll find a new job. I want to start over.'

'Of course you do!' He frowned, eyes upwards, thinking it through, then he beamed. 'I have a university friend who's been in Baku for years. He's from Ganja. He'll help, I'm sure. I'll call him straight away.'

He left the kitchen. I heard him speaking rapidly on the phone. His friend, called Suleyman, agreed to see me the next day.

'You'll come along with me and do the talking?' I said, wrapping my arms around his neck. I felt grateful that he had reacted so well to my revelations.

'Sorry, I can't, but…' he started, then paused and began again. 'I have to head back tonight. I have to see some patients in the morning, but…' he hesitated, 'I happen to know a former colleague of yours is in town.'

My heart lurched, surely not…?

'You remember Seva, don't you? She told me how much she misses you. I thought you would be pleased to see a friendly face. Maybe she is free to come to the meeting?'

I remembered Seva. Mahir's hand on her back, her laughter echoing from the other office, her provocative make-up and tight clothing. She was not my first choice for a chaperone. However, I knew too well that in Azerbaijan, going alone to a meeting with a strange man was pretty damning. It conveyed all sorts of messages: that no one had your back, that you were uprooted and vulnerable. This was true of me, of course, but I didn't want anyone to know that. No one functioned in isolation in Azerbaijan. I knew a person's survival usually depended on being connected to an extended family, who could offer support, guidance and comfort in times of distress.

Resigned, I called Seva. She actually sounded really glad to hear from me and miraculously was available to come and have lunch with Suleyman, the next day.

# 11.

# SULEYMAN

The February wind penetrated to my bones through my black leather jacket, as I stood in front of my block waiting for Seva. Once again, I regretted wearing my toe-tight, fashionable, leather boots. Their slim heels were so high I found it difficult to walk in them – they had cost me a lot in taxi fares – but I loved how they made my legs look and the inches they added to my height. I had dressed in Baku chic, to impress others and convey my success, even if that was bending the truth. I couldn't pace up and down to keep warm, so was getting increasingly impatient. Where was she?

Time was a fluid concept in Azerbaijan. 11am could mean 11am, but most likely 11:30am, if not midday. This man, Suleyman, might arrive before Seva, which would make my "reunion" with her pointless; but since I had called to confirm that I would be attending the meeting with a friend, she had better turn up.

After twenty minutes, Seva's curvaceous frame came into view. She ambled towards me, without a shadow of guilt on her face at being late. I stood glued to the spot, by my boots and the growing realisation on seeing Seva that I had made a terrible mistake. Despite the implications and possible dangers of meeting a stranger unchaperoned, I wished I had come alone.

Her make-up was as confident as her strut: four shades of purple eyeshadow competed with thick eyeliner, lash-curling mascara, rouge-plastered cheeks and a mouth virtually dripping with fuchsia gloss. I groaned inwardly at her gold hoop earrings, low-cut white shirt and a velvet skirt so tight that it fought her fleshy thighs every step she took. She trotted towards me, arms outstretched.

'Gulush! Where did you disappear to? We've been so, so worried,' she squealed before she even reached me. I had no time to respond as she engulfed me in a bear hug, kissing me on both cheeks. She reeked of some strong perfume. 'I'm so glad you're OK. You look fabulous!' Her hot breath tickled my neck.

'Yes, yes, I am fine.' I extracted myself from her arms. 'I just have this meeting with this man, Suleyman, originally from Ganja, who knows estate agents in Baku. I want… *my family* wants to buy a flat in Baku. He'll be helping me to find something suitable.' I lied so Seva wouldn't ask where the money was coming from.

She arched her eyebrows. 'What about the house in Ganja?'

Thankfully, just then, a smart black car beeped at us as it pulled up, which prevented Seva from asking any more questions. I did not want to return to Ganja, the house no longer felt like home to me and if Nana recovered from her treatment in Moscow, I knew she would insist on arranging me a marriage, which would undoubtedly lead to my death: I'd either be killed or take my own life, but either way I'd be damned because they'd all know about my transgressions. I wanted to make a life for myself, with a clean slate, and a lot was hanging on getting a flat.

A man in a dark charcoal coat and wool beret scuttled towards us from the car.

'Gulush?' he said, looking from Seva to me. I nodded. 'Good, good. I'm Suleyman.' He shook my hand carefully, then turned to exchange greetings with Seva.

'Thank you so much for agreeing to help me,' I said. Seva flashed her shark-white teeth in a smile. 'This is my friend, Seva, she's visiting from Ganja,' I added.

'Let's go discuss your plans somewhere out of the cold, with food and drinks,' Suleyman said, indicating his car. Seva headed straight for the rear door, before I could say anything. I noticed another man sitting in the front. 'I have a friend visiting today. I hope you don't mind him joining us,' Suleyman said, opening the other rear door for me.

'Leave your questions for later,' I whispered to Seva, as her lips started to move. I did not want Suleyman to know any of my business. He was from Ganja and might know someone – gossip travelled faster than cars in my experience. Suleyman's friend, Mr C, was also a complete stranger, and unremarkable in his appearance and conversation, despite Seva's efforts to chat. As we passed the Bayil mound on our right, I realised we were heading to the seafront near Shikhov beach.

Seva showed a childlike pleasure at being escorted into our private room in the sleek, modern restaurant. She would no doubt marvel, as I had once done at the lavish food and the sea view I predicted, cynically. Just sitting down at the beautifully dressed table brought a bitter taste to my mouth. I knew that behind the fabulous façades, each room held the potential of being a venue for secret and often harmful liaisons.

Today was different for me. This was a business meeting, and I was the customer, not the vendor. I sat primly upright as if it were my first day at university. I did not know what Suleyman's credentials were yet. My responses to his questions stayed clipped and to the point. I completely ignored his friend and avoided direct eye contact with Suleyman. Though Seva's presence detracted from the image I was trying to project – of a dutiful, homespun girl who was buying a flat on behalf of her family – Seva did keep Mr C occupied. Once she had decided someone needed drawing out of themselves, she seldom failed. Within a few minutes, Mr C was talking to her as if they'd known each other for years. They sat at the sea view end of the table, Suleyman and I at the other, separated by mounds of food. Although I could still hear Seva's louder outbursts, I knew she hardly paid any attention to my conversations.

Suleyman's questions were probing. He was trying to piece together a bigger picture of who I was. I kept steering the conversation towards his connections with estate agents and what sort of property I could hope to purchase in Baku, while he tried to navigate back towards details of my life.

I told him a combination of lies and truths to fabricate a plausible narrative. My dad was dead, I said, omitting the fact that I had never actually met him because my parents had separated when I was three weeks old. I did not mention my parents' political activities either. I stated that I now had younger siblings, which was why my mother could not be present. My remaining family, my uncles, were away in Moscow with my grandmother, in a bid to 'save her life, as the doctors were no good here'. That was the only time Suleyman showed any negative emotion.

'Not all of them,' he bristled. 'I am a doctor. My father was a well-known doctor in Ganja, and one of my brothers is also a doctor.'

I apologised profusely, saying I meant only the doctors who had attended Nana.

'Are all your family still in Ganja?' I asked politely.

'Yes, my mama still lives in our original family home; she's blind but otherwise in good health. My brothers live nearby with their families, as do my children. I'm separated.' He paused, as his shoulders hunched and he pulled his neck in. I had to stifle a smile. He looked briefly like a cartoon vulture.

'That must be hard for you,' I said, in the sympathetic tones I had used on the top civil servant and his ilk.

'No matter,' he said stiffly, recovering his composure. He sprang into action and busied himself filling everyone's plates with the food that had just arrived.

I resigned myself to his generosity without protest. The first course was chicken fillets served on a *saj* with tomatoes, potatoes and peppers. I ate mine slowly, while Seva tucked enthusiastically into her plateful.

'I hope you all like what I have chosen. I selected their most renowned dishes for us,' Suleyman said, as he tried to fill my glass with vodka.

'No, thank you,' I said trying to sound as pious and firm as possible. 'I never drink alcohol,' I said. Due to an unfortunate lull in their conversation, Mr C and Seva heard me. Seva nearly choked on her chicken and was ironically forced to drink water to stop coughing. I prayed that she had the sense not to blab to Mr C. I hoped she understood I was trying to make a good impression.

As the second course, a fresh salmon, was served, I reflected that I had more than one reason not to drink: I didn't like how it depressed my mood; I felt wary of being in another dining room with another stranger – however well connected; my breasts felt tender from the bruises, my period was late and I was periodically feeling nauseous; worse still, unexplained abrasions and a discharge had appeared on my genitals. There I was, too scared to consult a doctor, sharing a meal with one, who was oblivious to my worries.

Suleyman finally moved on to the subject of estate agents and flat hunting. He made a few phone calls on his mobile, while I pretended to eat. I thought he was at least forty, perhaps even older. He was balding but only slightly overweight and quite muscular. He clearly didn't believe that a beer belly was a good way to signify your wealth, as was the traditional view. However, his watery eyes remained as shrewd and calculating as his smile was broad and gold crowned.

By the time we had finished our meal, Seva and Mr C were quite tipsy and full, and Suleyman had agreed to take me to view a flat the next day. Once back outside my block, he produced two large buckets of flowers and two huge boxes of chocolates for us. I felt awkward receiving such gifts, but graciously accepted mine, while Seva whooped her thanks. She was swaying as we waved the car away.

It was still bitterly cold, but I found myself telling Seva that I had another meeting that day to fob her off. I ached to take my boots off. 'I'll call you tomorrow, so we can catch up properly.' A second lie, because I had no intention of ever seeing her again. Being around her had reminded me of everything I disliked about her. She smudged my cheeks with her lipstick as she kissed me goodbye and stomped off, cradling the chocolates and flowers to her ample chest. She didn't know my flat number and she never would. Clean slate, I reminded myself, clean slate.

*** 

When Suleyman picked me up the following day, at the same spot, I noticed he was wearing a smart but casual jumper and plain black trousers, which clashed with his mature, business-like features. I was puzzled as to why he had dressed down.

'We are going to Icheri Sheher. Have you been there before?' I feigned ignorance, even though I remembered visiting the Maiden Tower with Ilham, one of Nana's relatives, a few years before. I ached for my lost innocence, as I recalled Ilham's enthusiasm in telling me one of the legends of the Maiden Tower, built allegedly in the middle of the Caspian Sea to guard the purity of a rich man's daughter promised to a wealthy elder she despised. She was locked up in the tower awaiting her wedding as if it were a death sentence, when a handsome young but poor man she loved swam across the sea to be reunited with her. She mistook his steps for that of the elder, jumped into the sea and drowned. I wondered how my life would have panned out if I had married Ilham. He was so sweet towards me, but his family was even poorer than mine. Was it better to live in poverty with a man who loved you or have plenty of money but no love? I didn't have a chance to ponder the question, as Suleyman parked the car at the gates to the Old City.

Walking up the narrow winding streets and climbing the cobbled flights of stairs was a challenge, even in my more sensible boots, but Suleyman didn't even get out of breath and pointed things out to me as if he were a tour guide. 'This is the Old City of Baku, surrounded by a twelfth-century ten-metre fortress wall. It's a unique part of the city. Here's another set of gates in the fortress wall, there are five in total...'

*Blah, blah, blah* was all I heard as I trailed after him taking in the wooden balconies, hanging precariously above us with no visible support, and the narrow entrances to the sand-coloured houses, built centuries ago, presenting solid walls onto the street, their windows hidden within. After we had wandered through the narrow alleyways for seemingly twenty minutes, Suleyman stopped in front of one arched entrance, topped with once imposing, but now crumbling, decorative patterns.

'Here we are, *Italyanka*. You're likely to see the neighbours as we go up,' he said, ushering me in. What made this property Italian-style, I wondered?

We walked through into a small courtyard onto a scene that looked like an antique painting. It was packed with activity. There were two young women hanging clothes on a washing line, small children running about and three more women, their heads covered to prevent hair finding its way into the cooking, chopping vegetables, which they tossed into a large pan while gossiping loudly. This could have been Ganja, with Nana and her friends cooking over an open fire. Instinctively, I pulled my leather jacket down to cover my rear, straightened a little and then exchanged polite greetings with the women.

As we climbed the rickety wooden stairs to the top floor, my heart sank with each step. There seemed to be several families housed on each level. Those who were not in the courtyard, drew back their doorway net curtains to peer at us. By the time we entered the small grotty flat on the third floor, I hated the place. There would be no privacy. It was worse than Ganja. I had a sense that no one minded their own business here. Although I intended to keep my slate clean, my reputation would have to be impeccable to survive alone in this obviously tightly knit community.

A twisted, elderly woman showed us "around" the dimly lit one-bedroom flat. Everything here was dilapidated: the wooden floors had chipped paint, the formerly whitewashed walls were aged to a stormy grey, the furniture had passed its prime decades ago and was probably being eaten by woodworm. Once I saw the familiar sight of a large enamel jug and basin, presumably the flat's "bathroom", I let Suleyman do the talking, blanking out the words, impatient to leave.

He eventually noticed my lack of attention and rounded off the conversation with a polite goodbye. I was impressed by how easily he found his way back to the car. I felt completely lost in the Old City and the walk reminded me of my favourite Soviet comedy-crime-drama *The Diamond Hand*, which had been filmed somewhere amongst these streets. I smiled thinking of the hero's mishaps.

I didn't voice my opinion until we were idling in heavy traffic. 'I'm sorry, I hated it,' I said.

'I noticed,' he said drily. 'Those houses used to belong to one family before the Soviets confiscated them in the 1920s and converted them into Italian-style flats, hence the name. The community there is very… settled. The location is excellent, as you know. You're near Baksovet metro station, and within walking distance from the city centre…'

'I don't like it,' I said stubbornly.

'No problem.' He sighed. 'We'll keep looking, but after some hot tea, because I, for one, am freezing.'

I cast my old worries about visiting a café with a man aside, because I felt responsible for his feeling cold and was beginning to shiver myself. Unfortunately, that day I learnt that by "tea" Suleyman always meant a full meal, which I felt I could not refuse. He was so generous with his time and keeping him company was the least I could do to say thank you.


We went to Bayil the next day. It was close to the Old City, but here, though the houses climbed up a steep hill, there were some beautiful views of the Caspian Sea. I was relieved that the three-storey block of flats was a conventional Soviet-built one, with more privacy and no communal courtyards, but the flat itself was dank and dingy. It would need a complete redecoration. I dreaded to think what had caused the dark stains on the living room carpet. An oppressive smell like sewage hung in the air. Was this all my limited budget could buy me? Suleyman could obviously tell by my face what I thought, and we left after only a brief look round.

'Where's the next one?' I asked. He appeared to be driving the wrong way, out of the city.

'I need a cup of tea first, to take the taste away,' he said.

'Oh,' I said, thinking fast. 'I forgot to say, I have another appointment today. Just drop me, I'll catch a taxi.'

'What appointment?' He didn't sound like he believed me.

I elaborated on my lie, inventing a flat inspection and an electrician. He dismissed both phantoms. 'Let them wait, we're here now. You might as well eat first.' The restaurant was on the seafront. A piercing wind whipped up the majestic, steely waves of the Caspian Sea. In the face of this cruel beauty, I found myself agreeing with him. This time, I did not regret it. The fish-based menu was as fresh as the salt breeze itself.

For two weeks, Suleyman showed me flats all over Baku. We visited flats in the Black City – so named because that was where oil refineries once pumped out the soot and smoke that had cloaked this south-eastern neighbourhood of the capital. The flats there were tired and claustrophobic, like the area. Ahmadli yielded better prospects but was too far from the university. Being a car owner, Suleyman had no idea of the trials of public transport. Other areas either felt unsafe or too far from the city life I craved. Was this the reality of the housing market for a limited budget like mine or was Suleyman deliberately taking me to places that were no good, to prolong the process?

He insisted on a meal after every viewing. I assumed he was quite lonely in Baku and that my company cheered him up. His rampant generosity made me distrustful of his motives, because in my experience such "kindness" usually had to be paid for in some other way, but I did nothing to encourage him. I think I made it clear that a connection with him could not go any further than practical help with finding a suitable flat. I would mention my good friend, Dr Adil, every so often.

Suleyman was twenty-four years older than me, like my father, and had six children from two failed marriages. He wasn't a candidate for marriage, or for an affair. Sometimes his probing questions and shrewd expression made me feel so uncomfortable that I longed to find a flat and say my goodbyes. On the other hand, spending time with Suleyman was time away from my current home life.

Having cancelled all proposed outings for weeks – initially because of the assault, then because of my depression, the state of my genitals and my absent period – my relationship with Amina and the girls had continued to deteriorate. I had no one to share my dread of another termination with. I lost sleep at night over it but during the day obliterated my fears by keeping busy and out and about.

I was overjoyed in early March when we finally found the flat that seemed good enough. It was exactly what I needed, with a good-sized living room and a spacious bedroom. It was in a block of flats that was well connected with the city centre by public transport. It was on the ninth floor, sported a distant view of the Caspian Sea and had an old but functional lift. The price was good too, after Suleyman had haggled with the owner, an old man with two teenage children: eight thousand, nine hundred US dollars. I had enough left over from my "wages" for the legal formalities, furniture and to pay bills until I figured out my new life.

I beamed at Suleyman to show I liked the flat.

'We'll bring cash tomorrow,' Suleyman told the owner, and they shook hands on the deal.

'Tomorrow?' I said as the lift creaked its way down. 'What about the legal formalities?'

'They need to buy a new place to move into. Let's give them two weeks to sort things out.'

'But what would stop them from denying that they had ever received the payment?' My heart was pounding at the thought of losing it all.

'Me,' he said. I could not help but look up at him. Something in his tone, the set of his mouth and his eyes made me believe that no one would cross him.

Handing over the cash the next day felt exhilarating as well as frightening. I felt so proud to be buying my first flat on the eve of my twenty-first birthday. Mentioning that fact to Suleyman was a mistake because he insisted he would treat me to a joint birthday and flat celebration dinner the very next day. Given how much he had helped me with finding the flat, I felt compelled to agree and I knew I could not say my goodbyes to him until I was the legal owner of the flat. I insisted on lunch rather than dinner, though, as it felt more neutral.

I returned to my rental flat euphoric but determined to hide the news until I was ready to move out. Strangely, Nargiz greeted me sweetly and offered me a cup of tea, but Irada had her business face on and demanded I come speak to her in my bedroom. I reluctantly agreed, fully expecting her to interrogate me again about my whereabouts and plans. I had never actually said I wouldn't attend client outings again, but in the past several weeks I had come up with a range of reasons why not: I was depressed, I didn't feel well, I needed to study for my forthcoming exams, an unexpected timetable change, I'd got a strange rash. Usually, Irada listened to my excuses with patience; her young face had scrunched up with concern when I mentioned the rash, but her carefully plucked eyebrows arched cynically whenever I spoke about exams. There was no attempt at interrogation now.

'Amina said I should call her when you got home and pass the phone to you.' Her tone was stern, but her face looked concerned. I realised warning me about her cousin's demand was the only concession she could make for me. 'Amina's been very patient with you, until now,' she said, a trace of the old Irada in her liquid eyes.

'Well, why don't we say I didn't come back today, but I'll work tomorrow, and speak to her afterwards. Are there any outings that need covering?' I said, not wanting anything to deflate my mood.

Irada perked up. 'Yes. There's a client tomorrow who I can't do. Late afternoon, five o'clock. Here's the address.' Then she fluttered out of my bedroom, leaving me holding a pink Post-it note. I didn't care, I was feeling too happy to argue. What did one more client matter? Soon I would be gone.

★★★

The next day, I jumped into Suleyman's car, relieved that we were not going to be trekking to another viewing. It was a huge thing to buy my own flat, but for now I felt quite calm. I reasoned that it was not going to feel real until after

I had moved in. The meal was lovely, as I had expected, but for me it was overshadowed by the prospect of my five o'clock appointment. I hadn't recognised the name and Irada had no other details. The weeks spent flat hunting had obviously softened the protective shell I had built up inside. We finished the meal at three o'clock and Suleyman paid. I calculated I would have at least an hour and a half to freshen up and make my appointment, but then Suleyman said, 'I need to pop into my flat to pick up some paperwork. It's on our way. It will only take five minutes.'

'If it's just five minutes.' I felt I could not say no. 'I've got an appointment at five.'

The flat was a nine-storey block of flats near Ganjlik metro station. 'It was designed specifically for KGB officers and their families.'

I stopped breathing for a moment. 'You were KGB?' That would explain a lot.

'Me?' He laughed. 'No, no, but I bought it from one. It's a classic. Come and see,' he said.

It occurred to me that the last time I had gone nosing around someone else's house it had not gone well for me. I tried to think of a reason to stay in the car, but my mind went completely blank.

'Come on,' he said, 'I thought you were in a hurry.'

I sighed. This was Suleyman, a friend of Dr Adil, who had helped me find a beautiful flat, surely it would be all right. I got out of the car and followed him to the lift. It was much sleeker than the one in my block.

'I'm on the seventh floor,' he said. I decided to ignore the slight twinge of tension inside me. He was in such a good mood. His flat had a bright green door, made of iron.

'You can see the original Soviet design throughout. It's all very neatly done. Excuse the boxes, to be honest I'm still settling in,' he said.

The long kitchen with built-in dark-brown cupboards looked too dark for me, even with the hanging industrial-style lights switched on. There was no evidence of cooking activity anywhere. Perhaps he ate all his meals out? The big living room had a set of windows with a panoramic view at the far end. There was a large TV set, a wooden table and four matching chairs, but no sofas, just a mattress, covered in a decorative throw and two pillows.

'I don't know why I didn't buy the flat with the furnishings from the vendor,' Suleyman carried on speaking, 'it looked so cosy in here, but as you can see, I'm yet to find replacements that would really suit the flat.'

By contrast, the three bedrooms were light and airy. One had access to a large balcony, which overlooked the busy street in front of the metro station. It was the only bedroom yet to have a carpet, a dark-brown sea, with another mattress island, clad in a cream striped duvet and pillows marooned in the middle of it. I smiled; this lack of perfection made Suleyman seem more human.

'We need to go now,' I said, looking out into the busy street, but as I turned, I found him standing in the doorway staring at me, his face full of expectation.

'I thought…' He stepped towards me. I could hear him breathing.

Inside, I felt myself shutting down. *Oh no, not you as well*, I thought. As much as I wanted to push my way out of that room, I knew I couldn't, without causing myself more grief. I couldn't afford to piss him off. He was the key to my flat. What more did I have to lose? I had done this with so many men by now, it wouldn't kill me. If I had an infection and he caught it, that would be his problem, not mine.

I breathed in the scent of his expensive cologne, as he pressed me into his chest. Through his white stripy shirt, I could feel his strong muscles. He guided me to lie on the mattress, my head haloed by the pillows. Then he simply lay on top of me fully clothed and was still. I could feel his erection through the layers of our clothing, his heavy breathing next to my ear.

My heart beat the seconds away, like a stopwatch. Was he planning to stay like that all day? Perhaps this was his idea of getting my consent. I had that bloody client at 5pm. If I missed the appointment, who knew what Amina would do? I experimented with trying to wriggle out, but he tightened his grip. I was clearly not getting out of here until we had sex. It wouldn't take long. He was in his mid-forties, after all.

'Fine, let's do this,' I said, loosening my skirt and starting to push it down my legs. His hands joined in, peeling off the bottom half of my clothes before fumbling his belt and trousers open. He entered me quickly, before I was ready, but I was used to that, my vagina always seemed to go into spasm during sex, leaving the man to force his way in. I closed my eyes and made a selection of subtle noises as I went to the safe place in my imagination where my perfect phantom lover lived. Suleyman took a surprisingly long time to climax, for a middle-aged man.

When he was done, I grabbed my clothes and dashed to the bathroom. It was almost funny that I had managed to get suckered into this sort of mess again. When was I going to learn? Had he realised I was not a virgin? If he told the wrong person in Ganja about this… What about Dr Adil? I groaned in frustration as I sluiced out his semen with a small shower head in the toilet.

I had nothing to say as I rushed to sit in the car, or on the way to my flat. I just wanted to disappear. There seemed more shame in having sex with Suleyman than with someone I would never see again.

'You OK?' he asked, briefly touching my knee with his hand. He had never done that before.

'Yes, yes,' I said, trying to sound as if it were true. 'But I wanted to tell you about… you know… it was only once…' The words stuck in my throat. Did I even need to try and salvage my reputation? It was one thing not to be a virgin, but he mustn't suspect my experience was greater than one stupid mistake I had made in innocence. He'd be more likely to keep quiet about it then, I reasoned.

'Relax. I know everything,' he said.

I didn't know what to say. What 'everything' did he know? Had Dr Adil betrayed me? I didn't want to know. We had arrived at my block. The dashboard clock clicked onto 4.45pm.

'You'd better get going, my dear.' Suleyman suppressed a yawn before lighting a cigarette. 'See you soon.'

I couldn't reply. Shaking, I clambered out of the car and fled into the lobby. I didn't have time to go up to my flat, so hid in the shadows until Suleyman's car had gone. Then I emerged and fixed my make-up under the streetlamp, until a taxi glided up to me. The rest of that evening passed in a blur, as if I had been caught in a bomb blast. Everything, even voices, even touches, seemed distant and distorted, dominated by the ringing tinnitus of Suleyman's words: 'I know everything.'

★★★

I wanted to avoid meeting up with Suleyman for the fortnight leading up to the time when the legal formalities were due to be finalised. I dodged his invitations, with my usual range of excuses, from household commitments to my studies to my health. The latter was a real concern, although I still hadn't summoned up the courage to go and see a doctor. I thought I would do that once I was in my new flat. I also tried to stay out of the way of the girls, especially Irada and her pro-Amina speeches. I was on my way to a shop, a week later, adjusting my collar to keep out the March winds, when a voice right beside me shot through my thoughts.

'Gulush,' said Suleyman, from his car.

I turned sharply, a smile plastered on my face, trying to hide my surprise.

'How lovely to see you,' he continued, smiling back. 'Where have you been hiding? Why don't you get in the car and we can have a little catch up?'

'Have you been waiting for me?' My voice squealed a little. I didn't like to think of him parked in front of my block where he might see a client collecting me. I did not get in the car.

'I have come to arrange a time for the legal formalities to be finalised for your lovely flat. How about this Friday?'

'Yes, that would be amazing!' I said, relaxing a little.

'Good, good,' he said, blowing a smoke ring. He stared

up at me, curiously. 'So, are you avoiding me?'

'Of course not,' I said, as brightly as the morning sunshine, whose light was thankfully casting shadows over my face.

'It's just that since our... you know... I haven't seen you. You didn't like it?'

'It's not that, I've just been so busy, I told you. Staying with friends always complicates things, doesn't it?' I tried to sound casual.

'Let's go for a chat in my flat. You don't look like you're busy right now,' he said.

I didn't bother to say no. I couldn't have him feeling rejected. My flat was still in his hands. I had to play nice. Food, drink, compliments then expectations of sex: always the same.

At the flat, I noticed he'd even changed the bedding. Again, I hoped for a quick exit. Again, he kept going, until I had faked two orgasms. Again, he fell back panting while I rushed to the bathroom. However, when I returned to retrieve my shoes, I found him dressed but half leaning against the corridor wall, clutching his chest. He tried to say something, then lost his balance and toppled to the floor, as a confetti of one-hundred-dollar bills scattered from his torn coat pocket.

I stared in horror at his motionless body, cocooned in more money than it had taken to buy my flat. I had heard Amina and her co-workers talking about clients dying during and after sex, but I never thought it would happen to me. Moving nearer, I saw he was still breathing. I realised I didn't know the correct address to call an ambulance to, or even where the phone was. What should I do? Just as I started to panic, Suleyman stirred and opened his eyes.

'What happened?' he said weakly.

'You tell me,' I said. The shock had stolen my politeness. 'You're the doctor. You fell down.'

'Fetch me water,' he gasped. I assumed he had some medication he needed to take. Why hadn't he warned me that he had a health problem? I dashed to the kitchen and returned with a glassful, to find him already sitting up.

'What's all this doing here?' he said, as he started gathering up the hundred-dollar bills and stuffing them back in his jacket pockets.

Was this some sort of performance he had put on for me? Was it to show me that he had plenty of cash or to test my integrity and see if I would steal from him? He didn't say and I was too mesmerised by the strangeness of the situation to ask. He drank all the water, retrieved all the money and then insisted on driving me home. By the time we reached my flat, I had decided he was probably crazy and not fit to be interrogated. No one could have predicted this.

'Friday, eleven o'clock,' he said, as I got out of the car. 'Remember to bring your ID and cash for the notary.' Then he drove away without another word, leaving me dazed and confused on the pavement. Had I imagined it, or had he left smiling? It was all so bizarre, I almost laughed myself. Only a few days to go, and then, never, never, ever again, I vowed.

★★★

I woke with the dawn on Friday, the day that I hoped would change my life forever. After snatching breakfast in the deserted kitchen, with the girls still resting next door, I crept back to my bedroom and decided to start packing up my belongings. It was better than sitting counting down the minutes until my appointment. While the girls got ready to leave for school, I packed up my suitcase and hid it under the bed. I didn't want anyone to notice my preparations to leave. As soon as I had the keys to the flat, I would be ready to go, even if I had to put up with a lack of furniture. I could take my time choosing furnishings later. My mood was as buoyant as a party balloon, until, emptying my shelf of trinket boxes and make-up, I discovered that my remaining savings, my cushion of over one thousand US dollars, wasn't in its usual place. Feeling increasingly anxious, I went back through all the things I had already packed, through drawers, wardrobe, cupboards, on and under the bed and even behind the radiator and curtains, until I was sure: someone had taken all the money I had left.

## 12.

# NEW HOME

'Here's the key to your flat,' said Suleyman as soon as I opened the car door at 10.30am. He passed me a silvery key dangling from a simple navy keyring. I tried to suppress another sob; my eyes were already raw. Like a lure to a fish, it suddenly felt utterly out of reach. I felt I had lost everything I had worked for in the past months. I had sacrificed my health, sanity and future prospects for nothing! Suleyman hadn't noticed my face yet, only my suitcase.

'What have you brought that thing with you for? Do you want to go straight to your flat after the meeting? What about all your other stuff?'

I couldn't speak until I had climbed into the car, dragging the suitcase after me. Now he could see the state I was in.

'My savings… the money for the legal formalities…' I choked on my words. 'It's… it's all gone.'

'What do you mean? Who took it?' Suleyman erupted.

I didn't want to reveal the true version of events, so mumbled something incomprehensible while the morning's events flashed in my mind's eye.

Neither Irada nor Nargiz had picked up when I had phoned them after my discovery, so, fuelled by rage and panic, I had rung Amina. She, unsurprisingly, denied knowing anything about the theft. 'I have no idea where your money is. I wouldn't even spit on a mere thousand dollars. You are insulting me if you think otherwise. After all I've done for you!'

She was so vehement with her denial that part of me believed her. I felt so frustrated and nauseous that I couldn't stop myself biting back. 'Irada has been harassing me about paying you more for introductions. Did she take it for you, to punish me? I need that money, today. It's urgent.'

Amina's tone was icy now. 'Well, I don't have it and I think I have supported you enough over these past months. Perhaps… it's time… for you to move on.'

I might have grown to hate her, but I still remembered our first months together, when I thought she was my friend. The thought that she was discarding me, before I could choose to walk away myself, on top of everything else, unhinged my mouth. Angry words spewed out as I told her what I thought about her now and how she'd treated me and treated others, like Irada. She'd acted like my new best friend, showering me with gifts and kindnesses, but when she'd found out I had lost my virginity, I'd become disposable.

'If you don't like it,' she blasted through my monologue, 'then get out! I don't have to defend my choices to the likes of you.'

'It's your girls that need to go. I paid for this flat with my body!' I shouted, slamming the receiver down.

Suleyman shook his head. 'I don't think it's wise for you to go back. Once trust is gone, it's gone.' I don't know what he inferred from my explanation, but a part of me had wondered if he would save the day by paying my legal expenses. I was reluctant to ask him because I suspected owing him would be a hard hook to wriggle off. 'Besides, I have a solution to your temporary housing problem. Come and stay at my flat, until you legally own your home.'

I knew that sex would be involved if I went to live with him but, if I'd stayed in Amina's good books, that would also have been the case. Suleyman seemed the lesser of two evils.

'That is so kind of you,' I said slowly, trying to buy time for myself to think it through, 'but I don't want to get in your way.'

Suleyman did not have to ask me twice, but he seemed to understand my hesitation. 'I could have just lent you the money, but I do not believe, as a woman, that you should be indebted to anyone. It's not right to put you in that position. I am confident you will find a way to raise the cash, from family, in time.'

'You are right,' I agreed. 'My Baba always told me, live within your means; never borrow or lend anyone money. But if there's a delay, won't the vendors change their minds?'

'They won't dare.' His voice sounded so firm and self-assured; I took his word for it.

★★★

I had planned to stay at Suleyman's only briefly. I would call a couple of regular clients and Dr Adil, and make enough money to pay the legal fees, buy myself some cheap furniture and move into my flat. Every time I clasped the silver key, safe in my pocket, it felt like a talisman, connecting me to my future.

Suleyman treated me to a nice meal out on the first day and the evening ended, as I anticipated, with sex. Afterwards, he snored while I listened to the traffic whizzing by outside, wondering if I'd made a mistake by agreeing to live here. Eventually, I dropped into a dreamless sleep. When I woke the next morning, groggy and disorientated, Suleyman was already dressing, getting ready for work.

'You stay in and rest today,' he said, collecting his car keys from the windowsill. 'We'll go out again this evening.'

I was too exhausted to reply. I murmured goodbye and went back to sleep. All the stress and disrupted nights of the last few months had caught up with me. I was so grateful to have a quiet space where I was not disturbed.

When I got up, I had a long shower and dressed smartly in a pair of trousers and a black top. I drank tea, flicking through the TV channels. I was still feeling groggy, so I thought I'd go out for some fresh air and some food, as there was nothing in the flat, but I couldn't find any keys. The front door had two locks. One would open without a key, but I couldn't have got back in if it had shut. The other was locked from the outside. I started to feel a little agitated. Typical of a man not to think of giving me a key. It was a good thing I hadn't arranged any meetings already. What if there was a fire in the building? How would I get out then? What if something happened to Suleyman and he didn't come back at all? I made myself another cup of tea and paced the flat impatiently. I didn't like this feeling. It wasn't like I could climb out through the window on the seventh floor. By the time Suleyman turned up, only an hour later, the late afternoon sun was blazing through the windows and inside so was I.

'I need a set of keys,' I said carefully. 'I don't like being locked in. What if I had had to go somewhere?'

'One, I told you exactly when I was coming back.' I didn't remember this. 'Two, where would you be going?' he said, taking off his shoes.

'I might have had an appointment or something,' I said, as he walked to the living room.

'To do what? To fuck someone?' he threw over his shoulder. I gasped. 'I told you I know everything, everything you've left out of your stories.'

'I don't know what you mean.' I stopped at the threshold, supporting myself by gripping the edge of the door.

'Since we met, I have followed you to your "appointments". I know for certain how you've made that money.'

I couldn't move. He could tell anyone, even Nana. I was ruined. What could I do? Did he want me to beg him for his silence?

'You must understand,' he said slowly, 'that it's not normal to do what you have done. You are not to be trusted. You have to be protected from yourself. That's what I did for you today. And that discharge, it needs treatment, it could be serious.'

My face burnt with shame.

'The question you should be asking,' he continued, 'is are you really ready to leave that life behind and cut all contact with those whores and their clients?' My eyes filled with tears. 'Answer me!' he barked, walking towards me.

All my senses were screaming *run!* but all I could do was nod my head and mumble, 'Yes.'

'Good, good. That's a start,' he said, suddenly calm again, returning to rummage in the cupboard at the far end of the living room.

I moved gingerly towards the hall, my eyes on the floor. He didn't try to stop me, so I turned as I reached the door. 'If I'm so bad, then I think I should go. Thank you for all you have done for me, Suleyman,' I croaked. That voice didn't sound like me.

He remained in the living room as I stuffed my suitcase, put on my only coat and headed for the front door. I wasn't thinking straight. His words had broken me. I just wanted to get away from the shame, from all my mistakes. I expected that at any moment he'd come after me, but he didn't.

The lift was empty when it arrived. As the doors closed behind me, I burst into tears. I felt utterly alone and worthless. No one would really want me now, not even someone like twice-divorced Suleyman. As I stumbled out into the street, the fresh spring wind ruffled my hair, but I could not feel the warmth of the sun, I was cold from the inside out. I felt Suleyman watching me, from his balcony, before I saw him. It surprised me. Why would he care, after what he had said to me? I set off along the pavement, trying to look like I knew where I was going. At that point, I didn't.

Once out of sight of the flat, I hailed a taxi, climbed heavily into the back seat, and pulled out half a pack of Parliament cigarettes, Amina's favourite brand, from my handbag. I lit one and sat smoking, ignoring the disapproving looks of the driver.

'Where do you want to go?' he growled.

'Just a second,' I said through clenched teeth. I hadn't decided yet. I knew I only had a hundred dollars in my purse at best, which wasn't going to last me long, and the key. I reached to touch it. Perhaps? I gave him the address of my "new home" and collapsed into the cloud of cigarette smoke, until the driver asked for his fare, twice.

I didn't know if I had any right to be in the flat, but I had the key, I had paid the vendor and had no other choice. The previous owners had taken all their belongings, including the Soviet-made air con that had occupied half of the living room window. A sea wind howled in through the gaping hole. I shivered and, closing that door, I walked around the rest of the flat. The balcony of the main bedroom was not well insulated, so that room was cold as well. Its beautiful view of the city and the Caspian Sea twinkling in the distance was no use to me, so I headed for the small kitchen. The cooker and sink were still there, but there was no kettle or utensils. Next, I entered the much smaller, darker bedroom. It was the warmest and had a large built-in wardrobe, which, when I opened it, featured a shoe shelf that was sturdy enough for me to curl up on. I hugged my knees to my chest and started to cry again, releasing all my bitter fears.

My mind thrashed around in my sore head trying to come up with solutions for my many problems. Who could I call? I had to discount Dr Adil straight away. He was also a direct link to the past and Suleyman and I needed to leave it all behind.

I contemplated contacting Mama next, but quickly dismissed that thought because she was still unemployed, staying in her comrade's flat, the family surviving on what little work her husband could find. If I could just get enough money for the legal fees…? I imagined bringing them to live with me. That would be overwhelming and wouldn't help with my other priorities. I had just over a year of my university course left, during which I had a dissertation to write and an oral viva to pass. It was a daunting prospect, but I knew if I could put in the work I would pass.

I needed a job of some sort, although finding employment was practically impossible without connections or bribes, especially in Baku. If I miraculously procured one, there was still the challenge of life without male protection. It could be dangerous if people realised that I was living alone. I would be regarded as fair game by many. Being someone's lover seemed my only option – but without my sexual health that was going to be impossible. My potential future got darker the more I examined it.

The flat was still not legally registered in my name. What if Suleyman tipped the owners off? I had no written receipt for the money. Might they return and reclaim the property? I could end up homeless. I needed money for a termination as well as treatment for the mysterious infection. Until that was sorted out, I couldn't risk contacting old clients. Even if they didn't notice at the time, if I passed it on to one of them, that person might get sicker than me or angry enough to tell others.

It all seemed so hopeless. It was getting dark outside and in my unlit flat, but at least I was not on the streets, yet. I was thinking it might be more comfortable on the floor than the shelf when my phone rang. I fished it out of my handbag, ready to lie to any potential client. Who else would be calling me?

'Where are you?' Suleyman's voice sounded tense. 'Did you go back to those whores?'

'No,' I said. I didn't like him calling them that, even if it was true. For a while they had felt like sisters to me.

'Then where are you?'

'Why do you care?' I sighed. 'After the things you said to me…'

'That was the truth, but when did I say I didn't care?'

That was the nearest he ever got to saying he did, but at that moment, tired and desperate, trying to sleep in a wardrobe, it seemed enough to me.

'I'm at the new flat,' I sighed. I felt defeated by it all.

It seemed ages before he replied. 'Good choice. That gives me hope that not all is lost. But you can't stay in an empty flat. I'm coming to collect you.'

My pride wanted to stay, prove him wrong, lead an honest life without his help, but in my heart, I knew that realistically Suleyman was my best option. I didn't have the money or connections to go it alone, my family couldn't help and Amina would never forgive me for my rebellion. That lifestyle had destroyed me from the inside out. Being Suleyman's live-in lover surely couldn't be as bad as that?

On the way back to his block of flats, Suleyman outlined his plans for me. 'If you are serious about changing your life, you will have to follow my guidance absolutely. Is that clear?'

'Yes,' I said, miserably, catching glimpses of everyday workplaces as we whizzed by. Behind each garage, shop and office door, I imagined happy people who had made better choices than me, going about their ordinary lives, never realising how lucky they were.

'You'll have to disappear for a while. Let those false friends of yours forget about you. That means *no* leaving the flat by yourself. If we do bump into someone who thinks they know you, we will deny it's you. You'll need a fake name. You don't have to change it legally, but you need to be quick to introduce yourself by it.'

'I used the name "Parvana" once,' I said.

'Parvana, yes, I like that one. Your appearance must change too. All right?'

'It sounds like you have it all mapped out for me,' I said, feeling very tired.

'I have your welfare at heart, be assured of that. I'll look after your phone for now.'

'But what about my family? They'll be worried,' I protested.

'What about them? Where were they when you got into this trouble?' I tried to defend them, but he cut me short. 'You can call your Mama. Tell her you have got a job in the States, on a diplomatic mission, which means you can't contact anyone again, until you pass clearance. See, I can sort these things out for you.'

I thought it all sounded like a cheap spy movie, but I called the number Mama had given me the last time I saw her. The phone rang several times. I hoped she wouldn't pick up this first time, so I could keep my Motorola a little longer. It had made me feel connected to the rest of the world, even when I had no one to ring. Mama answered just before I was about to suggest trying later.

'Hello?' She sounded as weary as me. I could hear

children squabbling in the background, against the sound of a radio.

'Hi Mama, it's me. Listen… I've got a job in the… diplomatic service. I'm going to the US…' The lie felt too big to tell, so the words kept sticking in my throat, but Mama believed it.

'Wow, how did you get the job? That's amazing! When are you coming here so we can give you a proper send off?'

*With what money, Mama?* I thought bitterly. We had none.

'It just came up, but …' I explained about the mythical clearance process with its non-contact proviso. 'When I've passed, I'll have to leave immediately.' I tried to pump it all up, to sound confident, but I thought I sounded fake. I wanted her to see through it all, to come and rescue me and take me to their home; but I knew their home was not mine, nor was Nana's house and, for now, neither was the flat that I had bought with my own flesh and blood.

'So, this is goodbye then? For how long?' Her voice trembled.

I wanted to howl with grief and pain; instead, I said, 'I don't know, but I promise I'll be in touch again as soon as I can.'

Suleyman's hand squeezed my thigh, harder than he needed to, to show his impatience.

'Good luck, Gulush. I'm sure you'll do so well,' Mama said, tears in her voice.

'Of course, Mama. Tell Nana I'm safe.' I hung up before my tears joined hers.

Suleyman held open his palm expectantly. I surrendered my phone and turned away from him to stare out of the window with tearful, unseeing eyes. This was it. With the phone gone, all my exits were closed. There would be no going back if he deleted my phone book numbers and kept it switched off. Most people moved on if you didn't answer their calls. Feeling that things couldn't get any worse, I told him my only remaining secret. 'I think I am pregnant, Suleyman.'

'It's not mine,' he said tersely.

'I know,' I bristled. 'But it's been a while and I need to…'

'I can book you into a clinic. Do you want that?'

I mumbled my agreement.

'But first,' he said, parking the car, 'we need to treat that infection. I've already bought you some tablets.'

'How do you know what I need to take?'

'I am a doctor, remember?' he said, grimly. 'All you need to know is that it is treatable, if you do as you're told.'

★★★

I started taking the handful of pills that same day. I had no idea what they were. Suleyman prepared each dose and handed them over with a glass of water at 8am, every morning. He would watch till I had taken them all, then leave for work, locking the door behind him. He repeated the ritual after work, too.

I found that I slept soundly most of the day. The tablets seemed to knock me out. Suleyman said this was because my body was working so hard to fight the infection. Even if I woke up, after smoking a cigarette and grabbing a piece of bread and cheese, I usually went back to sleep, as I had no interest in being awake, to pace the flat alone. Most days I slept till 6pm, then showered and dressed up, patiently waiting for Suleyman to return and take me out to dinner.

The nights were the hardest times. Sleeping in the day meant I was wide awake as Suleyman snored by my side. My mind tormented me with horrific repeats of the past few months, in full technicolour, featuring all the experiences I had not been able to process at the time. Suleyman bought a double bed for the master bedroom, but that did not help me. Invariably, after he fell asleep, I would tiptoe to the spare room, curling up on the single mattress on the floor, so I didn't disturb him with my tears. The first three nights he came to find me, to comfort me, the only way he seemed to know how, with sex; but the fourth and following nights, he thankfully left me to cry alone.

I mourned the loss of my old life with Nana, despite its challenges. I knew she was due to return from Moscow in a few months. How would she manage without me? At least she couldn't insist on an arranged marriage now I was "away". I mourned the loss of my supposed friends and the good times we had had together. I mourned the loss of my steady job at the Prosecutor's Office, remembering the smiles and laughter amongst the frustrations and betrayals. In short, I mourned for my entire past life. What a waste, I thought, so much potential and yet now no future. My tears seemed never ending, almost hysterical. By the time the sun started to blaze through the now permanently locked balcony windows, I was usually exhausted again, crushed by the disappointment of surviving to face another day.

I think the situation was a strain on Suleyman too.

Within two weeks of moving me in with him, his charms had started to fade. As I lay, sleepless as ever one night, I remembered a tale Nana used to tell.

'A man goes to visit some relatives. They greet him warmly that first day and treat him like a God. They feed him delectable food and at night they prepare him a comfortable bed by laying down a flat-woven wool kilim, then a thick, silk and wool Persian carpet, then a striped wool mattress and finally a sheet, duvet and fine pillows. The guest sleeps like a baby on it. The next day, he goes to explore the town and meets some friends at a tea house. When he returns, the duvet and pillows are missing. No one says why.

'Ah, they are probably airing them, he thinks, as he blows out his lamp. He has another restful night on the remaining soft bedding. On his third day, he goes sightseeing at a local bazaar to buy his children some presents. When he returns to his relatives' house, his sheet and mattress have vanished. Again, no one says why, even after they have shared some soup.

'They are probably airing them too, he decides, curling up on the soft carpet and the kilim, which was still reasonably comfortable. Again, he sleeps well the whole night through.

'The next day, he is walking around the neighbourhood, reflecting on how strange it is that his bedding is gradually disappearing, when he meets an old wise man of his acquaintance. Soon their conversation turns to the vanishing bedding.

'"How long have you stayed there?" the sage asks him.

'"For three nights only, wise one," he replies. The sage smiles.

"'It is said that on the first day a guest is as gold, on the second day he is as silver, on the third day he is as bronze, but by the fourth day he goes bad. I would give thanks and take your leave, before tonight.'"

I had always laughed at this story, understanding that even your nearest and dearest can outstay their welcome. Suleyman's changing behaviour reminded me of that, except that I had nowhere else to go.

★★★

After taking me out for dinner every night for the first few days, Suleyman started bringing home takeaways of various kinds and we would sit in the living room and eat in silence; he seldom shared the events of his day and I had little to say about mine.

Then one evening, he arrived back with a shopping bag, stuffed with a selection of fresh ingredients and announced that he had already eaten. I was a bit rattled by this, but like the guest in the story, I didn't complain. I chopped some succulent tomatoes and ate them with cheese and bread. Although I had been Nana's little helper in the kitchen, she had never let me cook independently in case I spoilt the ingredients. I was there to chop, dice, pluck and pulverise, fetch whatever she needed, then mix, stir, fry or braise the ingredients. She was the one behind the spices and seasonings, combining everything together into splendid meals for the many or the few.

Suleyman, like the hosts in the story, didn't say anything about this development. It took my addled brain three days to realise that he wasn't going to be bringing me ready cooked food any more, so I started experimenting with cooking myself, trying to replicate some simple dishes from my memory. My attempts were not great at first: I overcooked or undercooked rice, some vegetables were soggy, others were stringy, and the meat or fish was either too spiced or bland as bread. Suleyman seemed pleased that I was trying to do something constructive with my day. At first, he would just taste the results, but then he started to join me and ate up everything I served him, even when my inner Nana was shouting 'a dog wouldn't eat that'. I began to redouble my efforts to improve, because at least his appreciation of my food got me some positive attention.

Without a washing machine in the flat, I ran out of clean clothes, so I had to wash my underwear by hand with household soap. I borrowed a long, chequered shirt from Suleyman's wardrobe that came down to just above my knees and wore that day and night for a while. I wasn't going out any more, so there seemed little point in making a fuss about my lack of clothes. It felt liberating not to be constricted in any way since my tiny belly had expanded. The waistline on my fashionable trousers had started to dig in. Since my genitals had begun to heal, the abrasions smoothed out and the discharge gone, my pregnancy had become my greatest night-time worry, but I didn't try to talk to Suleyman about it.

I got used to my new schedule: sleeping 8am to 6pm, cooking 6pm till 7pm, and then waiting for the turn of the key in the green metal door, as Suleyman returned from work. Sometimes I felt almost excited to see him, but that excitement was usually short-lived, since he preferred to eat in silence and would then change and slump down in front of the TV, on his new leather sofa, biting the collar of his favourite old track suit. He was usually exhausted after his workday, the details of which he never shared. He would say he'd had his fill of talking during the day and wanted to fill up on peace and quiet. I had little I could talk to him about anyway, apart from the TV and my cooking, but having been alone all day, I found myself craving some sort of connection, even with him. Apart from the occasional sex session, which I was now the main initiator of, nothing changed between us. I might sigh or even sulk, or make a point of going to bed early, hoping that he would notice and follow me to the spare room, which had become my domain. I was prepared to do virtually anything, by that time, to save myself from yet another night alone with my thoughts. He never came, but would sit in the living room and watch national TV.

Consequently, I was stupidly intrigued when he returned one night, carrying two bags. One contained the usual groceries, which he placed on the kitchen counter, the other bag was a flimsy plastic one. I reached my hand in and drew out, much to my surprise, an outfit even my Nana would have approved of, and probably worn. It consisted of a long cream skirt with minimal decoration and a loose matching knee-length chemise.

'Who is this for?' I said, thinking perhaps it was a gift for some relative, which he wanted me to approve.

'Put it on,' he said.

'What for? It's so long and shapeless.' I failed to hide my dislike.

'What do you want to wear then? The clothes that you prostituted in?' I flinched at his harsh tone. 'I don't understand why you would even keep all that shit. Does it tickle your fancy to think about how you peeled off these clothes for men's pleasure? Hoping to have another outing? Not on my watch! Go dress in your new clothes.'

Once on, the outfit was as unflattering as I had thought it would be, but there was no other choice and, inside, part of me thought Suleyman was right. I found myself mechanically gathering my expensive, fashionable clothes and more flimsy underwear into a large bin bag and leaving it by the front door for him to dispose of. After he had made approving noises about my new outfit, I went to my room, carefully took it off, put the chequered shirt on and lay down prepared for my usual sleepless night. I heard him switch off the TV and pause in the hallway.

'I have arranged your clinic appointment for tomorrow,' he said through my bedroom door. 'Be ready for 1pm.' He went off to bed without another word, leaving me with my suffering.

★★★

Dressed in my new outfit, my initial euphoria about stepping into fresh air for the first time in days was quickly submerged with dread, as Suleyman drove me to the clinic. Despite the bright sunshine, the April air was still chilly. Looking out at the dusty conifers and the bare trees, I chain-smoked, trying to suppress my tears of fear and guilt.

'If you really want to keep it, I would support you,' Suleyman said matter-of-factly, as we arrived at the entrance of an anonymous, modern building. 'But would you want to bring a child into a world where he would always be

246

regarded as a bastard?' His words had a sobering effect. I
stopped crying.

Unlike the last doctor I had had, this one was clipped
and dry. Her mouth was pursed unhappily, like a chicken's
bottom, Nana would have said. That idea nearly made me
smile, but her stern look dissuaded me. Suleyman had told
me how hard it was to find someone willing to do a late-
stage termination. I could have been as much as eighteen
weeks pregnant by then, which meant I had got pregnant
again soon after the previous procedure.

'Take off your leggings and underwear and lie on
the couch,' she ordered without looking up from the
paperwork.

Feeling awkward and vulnerable, I lay with my legs
wide open. I hadn't been offered any pain relief, so I braced
myself for the agony to follow.

'You've been smoking? You stink of it,' she said angrily.
'What kind of woman smokes anyway?' She continued to
rant on about it while stretching my vagina, as I whimpered.
'Quiet now,' she barked, 'I need to concentrate. You should
have thought about the consequences when parting your
legs for men.' Her words sliced through my brain. She had
instantly judged me, despite my prim and proper clothes
and freshly washed hair. I fought to supress any reaction,
biting my lip, clenching my hands into white-knuckled
fists. 'What a horrible, disgusting person you are,' she
continued as she operated on me. 'This foetus is fully
formed, with arms and legs. You want to see?'

'No,' I gargled through my choking tears.

'What on earth were you waiting for? Why leave it so
late? It's inhuman!' I was defenceless, horrified by her

cruelty. 'I have to remove a beating heart. You make me an accomplice to your sin.'

Her words cut into me sharper than her knife. My brain had gone past the point of being able to register the pain. I ached to die as I swallowed my emotions and tried to lie still, because every time I showed any sign of hurt, she ramped up her verbal outbursts. I think I may have passed out because the next thing I remember was her shaking me, ordering me to dress and get out of her sight.

Though dizzy, nauseous and shaking, I managed to dress without help. I dragged myself to the toilet, and then to the lobby where Suleyman was waiting for me. He said nothing but gave me the briefest of hugs and took me to the car. He clearly did not want to know how I was feeling, though he must have known the mechanics of the procedure. I tried to console myself with the thought that at least this time I wasn't completely alone.

★★★

Now that he thought my "major problems" were resolved, Suleyman decided to switch his attention back to his other priorities. The rhythm of weekdays remained unchanged, but the weekends, when he was mostly in, transformed. He started going to Ganja every weekend to tend to his elderly mother and visit his children and his brothers, leaving me alone, still confined to the flat. He also absented himself during all significant family celebrations, from birthdays, weddings, funerals to New Year and Novruz. His idea of involving me was to ring me up and let me listen to the faint sounds of musicians playing live music in the background, as people I would never meet chatted, laughed and sometimes sang along. It upset me to hear this other world I was missing out on. How long would this last?

I was a dirty secret he kept away from his family and friends. If I broached the subject of my freedom, he would only growl that my confinement was for my own good. When he locked the door, my only props were TV and ice cream. He now refused me all cigarettes. After several humiliating attempts to beg for some, I had decided to quit.

His much longer absences made me increasingly anxious. 'If there's fire in the building, I'll be trapped! I need a key,' I reminded him.

'Out of the question!' he snapped. 'Don't you get it? You're still not to be trusted. As soon as you're free, you'll be out of control again. It would be better to burn in this flat than in hell!' I started to protest, but one look at his stony face told me there was no point.

He did grant me one concession: he allowed me to call Nana from time to time, who had returned from Moscow, and tell her a pack of lies. Much to my relief, my half-sister, who had just turned eight, answered the phone the first time and told me she was now living there, 'So Nana isn't lonely.'

'It is such an incredible opportunity, Nana,' I enthused, as Suleyman listened in, 'I couldn't turn it down. I'm working at an embassy,' I said confidently. 'It's difficult to call anyone from here, the signal can be very bad and I have to fill in permission forms every time. It's all very confidential work, you see. Yes, I'm very well. You shouldn't worry about me. I'll come and visit you, as soon as I get back, but I don't know when that will be yet,' I promised her. This last sentence was not a lie, but a prayer.

I still worried about Nana's well-being. Suleyman had once said he would take care of her but had done nothing, so I was surprised, the next time I called, when Nana thanked me profusely for the generous load of shopping and the three hundred dollars an unknown man had delivered. The description she gave was unmistakably Suleyman.

'It's nothing, Nana, enjoy,' I improvised, while searching Suleyman's smug face. I suddenly felt overwhelming gratitude towards him, that he did that for her.

From then on, whenever he visited his family in Ganja, he would "pop in" to see Nana, with my "gifts" of food, money and once even a *putyovka*, a booking for a month's stay in Absheron Sanatorium in Mardakan. This was a little village adjacent to Baku where we used to visit Nana's relatives for my childhood beach holidays.

When I thanked him for that, he waved it off. It was not a big deal, he said, because the organisation he worked for supplied food to all the sanatoriums in Azerbaijan. 'That one specialises in digestive issues, so it is the best fit for your Nana. She can get prophylactic treatments and so on, which she needs to strengthen her body and her immune system to fully heal from her stomach ulcer.'

Despite his kindness towards Nana, I still felt suffocated in the flat, with Suleyman controlling my every breath. When he came home, he would press autodial on the landline to check if I had phoned anyone, although I only had Nana's number to call. I started dialling zero on the phone before he came home, just in case he forgot when he had used the phone and accused me. My paranoia was growing. I started speaking out loud about my activities, saying things like, 'Come on, Gulush, let's go and make a cup of tea,' then providing a running commentary of everything I was doing. My anxiety caused me to regularly patrol the flat checking Suleyman hadn't sneaked back in. I also looked for hidden recording devices. I had become convinced he had some means of watching me when I was alone, after he had come back one day and accused me of wasting my time masturbating, which I had become prone to do more and more obsessively in an attempt to create some meagre stimulation in the numbing boredom of my prison.

'What made you think I was doing that?' I asked him later, after he had calmed down.

'Because of your bloodshot eyes,' he said, staring at the sports news. I did not know if I could believe him.

Since my cooking had improved dramatically, food was my comfort and friend now. I put on weight so quickly that the respectable outfits Suleyman continued to buy me were now flattering because they covered up my larger belly and blooming breasts. My stylish short haircut had grown out and I now wore my hair in a ponytail. When Suleyman bought me some black henna to dye it with, my look was so completely transformed that I hardly recognised myself in the mirror. Suleyman started taking me out for walks and I was instructed to call myself Parvana if we ran into any of his colleagues or acquaintances.

Suleyman seemed intent on erasing my past without leaving a trace. He even managed to convince me to burn all my photos. 'Why do you cling to your past? It's not healthy for you,' he said repeatedly. 'When are you going to prove to me that you're done with it?'

One afternoon, I was looking through my favourite Polaroids of days out with Amina and the girls, which I had found in my handbag lining, and some family photos that Nana had sent to me via Suleyman when he had lied and told her he was visiting the States and might see me. I realised it made me sad to look at them, even though they were frozen images of happy times. All the smiles looked false to me, including my own. I took them to the kitchen and burnt them one by one in the sink. There were so many images still in my head. When Suleyman saw the pile of ashes, he made no comment, but I think he smiled.

★★★

Months morphed into each other with little change. I was still severely depressed and struggling to sleep at night, haunted by my past experiences and my current dilemmas. How long would Suleyman keep me captive? Was this forever? No amount of questioning had an effect on Suleyman. I asked him repeatedly about the legal situation with my flat and the promises he had made about it. Sometimes he got annoyed but mostly he did not even bother to respond. He took care of my day-to-day needs. There was always plenty of food, warmth, light and hot water. He bought me practical and comfortable underwear and outfits from the local flea market, which sprawled out near the entrance to Ganjlic metro station, nearby, but he never took me along to choose. He said I could not see myself as the world saw me, so he could better choose colours and patterns that suited me. I now looked the epitome of a respectable housewife.

He even took care of my educational needs, including the dissertation I needed to produce to graduate from Baku State University. He found someone at the university, who had no scruples about obtaining and selling me someone else's dissertation, written only a few years before.

'All you need to do is to copy it in your own handwriting, memorise a few facts from it and present them in front of a panel in June! It's that simple!' Suleyman said triumphantly.

I wasn't so sure. Surely, they would have noticed I hadn't been to any lectures, or been seen about the campus? How could I argue the case for something I hadn't done the research for? At least copying the dissertation gave me an incentive to get up earlier on weekdays and I mentally formed emotional connections with the TV soap opera families, which made me feel less isolated from the world, although their homes were far more glamorous and their lives more action packed than mine.

# 13.

# THE LURE OF MIAMI

The dissertation viva went far better than I could ever have imagined. The lecturers that had once intimidated me seemed so small and wrinkled sitting at their desks. I realised, as I stood there in my smartest, black, chemise-suit, that they could not scare me any more, I had been through far worse than this. I had swept out of Suleyman's car into the hall, ignoring all my previous classmates, most of whom did not recognise me, and put on my best performance yet. I had memorised my whole dissertation on Environmental Protection in Azerbaijan and was confidently answering all the questions, until a lecturer in a smart suit asked when was the Environment Day in our country. I tried to fudge my answer and made an unlucky guess. Much to my dismay, it was on 5 June, the same day I was passing my viva. What were the odds? Whether the lecturers decided that the omission was not significant or Suleyman paid them a bribe, I was awarded an excellent mark. Then, without a word to anyone, I marched back to the waiting car and was taken out for lunch.

Although I hadn't written the final dissertation, I knew I had worked hard to get this qualification and I ached to use my knowledge. I decided that I wanted to try and get a job.

I broached the subject with Suleyman, but his response was always the same: 'Look what working has done to your life! Why would you want to work? Haven't you got everything you need here?'

'No, I don't,' I would say. 'This is all yours, all earned by you. I want to sort out my own flat, not just leave it empty. Besides, what if something happened to you?'

'Great, you're now wishing me dead,' he said.

'I'm just saying I want to work.'

'And I'm just saying no!'

I kept raising the subject, every time it seemed appropriate, and eventually my determination seemed to have paid off. A few weeks later, he brought me some paperwork from his organisation. I examined the flashy logo "Sanatoriums Joint Venture" on what looked like a contract of employment.

'Here, sign this,' he said, handing me a pen. 'You'll be registered as my assistant. We have backdated your appointment, so there's no break in your employment history, after you left the Prosecutor's Office, and you'll have full pension rights in the future.'

I insisted on reading through the contract before signing the papers. I had a law degree, after all. It was with a sense of renewed excitement and anticipation that I managed to get up early and dressed in my cream outfit the next morning. Suleyman was surprised to share his breakfast with me, but even more surprised when I tried to leave the flat with him.

'Where do you think you're going?' He laughed, when he realised. It turned out that my new job was a sham, money without work to do. 'I told you,' he said, pushing past me to the door, 'a woman's place is at home, not on the streets!'

I did not need an enemy or blast from the past to be reminded of what I had done. No, I had him to do that for me.

After he left, I raged out loud, angry with him, angry with myself and angry with the world. Then my paranoia had me comb through the flat again in search of listening bugs. We never talked about our feelings, thankfully, but I did not want him to know my growing level of hatred towards him. His words had hurt me again, but he was starting to trust me a little bit. He had stopped locking both locks on the front door, but that still kept me from leaving, unless I left the door on the latch, risking the contents of the flat. Technically, I could slip downstairs and walk round the block, but the reality was I had nowhere else to go.

★★★

The summer of 1997 was sweltering hot. I remembered my times on the beach with Amina and the girls, in the days before my innocence was gone, but felt stupid missing them. I just wanted some fun again. The seaside on a hot day would have been lovely, but I didn't want to expose what I thought of as my plus-size figure to the world, and worry had doubled the age of my face.

Suleyman arrived that evening with a large watermelon. 'Here, cut this up, it's very cooling.' I took a large knife and expertly cut him the first slice. 'Oh, and this is yours.' He thrust a piece of paper at me to sign and then counted some money into my hand.

'What's this?' I was puzzled.

'Your salary,' he said, through the watermelon juice.

From then on, I was paid monthly without stepping a foot outside of the flat. I hid the money in my bedside drawer. I never had the opportunity to spend it, but I liked to know it was there. Suleyman still paid for everything when we went out.

★★★

I was now a fully functioning housewife, like the women behind the net curtains near my old job in Ganja, seemingly watching other people's lives go by. I could cook complex, delicious meals, which rivalled Nana's and surpassed Mama's. I kept the flat sparkling clean and our clothes impeccably starched and ironed. For a while, I thought I was content. I even entertained the mad fantasy of conceiving Suleyman's child, now the aftereffects of the termination had finally abated. He was ambivalent about it, so after a few false alarms, I gave up on the idea.

In the midst of this ocean of repetitive normality, an unexpected wave of change was about to manifest itself. Early in 1998, Suleyman bought himself a Mercedes. The owner was emigrating to the United States to live with his mother, who was currently paying him a flying visit. To 'seal the deal', Suleyman invited them out for dinner and, because they were complete strangers to both of us, he decided I could accompany him.

In the restaurant, I was amazed to hear Suleyman sing my praises to them. He seemed to be trying to impress them. 'She is a law graduate … She is my assistant at work ... She is a quick learner ... You should come over sometime to taste her delectable cooking.' I just sat, mildly embarrassed, and ate my food, until the mother, an ageing woman, whose face was plastered in cheap make-up, started talking about her life in Miami.

'It's a paradise,' she said, 'so warm, no winds there. I don't work all the time, only when I need some money. I just do the odd job here and there. It's not difficult to get manual work at all, if you're not fussy. I wash dishes, clean premises, look after pets, that sort of thing. Then I party the rest of the time.' She laughed and downed another shot of vodka. 'If you know anyone who fancies it, I could help them with the immigration people.' She seemed to be speaking to me, indirectly, sensing my interest. 'I've cracked a code on that. I've helped several friends get out of this hellhole. You need to learn English, though.'

*I can learn English*, I thought. My heart was beating fast. I glanced at Suleyman. He wasn't listening, he was absorbed by the live entertainment of some traditional singers. When he turned back, the direction of the conversation had changed. I felt dazed the rest of the evening, eager to get back to discuss my future.

After the meal, I returned to the flat transformed inside, with a sense of hope and purpose, a goal I could work towards. Why did it never cross my mind before? I just needed to get out of Azerbaijan and live in a place where no one knew about my past. The key to my freedom was to learn English, of that I was certain. I didn't want to spend any more of my life in the comfortable, safe cage Suleyman had created for me. I was tired of having conversations with myself. I wanted to talk to the world.

From then on, my nightmares were replaced with dreams of living in Miami. I might have to sweep the streets before sunrise and wash dishes in a dim café kitchen in the evenings, not the sort of work I had anticipated when I did my law degree, but if that was what it took to be free, that's what I'd do. There was no point in feeling sorry for myself any more. I longed to be my own person, to do what I pleased, to go out and about without the constant anxiety of running into a past client who would recognise me and could expose to the world my shameful past.

I begged Suleyman to buy a satellite dish that could let me access films and programmes in English. After a brief hesitation, he conceded to my request. I started watching anything I could find in English that our satellite dish could pick up. I was particularly struck by Will Smith's 'Welcome to Miami' song. I gorged my eyes on it every time they showed it, trying to imagine what it would be like for me to live there. It looked like they had glorious beaches and a vibrant nightlife. I realised my new life wouldn't start like that, but I was determined. I really enjoyed music in English, and even transcribed some songs, such as Des'ree's 'You gotta be', which I performed repeatedly to my invisible audience. Sometimes, I recorded my performances on a small camcorder dressed in a white knitted top and grey miniskirt, which I fell in love with when I was in a shopping mall with Suleyman. He reluctantly bought it for me with strict instructions to only wear it at home. Making videos was fun but mechanically memorising and mimicking words without understanding them was not the best way to learn the language.

'I would like to study English properly. Can you please

get me some books?' I kept asking Suleyman. 'I need something to keep me occupied. You're away so much these days.'

At first, his only response was to laugh and continue watching TV as if I had not spoken at all. After that, he simply ignored my requests, but I kept pestering him. I made extra efforts to please him in any way I could. When he came home with a heavy box one day, I did not dare hope my wish had been granted; but it had, in a way. Inside the box there were thirty paperbacks in English, most of them Agatha Christie's crime novels.

'And you'll need this, too,' he said, passing me a small, bright-yellow volume.

It was a Russian to English/English to Russian dictionary. I squealed with delight and hugged him. After dinner, when he was fully occupied watching international football, I retreated with my new treasure trove to the bedroom and started trying to read *Death on the Nile*.

★★★

My progress with English was painfully slow at first. Reading mystery novels at a snail pace was very frustrating. I wanted to know who had done it. Whether it involved piecing together Hercule Poirot's clues to the complicated cases, investigated by Inspector Japp, or interpreting Miss Marple's harmless nosy remarks as she poked around her neighbourhood, I tried to predict the outcome of each book before its end.

Typically, out of six words in a sentence, I did not know five. I diligently looked up every word and carefully wrote its meaning in a notebook. I leafed through the pages of my dictionary so often that the English to Russian section started to grey. Using the dictionary was not straightforward because often a word had many meanings, so I had to guess what it actually meant in the context of the story.

I didn't mind that Suleyman was out, every day and at weekends, any more, because I could completely disappear into my new world. I tried to read for twelve hours a day every single day. Whether it was my curiosity or diligence that drove me, my reading speed increased dramatically in only a few months and my previously non-existent English vocabulary had expanded to the point where I did not have to look up every other word.

Once I was done with the mystery novels, I moved on to consuming anything else I could lay my hands on, including the *Azeri News* weekly, which was published in English. I read about how President Heydar Aliyev had been re-elected to a second term in October 1998. I remembered him being elected for his first term in 1993, after President Elchibey had fled the country as a result of the losses in Nagorno-Karabakh. It felt like a lifetime ago now. Although the weak opposition parties accused Heydar Aliyev of voter fraud and the international community condemned the elections, he increased oil production, boosted the economy and remained in power. It seemed the political climate had at least stabilised. The ceasefire continued but, despite the efforts of international organisations, there was no resolution to the conflict. I started to recall the day the ceasefire was achieved, but had to shut the door on that memory because it was attached to my time at the Prosecutor's Office.

English was my project throughout the year. Generally, I found the news boring, but I persevered, reading the newspaper in English religiously. It was early 1999 when I came across a piece of news that lit me up from the inside out: Western University, a private university in Baku, was opening its admissions for the masters' programme in international law, taught in English. I pointed the advert out to Suleyman during dinner.

'Look at this. I'd love to study for that.'

'Why? You already have a law degree from Baku State University.' He waved me off.

'Learning it in English will enhance my qualification,' I persevered. He didn't know that my dream of emigrating was still very much alive. Suleyman had ignored all my ideas about leaving the country. Now he sat frowning. He pushed his empty dinner plate away.

'I won't pay for that course. You realise that it's a paid course, right?'

'I don't care. Let me work, make my own money and pay for it myself.' My frustration started to show. 'And while we're at it,' I said bravely, 'let me have my own home, too. It's been three years now. No one remembers what I was any more! I don't remember who I was any more! I've had enough. I want to live out there again!' I turned and ran to my room, leaving the dishes unwashed.

★★★

Suleyman usually ignored my angry outbursts. He would simply blank me until I stopped mentioning whatever it was, especially when it came to what had happened to my flat. However, my plea for work had an unexpected result. A few days after my outburst, having finished his dinner, he asked me to be ready for 8am in the morning.

'Where are we going?' I yawned.

'You wanted to work? That's great. It's time for you to show up for the money that you've been making in the past couple of years.'

I couldn't believe it. He had never offered to take me to work before. I did not even know that was really an option. I hid my excitement this time, fearing there must be a catch.

The next morning, we drove off through the Black City, for forty minutes, to his workplace. I had dressed in my most modest outfit. I kept my head down. I wasn't sure how I was supposed to behave in this situation. Suleyman led me to the left wing of a large building.

'This is where the procurement office is located,' he announced. 'The rest of the building is dedicated to the management of the seven sanatoriums. As you know, they all have a different specialism and treatments, from heart disease to digestive issues, from curative mud baths to hot mineral springs. You won't deal with the sanatoriums directly. I'll take care of them. Your job will be to manage the two accountants you are about to meet.'

One was a young man in his late twenties, skinny and sickly looking. He seemed in awe of Suleyman, brought him a chair and made him tea, just the way he liked it. I politely declined tea and, perched on a chair nearby, occupied myself by gazing around the room while Suleyman caught up on work matters with the young man. The décor was old. The room felt depressing from the lack of light.

When they had finished their discussion, Suleyman led

me to a separate back room, which was apparently going to be my office. It felt cold and uninviting, with its naked shelves and dim lights, but I sat, as instructed, behind a large plain desk facing the door to the main office. Through it, I heard a woman's twinkling voice.

'Bahar *khanim*,' Suleyman called. 'Please could you come through here?'

Bahar was only a couple of years older than me. She looked smart and professional in a brilliant white shirt and navy-blue pencil skirt, with a black bob framing her round face.

'Bahar *khanim*, I need you to teach Gulara *khanim* the basics of our accounting system. She'll be overseeing your work.' It was nice to be introduced by my real name for a change; I figured it was unavoidable given that I was registered at work as Gulara.

'Yes, of course,' she beamed at Suleyman self-importantly, obviously eager to take me under her wing and share the benefits of her knowledge.

***

Although work at the procurement department was dull, it was a major improvement on my flat-bound existence. Within a week, I realised that I needed to take a proper accounting course, not what Bahar had to offer. Although she was obviously a knowledgeable accountant, I didn't think she relished the thought of me overseeing her. An unexpected bonus of my willingness to learn, apart from pleasing Suleyman, was that the part-time accounting course was in the city centre. Twice a week, I had a chance to step into a different environment with people I didn't know. I kept myself to myself in case Suleyman had me under surveillance. I thought he might use anything that he deemed to be an indiscretion as an excuse to lock me up again.

As I learnt the foundations of accounting and began to examine the company paperwork, a clearer picture started to emerge. Suddenly, all of Suleyman's lavish purchases, including his Mercedes, cars for his brothers, expensive shopping habits and extravagant restaurant food, made sense. I did not need a degree in accounting to spot what was going on.

Since Suleyman was responsible for purchasing hundreds of kilos of produce each day, he could negotiate the price with the wholesalers. He also had many connections with the suppliers. He spent his days driving around, perusing produce and deciding how much product the organisation should buy. The produce, which included meats, fresh fruit and vegetables, canned goods, dairy products and sweets, was then shipped to storage units in the Mardakan district of Baku, a short drive from the office. Another employee, working in Mardakan, was responsible for the distribution. The drivers from various sanatoriums would drive to the storage depot and collect the allocated supplies, which were then prepared at the resorts for the clients. But the figures our office published were not representative of the actual money spent. That difference was currently being split between the head of the organisation and Suleyman. I did not know the specifics, only that I didn't feel comfortable being involved, even when Suleyman admitted I was correct.

'I'm happy just to do the office work,' I said firmly. 'What you and your boss get up to is your business, not mine. There's something that could instantly make a difference, though. I notice everything in the office is still done manually…'

'You know how to work a computer?' Suleyman said, for once interested.

'No, I was thinking of a typewriter.'

'Really? Think bigger! Let's buy you a computer,' he said grandly.

'But I don't know how to use one.'

'We'll sign you up to a course at the Academy of Sciences. Someone mentioned taking computer courses there.'

I could feel my cage blowing wide open. I was willing to learn, whatever it took to escape.

★★★

I did not even have a computer when I signed up to the computer course at the Academy of Sciences. The teacher, a lanky man with a mop of dishevelled black hair and thick glasses, spoke fast with enthusiasm about the technology. I diligently memorised everything he taught us, practising at home on a piece of paper I had drawn the layout of a keyboard on. The teacher became impressed that I could remember the various key combinations, without having a computer. I really enjoyed using the computers, so as soon as I had mastered the basics, Suleyman took me to a computer shop, where an eager assistant helped us to choose the best laptop there was.

I soon started to digitalise the office paperwork,

partly to show Suleyman how capable I was. He seemed pleased with my efforts, encouraging me to take on more responsibilities. 'You could make some of the regular visits to Mardakan to check on the quality of the produce,' he said one day, after just two months of me starting work.

'I'm not sure about that. It's one thing to deal with paperwork, quite another to manage quality control. How will I get there?'

'You can have a driver for such trips. It's up to you how often you go, but it would make a significant contribution to our processes.'

It only took one trip to the Mardakan office for me to accept this was a good idea. The storage depot was a vast warehouse run by Akbar, a good-natured man in his fifties, who unloaded and kept all the products organised. He seemed to be terrified of Suleyman, but was kind and reverent towards me. When I visited, he would come out of his little office and busy himself checking the produce, while I sifted through the paperwork. Sometimes I would examine the produce too.

Away from Suleyman, the Mardakan office was an oasis of calm for me. It had a large courtyard where my driver parked the car and sat outside smoking. The storage unit was only a ten-minute drive from the best beach in Baku, and on hot summer days, I got the driver to take a short detour for me to have a paddle out of sight, while he waited in the car.

The drive to Mardakan gave me daytime head space to reflect on my life. I still wanted to do the masters' degree at Western University. Now I had proved to Suleyman that I was capable of office work to earn money, wouldn't he relent and let me study? I could enrol straight away, if I used up the money I had saved, but I still needed his permission. It seemed my diligence was paying off because his attitude to me had started shifting. He no longer ignored me at home. He talked about work and asked for my views sometimes.

★★★

One afternoon, Suleyman, without saying why, drove me to the flat that I had paid for, all those years ago.

'Why are we here?' I said, because I had given up mentioning the flat by this time.

'It's a surprise,' he said, bouncing out of the car. 'Follow me.'

When we got to the flat door, I hesitated, momentarily remembering my last visit, curled up in tears on the shelf in the built-in wardrobe. I shivered with apprehension, but Suleyman unlocked the door and insisted I walk in ahead of him. Then I gasped in shock. A smell of fresh paint hung in the air, the walls were covered in a tasteful, new wallpaper and the windows had all been replaced. Everything about the flat had been transformed. It was fully renovated and furnished.

The living room had a large, brown floral sofa, a TV set on a smoked-glass stand and a smart, square table with four matching chairs. There was a comfortable-looking double bed in the bedroom, complete with a thick duvet and pillows, a small dressing table and a walnut-coloured wardrobe had replaced the built-in unit. The small kitchen had a little table with stools by the window and all the necessary equipment to make a cup of tea or cook a meal.

'Why? How? When?' I marvelled, looking around.

'Do you like it?' Suleyman's eyes actually sparkled.

'Yes! I love it!'

'Do you want to live here?'

I gulped. I had been waiting for this moment for so long, but now that it was finally here, I felt scared. What if I was not ready for my independence? What if I made more mistakes? What if he had been right and I was not to be trusted?

'I'm not finishing with you,' he said, misinterpreting my hesitation. 'It's just that now we're working so closely together, I thought maybe it would be a good idea for you to have your own space.'

I nodded. I was so surprised, I asked, 'What about the legal formalities?'

He sighed, possibly at my impatience. I hit my head inwardly. He had just transformed this flat from bare walls to a habitable home for me and I had asked for more. I tried a softer approach. 'I wanted you to know that I already have the money for the fees. All the salary you have given me over the past two years, I haven't touched a dollar of it. There's even enough to pay for the first year of my masters' degree: can I do that?'

'It's your money, you should do with it as you please,' he said, betraying no emotion. 'But first, let's go pack your bags.'

***

Although Suleyman did not explicitly agree to me doing another course, his lack of opposition was good enough for me. The next day, when the driver arrived at my own flat, I asked to take another detour, via Western University, where I could formally apply for a masters' degree in international law.

The admission process was reasonably straightforward. The dean, a green-eyed lady in her early fifties, handed me three sets of forty questions, one for each subject: English, civil law and constitutional law. I had to be prepared to answer any of those questions during an oral examination starting on the 1st of August 1999, so I had three weeks to prepare.

Though my English vocabulary had greatly expanded due to all the reading I had done, I was less confident about my spoken English. I might be able to recognise the meaning of words, but could I string individual words together into coherent sentences? I was prepared to take the risk, especially because the masters' course included three months of intensive English tuition. Western University had a small but well-stocked library, which I was allowed access to, so I visited three times a week to make notes and photocopy materials. I would sit amongst the book-crammed shelves, feverishly preparing answers to all the questions and, within two weeks, I was feeling better equipped be able to answer any of the questions to an acceptable level. Being amongst students again, although I spoke to none of them, reminded me of the days I had spent studying with Lala by my side. If she hadn't betrayed me, would I still know her now? It still hurt to think about her.

★★★

On the 1st of August 1999, I arrived promptly at Western University, nervous but excited. I hadn't told Suleyman about the tests, I wanted to pass them first. My first test was English and I was delighted to discover that not only could I understand the examiner but I managed to convey my ideas fairly well. I did make a few mistakes and was lost for words at times, but the teacher, a kindly, curly haired, petite woman, seemed satisfied and said I showed a lot of potential, and that she looked forward to seeing me in English intensive class in the first term, if I passed the other tests. Her confidence and fluency in English were inspiring. I found myself looking forward to becoming her student.

My next examiner, for civil law, was the green-eyed dean herself. She looked rather motherly and radiated kindness. Baku State University had been a largely male domain, so I was pleased that Western University had predominantly female staff. Encouraged by her warm greeting, I eagerly answered all her questions. She too seemed satisfied with my level of proficiency.

Later in the day, when I arrived at my constitutional law grilling, I was pleased to find that my examiner was the same green-eyed dean. I felt very relaxed and rattled out all the answers I had memorised, as well as responding to supplementary questions. The dean was very pleased with me and so was I when she told me I had passed all three tests.

The next step was to pay for the first year of my studies and get ready for my classes to begin in September. The dean introduced me to the admissions officer, who determined that based on my grades from Baku State University, I only had to pay 1350 USD per year, as opposed to 1950 USD for those who had not performed as well in their first degree and did not have an average mark of four out of five. I was thankful that the bribes I'd paid to pass my last set of exams had earned me the discount.

'Classes commence on Monday the 6th of September,' the administrator said, as I completed the official forms. 'Your lectures will be daily from 6:20pm till 9pm.'

I had not realised they would finish so late. I felt a bit anxious about Suleyman's reaction, but comforted myself with the fact that it would not disrupt my work schedule.

★★★

As it turned out, shortly after moving into my own flat, Suleyman reunited with his second wife and their two young children, bringing them, as well as his four children from his first marriage, back to Baku. It seemed I was not the only one of us who had been incubating plans. I found myself strangely jealous, even though I probably wouldn't have wanted to marry him, if that had been possible. Becoming a respectable married woman would not have been worth the eternal enslavement.

However, I did feel like I had been used by him and then abandoned. I discovered, through chance remarks he and his colleagues made, that he had been in regular contact with his second wife the whole time I'd lived with him, taking her shopping and going out with his children weekly. It was not that I objected to any of this, they were his family, after all, but it was that he had never told me. I wondered what else he had hidden from me.

One thing I was clear about was that I did not want to have sex with him any more. Now we had separate lives, I wanted to move on. Marriage might still be out of my reach, but forming an intimate friendship with someone might be possible. I wanted to keep my options open. Suleyman obviously had different ideas. He expected me to report my whereabouts to him, at all times. If I did not respond to his messages immediately, he would flap like Nana did in the old days.

I missed Nana so much during this time, aching to share my new successes with her, but I was not quite ready to face the realities of Ganja yet. Thankfully, Suleyman continued to visit her with gifts of shopping and money on my behalf and I phoned her once a fortnight from "America", so I knew she was doing well. Mama, however, was nowhere to be found. The last number I'd had for her was no longer in service. Though I was worried, I felt I could not risk antagonising Suleyman by looking for her, at this time. Nana assumed I was in contact with her, however, so I had to add more lies to the ones I was already telling her, so she wasn't worried herself.

As soon as I moved to my flat, I decided to adopt a healthier lifestyle. Since I was no longer obliged to cook fat-laden treats for Suleyman, I could eat what I chose, with salads and *dovga* – yoghurt soup with finely chopped fresh herbs – becoming my favourite options. Suleyman agreed with me signing up to an aerobics class at a studio near my flat. I took immense pleasure in sweating off my extra kilos to "The Rhythm of the Night" by Corona and "Larger Than Life" by Backstreet Boys, gradually regaining my former shape. I updated my wardrobe with still modest but more stylish clothing, which suited me. Discarding the clothes of my captivity felt like shedding a chrysalis to become a beautiful butterfly.

My rejuvenated appearance had a disturbing effect on Suleyman. He was still visiting my flat regularly, to check up on me, I thought. He usually came on the pretext of needing to discuss a work issue, but one evening, he tried to kiss and hold me. I pulled away, astonished.

'You have your wife back. I don't want this.'

My words of rejection had the opposite effect. He seemed excited by the challenge. First, he tried to sweet-talk me into being intimate with him, reminding me of his many kindnesses towards me. Then he lost patience and chased me round the flat, knocking a chunky vase flying, as I tried to reason with him. It was pointless. When he finally caught me, he easily man-handled me to my bed and took me against my will as I struggled beneath him. I quickly learnt that the more I resisted him, the more it excited him. If I dropped the resistance, his interest waned. One step forward, two steps back, I thought, as I absented myself from each encounter by focusing on a vision of a better future. This was just another normal to get through.

★★★

A week after he had forced himself on me, Suleyman rang and instructed me to be ready to meet him early the next morning in front of the building. 'Bring your ID,' was all he would say.

He drove us to a municipal building I had never seen before.

'What's this place?' I asked, assuming it was work-related.

'You'll see,' he said. A smile was leaking onto his face.

Inside, an old man who looked vaguely familiar, wearing a crumpled suit, shook Suleyman's hand.

'I'm so glad you're ready to do this, at last,' he said to both of us.

What were we going to do? I was unnerved by trying to place the man whom I had definitely met before. I tried to smile politely as I searched my memory for some clue to his identity. We waited in the foyer for a few minutes before the receptionist ushered us into a large, musty, wood-panelled room.

'Gulara Guliyeva?' The official behind an imposing table stared at me, given that I was the only woman in the room. I nodded and stepped forward. 'Sign here,' he said, pointing to a dotted line on a document laid out on the table.

What was I about to sign? I turned the piece of paper over to read it.

'Signature and date, please, I don't have all day.'

Ignoring the man's urgency, I stared… at the legal deed to my flat. That was why I had recognised the man in the corridor – he was the former owner. I had waited for this moment for nearly four years, and now that it was finally here, I was stunned. The fluted edges of the fountain pen started to cut into my hand as I clutched it. *Finally, finally, finally!* I sang the word in my head, until Suleyman nudged me, then I signed the paper and passed it back to the grumpy official.

The previous owner was next to put his signature

down and Suleyman paid the fee. These long-awaited legal formalities were completed in under five minutes. Suleyman and the vendor shook hands and patted each other on the back like they were old friends, before the man hobbled towards his battered car and we headed for Suleyman's. I clutched the papers, thinking them my ticket to absolute freedom as we sat in the car, silently watching the dark grey clouds painting a dramatic setting above us.

'Are you not going to thank me?' Suleyman said.

'Thank you?' I swivelled to face him. I could almost have laughed but I was suddenly so angry. 'I have waited for this day for years! Do you have any idea how much time and energy I spent worrying about this one piece of paper? For so long that eventually I gave up... all... hope! Yet, it only took five minutes to finalise the sale! Just five minutes! But you had no problem tormenting me about it for years!' I raged on and on. *Now I have it*, I thought, *I don't have to be nice any more.* 'Do you remember all those times I begged you to get it done? I pleaded like a street beggar, but you showed me no mercy. You ignored me. You wouldn't respond; but now you think I should thank you? I won't be doing that! The truth is, I have learnt to hate you! And I always will!'

Suleyman's expression was now like a forlorn child's.

'It was for your own good,' he whispered, feeding me his usual line.

'What was for my own good? You owning me?' I shouted, exploding like hot flames from an oil seam. All those years of repressed pride, of abuse, of shame fuelled my anger. I unleashed it all onto him, my voice rising, my heart bursting open with shuddering emotion. Then before he could start the car, the rain came tumbling down. He drove through a downpour to my flat. When he pulled in front of the building, I leapt out, clutching the deed to my chest to protect it from getting soggy and stomped away. Even the lightning strikes and the crashing thunder around me did not frighten me. I felt freedom tingling electric through me.

14.

# JESSUP

From September 1999, I worked from 9am till 5pm at the Sanatorium Joint Venture, then dashed home for a quick bite and a Cinderella-like transformation. I swapped my sensible work clothes to skin-tight tops and trousers or occasionally even a miniskirt when I knew Suleyman was in Ganja, I applied my make-up and turned up at Western University at 6:20pm looking how I thought a twenty-four-year-old student should look like. The majority of my classmates were young women of roughly my age, so I didn't feel threatened to let my beauty shine. I came home tired, but glad to have been out all day, although I still struggled to connect with people. I felt distant and reserved, anxious not to reveal too much about my past. Just like at work, I kept myself to myself at university.

The first term was dedicated to English. I understood a lot, but still felt self-conscious speaking. I envied my peers, women like Ayna and Natalia, who expressed themselves with more confidence in English, due to working at places like British Petroleum (BP), until my determination and ability to devour any amount of homework started paying off. My competitiveness spurred me to stay up late at night, repeating each phrase out loud, over and over again, plus completing all the written assignments on time. Even my daily expeditions to Mardakan to check on the procurement operations gave me some learning opportunities: I spent each return journey practising English phrases and idioms under my breath.

As I gained confidence in English, I gained confidence at work. I was teamed up with another colleague overseeing the food quality at the sanatoriums during regular inspections of their kitchens. I felt more authoritative and knowledgeable now. Suleyman said he was pleased about my initiative because now there was someone to support the product choices he made.

I still didn't feel entirely safe around Suleyman out of work. On the weekends, when I was deep in study, he would still show up unannounced. I kept to one side of the kitchen table, with my books, while he nursed a cup of tea on the other. He would ask me about my university experiences. To be honest, it was nice to share them with someone, even him.

'I love it!' I beamed at him. 'It's fascinating to learn about the make-up of international organisations. I hope one day Azerbaijan will become a member of the Council of Europe, it's a human rights organisation. My favourite one is the European Union. Most people in the class find it difficult to understand because it's so complicated – the institutions, the way it operates, its history – but something in its complexity really intrigues me.' What I didn't say was that I was still harbouring hopes of leaving the country and, the more I learnt, the more my dreams intensified.

Suleyman seemed to listen intently, but I think he was only trying to read between the lines, waiting for me to mention some student, some other man, once too often. I don't think he believed I was speaking the truth: to me, studying again was exhilarating enough. My main challenge these days wasn't a recipe, or trying to find a friend, it was mastering subjects I already understood, in English, to the highest level. This was not easy. I now found the number of available textbooks in the library limiting and had realised that the majority of my tutors only had intermediate English. Given that my main reason for wanting to go to Western University was to master law in English, this was a significant setback, which I did not share with Suleyman.

★★★

As my studies progressed, I was able to relax into socialising at university. A girl called Farida started being friendly with me. She had spent her final year of secondary school in America as part of an exchange programme, so her command of English was exceptional. Although quiet and reserved, she had a lot of insight on many topics. She worked for BP. I was flattered by her wanting to get to know me and was relieved to have a peer to talk through our studies with. Not only could she grasp information effortlessly, but she questioned everything, trying to find the rationale behind the facts. I admired her independent thinking. I seemed to have lost some of my capacity for that.

That first year passed in a blur, I was so busy; unlike the previous years in Suleyman's flat, which had crawled by so painfully. I was pleased with my progress. When Farida approached me with a proposition to stretch myself even further, I was interested. 'Have you heard of the Jessup Moot Court Competition that the American Bar Association runs every year?' My blank face answered for me. 'They give you a case scenario and you act as lawyers to argue the case,' she explained. 'It's all about international law, and you are good at it. If we form a team and our team wins, we'll get to go to the States. The next round of the competition is in Washington DC! Baku State University has been winning the competition pretty much every year; perhaps we could change that.'

'I got my degree by part-time study,' I said, nervous about competing against a team from my previous university. 'The full-timers get a much higher standard of tuition. Plus, my spoken English isn't as good as my written reasoning.'

Farida waved away my concerns. 'All that matters is the strength of your written arguments. If you learn them by heart, I am sure you'll make a great oral presentation. It will really spur on your learning. I've attended a few of these competitions. I was impressed by the panel of judges who mostly studied abroad and asked excellent questions. I know you can do this, I'll help you.'

I didn't know how I could fit more work into my packed schedule, but Farida's enthusiasm was infectious. Soon every conversation we had was about the competition; when and how we could register for it, how to go about the division of responsibilities and a myriad of other things. Farida took care of the formalities in the background and set some preparatory work for us to do over the summer holidays. We agreed to meet every week to bounce ideas off each other ready for the competition.

I kept my friendship with Farida hidden from Suleyman because I was sure he would interfere in some way. I wanted time to nurture this connection, the first of my new life, so I always arranged meet ups with Farida for days when I knew that Suleyman was preoccupied with his family in Baku, or Ganja.

★★★

Although I didn't tell Suleyman about Farida, I was, of course, transparent when it came to work matters. I got on well with the accountant, Bahar, but I was careful about what I said to her as I thought she might be reporting back to Suleyman. However, it still felt like a friendly connection. In November 2000, when Bahar invited me to her friend's birthday party, at a restaurant, I told Suleyman and let him decide if I should go or not.

'Sure, you should go,' he said, 'I'll give you a lift there and back.'

I wore my best evening outfit: a silver top with an open neckline, teamed with a metallic short skirt, long leather boots and my favourite silver necklace. I applied some subtle make-up and blow-dried my hair. Suleyman smacked his lips when he arrived to take me to the party at 7pm. The wind was piercing, so I slipped on my new leather jacket, though I was not that worried because Suleyman's car was warm.

Bahar's friends were an unexpectedly lively mix. The birthday girl, Gultekin, two years older than me, loved having fun. We were in a separate function room, where waiters brought enough food to feed twenty people, not the ten who were there. Bahar poured champagne in all our glasses, but I refused. I had not drunk alcohol for years, plus I feared Suleyman might find out and not approve. My paranoia was always lurking in the back of my mind.

'You have to drink to a birthday girl,' Bahar insisted.

'How about I make a toast, and you drink it,' I said, though I was not sure that Suleyman would even approve of that, especially since the party was being videoed.

Bahar agreed. I paused, trying to recall one of the toasts I had heard when I used to go out with Mahir. These toasts were often long-winded, but I liked this one because it felt like a story: 'There were four men sitting under a magnificent tree drinking vodka on a summer evening. They kept toasting each other and their loved ones, but eventually they ran out of toasts. Suddenly, a leaf fell off the tree and landed in one of the men's drinks.

'"Let's drink to this leaf!" the first man exclaimed.

'"No, let's drink to the branches that grew the leaf," suggested the second one.

'"I toast the trunk. It holds all the branches from which the leaves grow," said the third.

'"The right thing to do is to drink to the roots of the tree. They hold the trunk, branches and the leaves," the fourth man announced wisely.

'Let's drink to your roots, to your family!' I concluded, raising my glass.

Gultekin, her three sisters, Bahar, her siblings and their friends repeated my words and cheered themselves, while I pretended to take a sip of champagne.

The party began to sparkle as people started dancing barefoot in the middle of the room. I enjoyed watching to start with. When I was finally persuaded to join the revellers, I kept to the edge and danced slowly and elegantly. As Bahar's superior at work, I thought I should be more reserved. When a rope was produced and people started to take turns holding the rope taut for others to bend backwards and shimmy under it, I sat back down in wonder. In the whole of my twenty-five years, I had never played that game. It was thrilling to watch. I didn't think I had ever been as bendy as the birthday girl and shimmying under a rope in a short skirt would be too exposing.

When the waiters brought in Gultekin's birthday cake, with her name and age on it, decorated with colourful flower patterns, I thought the party was soon to end. The cake tasted freshly baked, walnut with a delicious cream filling. I allowed myself a whole piece. The clock showed that it was just gone 10pm when Bahar and her friends laid a thick cloth in the middle of the room and started breaking bottles on to it. Bewildered by the activity, I tried to make my excuses and leave, but Bahar insisted that I had to wait and see what came next. 'You don't want to miss this,' she slurred.

I stared in amazement as everyone gathered round the now pummelled shards of glass, which had been arranged into a narrow path. When the birthday girl stepped on them barefoot and started to walk across, amid cheers, I gasped out loud. Simultaneously, I felt as if a giant had picked up our room and shaken it like a matchbox. How did they do that? For a few seconds, I thought that it was all part of the performance, but everyone started shouting, in our room and others.

My gut instincts kicked in and, grabbing my bag and

jacket, I ran out of the room towards the entrance. The corridor was moving as if I was drunk, swaying from side to side. I was completely disorientated. When I reached the door, part of me realised I hadn't even said goodbye. I hesitated, looking back to see where everyone was, when I heard Suleyman calling me: 'What are you doing? Let's go! Do you want to die? It's an earthquake.'

'What? I have to see what's happened to everyone. I have to say goodbye!'

'It's not safe!' he shouted after me.

The door of the function room was wide open. As I reached it, the whole building seemed to lean again like a ship tossed on stormy seas. Inside, there was absolute chaos, staff and guests scrabbling around, but Suleyman grabbed me and pulled me away.

'We all need to get out of here!' he shouted, pushing others forward as he dragged me back to the street.

Once in the car, he started to rant about how he had nearly died at the wheel as the road had moved underneath him. He was clearly shaken and drove like a madman, dodging through the streets as everywhere people spilled out of all sorts of premises onto the pavements. The traffic kept building up, as the residents of multistorey buildings made their way to safer locations. As my nine-storey block loomed ahead, I saw my neighbours swarming into the courtyard like bees from their hive.

'I go out for the first time in ages, and this happens!' I sounded like my mouth was full of hazelnuts.

'I have to go,' Suleyman said, as soon as I had exited the car. 'Keep out of your flat,' he shouted as he sped off.

I watched, stupefied, as his car disappeared round the

corner. Was he going to leave me here? Families and friends were congregating together, offering each other blankets, food and water, while I shivered, in my leather jacket and thin party clothes, utterly uncomfortable, the only person standing alone.

The night deepened. One by one, my neighbours left, heading for their summer houses or the private homes of others, and the busy courtyard gradually emptied until I was the only person in the darkness, choking on my fear and rage. When push came to shove, Suleyman had naturally put his family first, abandoning me at the first opportunity. What if there was another stronger tremor? Where could I go? What could I do? My bitter tears dripped onto my freezing chest. Then I thought of Mama. I still didn't know where she and my siblings were. Had the earthquake reached them? Here there were just tiles dislodged, windows broken and old buildings left unstable, but with no phone signal, I had no idea what was happening elsewhere in Baku. I had heard my neighbours talking, saying people had died and many were in hospital. What if one of them was Mama? I longed to find her, put my arms around her, for all of us to be safe together. These thoughts so depressed me that, after what felt like hours in the late November chill, despite the warnings not to go indoors, I decided that if I was going to die, I would rather do it in the warmth of my own bed. As I dragged my weary feet up the stairs, I made another decision: I was going to break free from Suleyman, as soon as the opportunity presented itself.

When I got to the flat, I discovered the power was out in the block and the flame on the gas cooker was at a lower pressure than usual, as I boiled water for a warming tea, by candlelight. My little battery powered radio told me that was because of a fear of fires. Twenty-six people had been killed and over 400 taken to hospital. It was the strongest earthquake since 1842 and had affected other smaller nearby cities. Estimates were that over ninety buildings and apartment blocks had been seriously damaged, including the Opera and Ballet Theatre and the Taza Pir and Blue Mosques. Luckily, there had been no damage to the offshore oil rigs. People were still being advised to stay out of their apartments, as a further tremor was thought possible. Looking out across the neighbourhood, I could see that most of the area was shrouded in black, except for the distant glimmer from ships out at sea. I went to bed fully clothed, in case I had to bolt. It reminded me of long winter nights in Ganja, when Nana and I slept in our coats to survive the cold.

***

Who would succeed Azerbaijan's ailing president, Heydar Aliyev? That question had dominated political debate in 2000. On a course like international law, we students knew how crucial this was. Some feared his death would create political instability in our country and the war in Nagorno-Karabakh might reignite. Technically, the speaker of parliament was next in the line of succession. The parliamentary elections held on the 5th of November 2000 had been fraught with difficulties. So many irregularities had been discovered that the government had had to organise reruns in eleven constituencies. These took place on the 7th of January 2001.

Like many citizens, I did not know what the point of the reruns were because the authoritarian Aliyev regime had already banned seven opposition parties from contesting the elections. They had also cracked down on critical journalists and media outlets, with many political activists being imprisoned just for disagreeing with the regime. *Is Mama at risk?* I worried in the back of my mind incessantly.

When Azerbaijan became the forty-third country to join the Council of Europe on the 25th of January 2001, the response in the country and the international community was mixed. Some believed that the ratification of the European Convention of Human Rights would have an impact on the widespread human rights violations taking place in Azerbaijan, but many were unconvinced, given that the corruption in the law enforcement agencies made it virtually impossible for justice to be served. I knew this from my experience at the Prosecutor's Office in Ganja.

The government continued to drag its feet in fulfilling one of the preconditions of membership: the release of political prisoners. I kept a close eye on that list. Was Mama safe as a member of an opposition party? Although the government had replaced Soviet ideological terms with those of a Western democracy, the essence of the old regime survived in all its institutions.

As everything was in a state of flux around us, Farida and I concentrated on our studies and were kept busy preparing for the 2001 Jessup Moot Court Competition. This round of the competition was all about the Seabed Mining Facility, which was right up Farida's street, given that she worked for BP. She had full access to some amazing human and written resources there, but in contrast, I felt out of my depth.

288

As Azerbaijan, Georgia and Turkey reached an agreement on oil and gas pipelines linking the Caspian Sea's oil fields with Turkey, with a view to selling its resources in the European markets, Farida and I explored the intricacies of international law that applied to seabed mining.

As part of the competition, we had to prepare an applicant country's memorial, testimonial affidavit, claiming a violation of international law and a respondent country's memorial, justifying their actions as lawful. The task felt insurmountable to me, at first, but Farida's help soothed my worries. Suleyman was fully occupied with his family and usually away from Baku at weekends. I went to Farida's flat several times to go over the arguments and start drafting the documents.

It was on one of those visits that I first met her brother, Polad. He was tall, dark and mysterious and five years older than me. A perfect age gap for a marriage, I thought wistfully, before pushing the thought firmly away. That path was closed for me, and I did not want to undermine my friendship with Farida.

When I showed up dutifully with all my notes at Farida's flat the next time, I could not help but notice Polad, sitting on the sofa with his long legs crossed. He greeted me with a lazy smile. I managed a simple 'hello', before turning away to hide my blushes as I fumbled with my coat buttons. Then I retreated to Farida's room where I found it difficult to concentrate on our studies. She didn't notice. I was both relieved and a bit disappointed when I left a few hours later and he was not there. I told myself off for imagining he might have any interest in me, but decided to test my theory out and come back exactly a week later, even though Suleyman would be in Baku then. Even though I lived by myself now and he lived with his family, he still expected me to check in with him regularly.

My plans were quickly shattered when I showed up at Farida's the next Saturday and found Farida's mother, instead of Polad, in situ. She insisted Farida and I take tea with her before our study session. I sat nervously at the table as she smiled reassuringly and dispensed the tea from an elegant tea pot into traditional tulip-shaped glass cups. I clasped mine tightly to thaw out my cold fingers.

'It's so nice to meet you,' she said. 'I hear from Polad and Farida that you've been visiting for the past few weeks. Since I was out on those occasions at meetings and on other errands, I wanted to make sure I saw you today.'

Polad had mentioned me to his mother? The thought cannoned around my head.

'My oldest daughter Nigar is away this weekend. Have you met her?' I shook my head. 'She works for the American Councils for International Education. She's so very bright.'

I looked questioningly at Farida, over the other side of the table. Why had she never mentioned her sister? Farida shrugged. I wondered if they didn't get on. As Farida's mother chatted cheerfully about her many activities, I remembered that I barely ever spoke about my family either. I hoped she didn't ask me about them. If she did, I couldn't tell the whole truth: that I had told Nana I lived in the States to avoid the nightmare of an arranged marriage; that since Mama had moved flats and changed her phone number, I had no idea where she was; that I had lost touch with my uncles, my cousins and my former work colleagues; and that now I was alone in this world, apart from a dubious pseudo-friendship with my boss, who was also my ex-lover and gaoler, with no hope of ever having children of my own. It was best to avoid the topic of family altogether. Apart from the fact that I had told Farida that Suleyman was my uncle, after she saw him dropping me off at university once, I hadn't mentioned any of this to her.

'Did Farida tell you that there's a vacancy at Nigar's office at the American Councils for International Education? I hear your language skills have improved a lot. Perhaps it might be worth going for it.'

I could hardly breathe. The prospect of working in an international organisation and practising English every day felt too good to be true. I grunted a response, acutely aware of how self-conscious I felt.

'Gulya can be shy with new people,' Farida said coming to my rescue. 'I can help you with the job application, if you like,' she added.

I smiled at them both with gratitude. Inside I felt uneasy. How would Suleyman react to me attempting to leave my job? Yet, it was something I had been planning to do and the prospect felt so tantalising that I even forgot about the absence of Polad, for a moment, until his mother said, 'You've met my son Polad, haven't you? Well, he runs a resort up in the mountains, mostly for foreigners, but it's so peaceful in the woods and we are going for a few days in the summer. Farida and I wondered if you would like to come with us. What do you think?'

I felt thrown by the invitation but nodded to show my appreciation. It seemed odd that they wanted to take me on holiday with them. Or was that normal in their world?

Suleyman could never know. I would find a way and, if there was a spark between Polad and me, it was the perfect way to find out.

Farida nudged me to return to our studies and I followed her after thanking her mother profusely for the tea, the invitation and the heads up about the job opportunity. My head felt crowded and, much to Farida's frustration, yet again I found it hard to concentrate on our work.

★★★

I didn't go the following week. I needed a break because I felt things were moving forwards too fast for me to keep up, in my studies, my friendship with Farida and my attraction to Polad. I knew I needed to tread carefully. Polad might tick a number of boxes as marriage material for me, but there was no way I could for him. I didn't want to make a fool of myself, so I threw myself into work and study matters. I managed to complete the first draft of the written submission for the Moot Court Competition by the end of the weekend and I emailed it to Farida, who seemed pleased.

'I read your draft,' she said when we met up for a class. 'Let's finish it at mine, this weekend. The deadline is very soon. We can do your job application for the American Councils for International Education at the same time. Apparently, the boss is great. He's an American and a really lovely person. You will love it there.'

I agreed, though a little reluctantly. There were no gaps in our timetable that week. The competition work had to be done over the weekend. As for the job opportunity, I didn't think I had much of a chance, so perhaps there was no harm in applying, as a practice for the future.

When I arrived at their flat, Farida's mother was waiting for me.

'Welcome, welcome!' she said, again warm and hospitable, with a plate of fresh baklava to go with our tea.

She quizzed us about our progress on the competition materials. She clearly was used to talking to her children about everything they were up to. I wished I had a parent like that. After we had finished tea, before I could follow Farida to her room, her mother told me to stay put a moment and disappeared next door. She returned carrying an outfit.

'Gulya, I bought this suit in America when I was travelling for work. It was for Nigar, but she likes a closer cut. I bet it would be perfect for you. Would you like to try it on? If it suits you, it might be ideal for your competition appearance.'

I was embarrassed to be offered such an expensive piece of clothing by her. Should I accept it? However, when I put the dark green jacket and skirt on, in the bathroom, the suit looked like it was made for me. The skirt was shorter than anything I currently wore, coming to just above my knees when I was standing up and climbing up my thighs when I sat down, but I looked very smart in it. Amina would have said, 'You look expensive.' Delighted, I twirled in front of the mirror and came striding out to show it off to Farida's mother; but my thanks froze on my lips, as to my surprise, I saw Polad was there. I was so startled that I turned to dash to Farida's room, feeling awkward in my new outfit.

'Don't go,' he called, 'that looks great on you!'

His attention was flattering and reassuring, so I gingerly came back to the living room where his mother cooed her own appreciation. Was I misreading the situation entirely? There seemed to be something going on behind the scenes with this family. Again, I wished there was someone I could talk to who might give me some sound advice.

★★★

Finally, the national round of the Jessup Moot Court Competition was upon us. The competition was held in a building right next to the imposing walls of the Maiden Tower. I stood outside waiting for Farida and examining the golden plaque on the door. It had ABA-CEELI in large letters, with the full name of the organisation in smaller font size: American Bar Association – The Central European and Eurasian Law Initiative.

Farida seemed at home in this environment as she confidently led the way to the airy and spacious ABA-CEELI office. The competition was held in a large library. A panel of three judges, wearing formal black gowns, sat at the far end of the room. Two competing teams sat at separate tables, facing the judges. Behind the teams, there were five rows of chairs for the audience, mainly friends of the participants.

We had to compete against a team from Khazar University first. They were a rival, private institution that ranked below Western University in results. As far as we were concerned, we stood a strong chance of winning because, although I still lacked confidence in my spoken English, our material was solid and I felt my appearance would make a good impression on the judges. We won the first round.

The second round was against Baku State University. Having won the Jessup Competition in the past few years, their team was determined to have another trip to Washington DC. The five young men on the team had a good command of English and plenty of arrogance. They were sure that they would win again. Farida rebutted their arguments effectively and answered the judges' questions with a quiet self-assurance that made the result a close call. I did well at presenting my arguments, but when it came to the questions, I had a brain freeze trying to find the right words.

Baku State University won, although their team was so impressed by Farida that they asked her to join their team representing Azerbaijan in the international round in Washington DC. I was not sure what I would have done if they had asked me, but Farida declined with dignity, since she wasn't really bothered about the outcome.

'It's the experience that matters, not the result,' she said, as we left the building afterwards. I still felt upset about our defeat.

With the competition over, the next academic hurdle to face was exams. They seemed much less stressful in comparison. From late spring and to early summer 2001, I didn't see much of Farida or her family. I missed her warm, quiet companionship, and I missed the excitement of seeing Polad, whether or not he was interested in me. I was lonely, despite my work and my studies. I knew it was for the best, really. There were too many things I wouldn't want to share with Polad or his family.

I graduated from Western University with honours in June 2001. I loved the graduation ceremony, which was organised in Kirkha, a Lutheran church in the city centre built in 1889. Unusually, the Gothic-style church survived the Soviet regime, and made a grand venue for the ceremony. When I emerged from Kirkha with my degree certificate, Suleyman greeted me with a large bucket of red roses. I didn't like him showing up there unannounced, but he charmed me by saying, 'I had my reservations about your studies, but you did well. Honours in international law in English is pretty impressive.'

★★★

Two weeks after graduation, I received a call from the American Councils for International Education (ACCELS) inviting me to an interview. The invitation came as a shock because I had not anticipated getting on the shortlist. *This will just be good interview practice*, I told myself. I had zero expectations of getting the job.

On a hot July morning in 2001, I made my excuses at work and headed for Akhundov Park near central Baksovet metro station. I found the office easily. It was only two blocks away from Western University. A tall man with a ponytail, round glasses and a kind smile introduced himself as Jeremy and shook my hand. He first asked some questions in English. Then I was surprised to find that he also had a decent command of Russian, so some of our conversations took place in that language too.

'I'd like to hire you to run two programmes,' he said finally. 'One is for English teachers who spend up to six weeks in America studying teaching methods. The second programme is a civic education project open to all primary school teachers who have a reasonable command of English. Neither of these programmes have been run here before. They are brand new and I want to put you in charge of them. We have had another candidate who has excellent English skills. She's done a masters' degree in law in the United Kingdom. I will offer her a part-time job to support you in this role.'

I was completely awestruck that they had chosen me for the job and that they wanted me to run two high profile programmes. Surely, someone with better English who had a degree from a British university would have been a better choice? Had Farida's sister pulled some strings to help me out? I decided not to question my new manager's decision. My gratitude was overwhelming, but under my beaming happiness, a very different set of emotions was brewing.

Now I would have to deal with Suleyman.

15.

# BRIBES

That afternoon, as a cool seaborne breeze wafted in through the windows of my flat, momentarily displacing the heat rising from the streets below, I had gently circled around the subject of my new job. Suleyman listened disinterestedly, cradling a glass of black tea, as I told him how working in a procurement department was no longer the right role for me. Since he had heard me talk this way many times before, he was mostly gazing at the cloudless blue sky, until I spoke a bit louder, saying, 'Suleyman, I want to leave my job.'

'What are you going to do?' he snorted, spilling his tea. 'Do you want to go back to selling yourself?'

It had been nearly five years since I'd met him, but I still flinched when he said things like that.

'Perhaps I don't need to work with someone who delights in constantly reminding me about my past?' I could feel myself collapsing mentally, but this time I didn't let him see it or allow the usual tears to come into my eyes. I simply poured myself another cup of tea and stood by the window watching the sea of fast moving cars flowing by.

'I'm just saying,' he said, sounding surprised by my non-reaction, 'you've got to be careful. You know you have a tendency to follow other people who don't have your best interests at heart. You have worked so hard at our company. All your colleagues respect you and you are making good money. In fact, that's why I came here today. There's something here for you from the boss himself.' He reached into his inside pocket and pulled out an envelope. 'Why don't you count it?' he said, tossing it onto the kitchen table.

I opened the envelope and counted the contents. There was three thousand dollars in there! Suleyman had given me the occasional cut of his 'extra earnings', but never this much. I had never had a bonus direct from the boss before. I seldom even got to speak to him.

'He wants to make you a partner,' Suleyman said.

'Really?' I said, amazed. I was suspicious that Suleyman was lying. Had he just improvised, giving me the money he'd meant to buy some products with, so that I would reconsider my plans? I replaced the money in the envelope and put it down next to me. I still wasn't privy to what went on behind the scenes at the company or what arrangements they had in place, but I considered that I had earned that money fair and square, for what I had accomplished in the past two years. It could give me some breathing space in which to continue to rebuild my life.

'Well, what do you think, Gulush? Being a partner, a female partner in a business such as ours. Quite an honour,' Suleyman said, lighting a cigarette and inhaling deeply. I could see by his face that he was smugly confident about his response to my announcement.

'No.' I shook my head slowly. 'I don't think so. I still want to leave.'

'You can be so unreasonable and stubborn sometimes,' he said, sitting up. I could see the lightning flashes of temper beginning in his eyes. 'Where else can you make this kind of money?'

I calmed myself with a quick mental calculation. My new job would pay four hundred US dollars a month. Suleyman had just handed me over seven months' salary.

'Probably nowhere,' I conceded.

'Exactly,' he said and relaxed again.

*It's not about the money*, I wanted to cry out. *It's about breaking free, reclaiming my life, perhaps even getting married one day, however implausible that might seem. It's about you, constantly trying to control my life, suffocating all the vitality out of me, you fat pig!* Of course, I didn't say any of that. I just pushed the envelope back towards him.

'I do want to leave, Suleyman,' I said with a calm outward composure. Inside, my little self got ready to run; but she didn't have to. Something had changed between us. Whether it was my recent academic success, my prowess at work or just because I was now older and wiser, Suleyman's obvious anger at my words turned cold, not hot. He stood up and stared at me as if seeing me for the first time.

'Well, then, that's it,' he said, 'but you'll have to tell the boss yourself, especially after the bonus he's given you.' With that, he picked up his cigarettes and walked out of the flat, leaving me at the table, with the envelope of money, to contemplate whether I could handle my own independence.

The next day, I took my letter of resignation to the boss. Somewhat to my relief, I was told that he was out all day, so I left the letter with the receptionist. Then I went to my office to deal with the day's paperwork and start making sure I didn't leave too many loose ends for my possible successor.

Suleyman was in the main office, heavy as a dark cloud. He was unusually abrupt with the staff and ignored my presence. I didn't want to part with him on bad terms because he could be a dangerous enemy and had a long memory when it came to keeping grudges. Suppressing my anger with him for being so selfish, I made him some tea as a peace offering. He looked up, his watery eyes full of reproach and his mouth tightly set under his moustache.

'Do you have plans after work?' he said, as I was about to disappear into my room.

'No,' I replied, reluctantly.

I reasoned that I had to have a few more conversations with Suleyman before he accepted that I was leaving and leaving for good, because in my mind, this job and Suleyman were intertwined. Leaving one behind meant saying goodbye to the other, too.

'I'll be done here in an hour,' he said. 'I'll take you home.'

I finished my paperwork absentmindedly, preoccupied with the choice of words I would use to convince Suleyman not to make a fuss. I still feared that if I did something against his will, he would find a way to punish me. Our relationship had to remain amicable, for now.

I made no comment when, instead of taking me home, he drove to the city centre and parked by a row of expensive-looking shops. I assumed he wanted some advice on a present for his daughters, as he had done before. As we got out of the car, the wind from the Caspian Sea soothed the evening heat on my skin.

'I've seen some clothes in here that you would absolutely love,' Suleyman said brightly, as he led me into one of the designer shops.

Really, I thought, how life has changed for us both. This bizarre journey from the unflattering rags you bought from the flea market to the designer shops of central Baku had been long and arduous.

The shop assistant was so helpful it was almost too much. She brought out one stunning piece after another as my eyes lit up. I tried them all on, coming out periodically from the velvet-shrouded changing room to show them off to Suleyman. It was like a scene from the film *Pretty Woman*, except I was done prostituting.

There was a pale orange summer suit with a short-sleeved buttoned top and a long skirt that emphasised my figure; a grey jacket and skirt suitable for work meetings; a colourful magenta and cream top and a matching skirt, which hung in soft, flattering waves; but my favourite piece was a lightweight jacket with a real fur collar. The inner layer, attached to the fur, was removable, making it possible to wear the jacket in spring and autumn. The jacket alone was seven hundred US dollars. I knew it was extravagant to spend that much money just on clothes, but I thought I would buy it for myself. I deserved a treat for getting a new job.

'Do you like them?' the assistant asked.

I did not have time to answer because suddenly my phone rang. The number looked familiar, but I could not immediately place it.

'I'm sorry, I need to take this,' I said, moving to a quiet spot near the door.

It was the dean of Western University.

'Hello, Elmira *khanim*.' I was glad it was a woman calling. Though I had my back to him, I could sense that Suleyman was listening as best he could. 'What? You want me to teach International law and European law to masters' students? Yes, I'd love to teach in English. No, thank you, I don't need time to think about your offer. Those two subjects are my favourite. I'll start teaching in September, no problem.' I rang off and returned to Suleyman.

I couldn't believe all the opportunities life was currently sending my way. Then the shop assistant handed me two bags.

'Enjoy,' she said, smiling wistfully.

'What's this?' I asked.

'All four outfits,' said Suleyman, grinning. 'I thought you looked amazing in them.'

'But Suleyman, they cost a fortune! I can't afford them.'

'My treat,' he replied. 'You know you are so worth it,' he added, as we returned to the car.

A familiar unease crept over me. He was obviously trying to buy me out of leaving. This was not going to end well. The wise part of me suggested handing the bags back, but I ignored it and instead hugged the gifts to my chest as joyous as a child at Christmas in American movies.

Much to my relief, he dropped me off by my block of flats and whizzed off to his family. Perhaps it was a genuine gift, I tried to convince myself unsuccessfully. I dreaded the consequences of accepting the bait, but was determined to rebuff any sexual advances or other demands. I was going to a new job, no matter what.

★★★

The next morning, I was summoned to the boss's office. I did not particularly like him. He was often rude to the staff, even swearing at colleagues in front of everyone else. The first time I witnessed that behaviour, I had vowed that I would not give him a reason to treat me like that. Today was different, though. He was not going to be happy with me and Suleyman had made it crystal clear that I was on my own with this conversation. For once, he would not have my back.

'What's this?' Without hello or any preamble, Arif *muellim* waved my letter of resignation in the air. 'Where do you think you're going?'

'I've been offered a job.'

'What job?' His face was contorted with anger, his mouth hanging open, exposing uneven, yellow teeth.

I didn't want to disclose my position at ACCELS to anyone, so I hesitated for a minute before remembering that I had a perfect excuse.

'I have been offered a teaching position at Western University.'

'Teaching position?! Huh! And you think you can survive on pennies? That's the stupidest thing I've ever heard.'

I didn't tell him that his arrogant behaviour was amongst the many reasons why I did not want to stay another day in my present job, but my silence spoke volumes.

'You are serious, aren't you?' His shrewd eyes peering from under his bushy eyebrows were incredulous.

'Please sign me off. I don't want to miss this opportunity.'

'Well, if you are this stupid, I don't want to have you here anyway,' he snapped. As he signed the letter instructing human resources to release me from my contract, I prayed that I would never see him again.

I left his office riled by his attitude, but still happy. I would have to work through August, when all the sanatoriums were packed, but with my leaving date the 1st of September 2001 when my two new jobs began, I was willing to put in the work and finish on a high note.

Suleyman was pacing back and forth outside.

'So?' he said as I emerged.

'He signed it,' I said simply, hiding my elation from him because I felt sure he was still hoping that I would change my mind.

I was right. Suleyman groaned, 'It's not too late to come to your senses, you know. You've got a month. I'm sure we can undo this.'

I shook my head, almost feeling sorry for him.

'You've been in your job for ages, long before I started helping you. You'll manage fine, without me. The new person might be even better,' I said.

He shook his head. 'You don't understand, do you?'

'Don't understand what?'

'We can't talk properly here. I'll explain after work,' he said, stalking off.

I still felt so entangled with Suleyman, but I didn't understand why. Was it the fear that being alone I might 'make another mistake' as he put it? He had plucked me from one type of hell and plunged me into another, but the shared experience seemed to have almost merged me with him. I had learnt to read his moods and the familiarity of

305

being with him had been close to comforting at times, even though I had never loved him. Might something worse happen to me if I separated from him? I was terrified that there was no one else who would stand by me; but I didn't think I could stay his secret lover on the side and his slave at work any longer. I needed to live my own life.

We were both lost in our own thoughts as Suleyman drove me home after work. I could tell he was confused – having used all his usual tricks – that he hadn't changed my mind, but I knew he wouldn't give up. He had been raised to have things his own way, like most men in Azerbaijan. I had to stay strong. I had no other choice.

I wanted to object, when I saw he was driving towards the city centre again, to say that I did not want any more gifts, but I might have been mistaken. Anyway, it was pointless to fuss. When he stopped the car, I sat still, hoping he would pop out to run an errand, but he said, 'Come on, I've got something to show you.'

I followed him up to the second floor of a busy department store and into its jewellery department. There was a dazzling display of beautifully crafted necklaces, earrings, bracelets and rings sparkling under the artificial lights, cleverly positioned to show off every piece. I was puzzled as I waited patiently for Suleyman, who was having a conversation with a member of staff. Then he called me over. 'I thought you might like this,' he said. The man clicked open the lid of a velvet-lined case to reveal what looked like a perfect emerald and diamond necklace. I was stunned. In five years, he had never bought me a single piece of jewellery, not even for my birthday. He couldn't be serious? 'Try it on,' he said, deftly removing the necklace from its case. Though the touch of his hands and his hot breath on my skin prickled me with discomfort and unease, I submitted. 'Look at yourself, it's magnificent,' he said, tilting an oval mirror towards me. 'And that's not all,' he said. 'Close your eyes and give me your hand.'

'What for?' I asked, startled by his excitement.

He took my hand unceremoniously, slipped a ring on it and, before I could pull my hand away, a second followed.

'Now,' he said, breathless by my side.

I could tell by the way the light chased off them that they too were diamond.

'Do you like them?' he said, expectantly.

'I suppose so,' I said slowly, as transfixed by the glamour and glitter of the jewellery, as I was confused by his actions. Had I not made it clear that I was leaving the company and, by extension, him? I hadn't been as explicit about the latter decision, but surely he had realised by now?

'I can't accept these,' I whispered.

'Why ever not?!' he said, handing what looked like several thousand dollars to the assistant, who was overjoyed.

'I won't change my mind about the job, Suleyman,' I said quietly.

'I wouldn't expect you to,' he asserted, but his eyes told me he thought he was winning me over, bit by bit.

Though I knew I had to hand over all his gifts, part of me foolishly thought I had earnt them. A saying of Masha's popped into my head: 'When given take it, when beaten run away'. I was playing with fire. The right thing to do was to reject all of it, but I knew Suleyman hardly ever took no for an answer; in fact, it only spurred him on. I would accept the gifts with good grace, but keep reminding him that my decision was already made.

★★★

As I worked hard throughout August, Suleyman drifted around the offices like a lost ghost. I tried not to worry about him; after all, he had his large family to fall back on. The night of the earthquake had shown me that. I needed to find my own special people to turn to in times of crisis. It was selfish of him to try and hold on to me.

On the Monday morning of my last week, my happiness feeding my humanity, I asked Suleyman how his mother was, knowing he visited her every weekend.

'She is OK,' he said, not looking up from his work. 'I've been advised that applying leeches helps improve the eyesight, via the circulatory system, so I've been trying that treatment with her.' He lapsed into silence again. Something else was bothering him. I had assumed it was me leaving, but maybe not.

'It's Rena,' he said. His shoulders slumped.

'What's happened to your sister?'

'I don't have a sister any more,' he replied, staring ahead.

'She's only just turned thirty, and she's died?' I was horrified.

He seemed to wrestle with his words before speaking again. 'It's worse than death. In fact, I wish she were dead, instead of bringing shame on the family.'

Had she been raped? Was she involved with a married man? Or had she become a prostitute? I couldn't imagine that any of those things had happened. Rena was a very pious woman.

'She's eloped with someone against the family's wishes,' Suleyman said bluntly.

That was all? People who were in love eloped sometimes, when the family didn't favour the marriage. My parents had, when Nana and Baba opposed their marriage. It hadn't ended well for them because they were only eighteen and twenty-two respectively, but Rena surely knew her own mind at thirty. She had probably been written off as a spinster, destined to be her mother's carer, anyway. Didn't he want her to be happy?

I did not know what to say, so I just patted him on the back.

'And I don't have a wife any more, either. She gathered all the gold and money she could lay her hands on, took our two kids, and left the flat, while I was visiting my mum with the older ones. It's such a betrayal, I can never have her back,' he said, lighting a cigarette, his hands shaking.

I remembered what it was like living in that claustrophobic flat, with no friends or outside connections. Personally, I could not blame her. If I'd had somewhere else to go, I would have left myself.

'Now you are deserting me too,' Suleyman moaned, 'at such a difficult time for me! My oldest two are teenagers now. Who will be there to help me give them guidance?'

Surely, he couldn't expect my help with that, after he had criticised my life choices for the past five years? Although my compassionate side wanted to comfort him, my pragmatic side seized on the opportunity to confirm his worst fears.

'You are right, Suleyman,' I said, calmly. 'I'm leaving you too.'

His eyes looked like those of a wounded animal. It might be the last straw for him, but it was also the truth, finally, clearly spoken.

'But you can't leave me. Not after everything I've done for you.' It was his turn to whimper now.

'We are even, Suleyman. You did all those things for me, and in return I was your sex slave, cleaner, cook and then employee. I have paid you back with my body, my tears and my time. I don't owe you anything.'

'It wasn't like that. I don't understand how you can say those things.'

'I don't want any more contact with you, Suleyman,' I said, my heart feeling surprisingly heavy saying the words. 'This is it. This is goodbye.'

I waited for him to erupt, to say something in desperation, but he stayed seated, collapsed in on himself, a shadow of his former cocky self. My footsteps echoed in the empty corridor, as I walked away and I remembered the sound of Mama's stilettos when she left me on my first day at the Prosecutor's Office nine years before.

★★★

I started my job at ACCELS with enthusiasm. This was a clean slate. I was daunted by the prospect of managing two programmes that no one else had run before, but I felt hopeful. My responsibilities included contacting secondary school teachers and telling them about the two competitions: one for English language teachers and another open to any subject that could incorporate civic education into their curriculum.

I shared my office with Mehdi, the young man who managed a US study programme for secondary school students, and my co-worker Emiliya, who was the part-time employee with the degree from the UK. I immediately delegated all the correspondence with the DC office to her and concentrated on arranging meetings in local schools. To my utter delight, after speaking to a local headteacher, I managed to arrange my first presentation for the staff.

When I entered the school hall that hot September morning, it was packed. I had not expected a full attendance. I enthused about the programmes, about the amazing opportunities that awaited them in America. The murmurs in the room told me many were interested, as I assured the audience that I would be personally available to help anyone who struggled with the application process. Leaving a generous stack of application forms and my brand-new business cards, I returned triumphantly to the office to call the next school on my list. I was determined to make the programme a success.

A few days in, Suleyman rang. When his phone number flashed on the screen, I quickly turned the sound down. I did not want to answer it, but thinking he would find another way of reaching me, perhaps in person, I reluctantly answered. I hoped Mehdi did not speak to me while I was on the call, fearing that would spark Suleyman's temper. His voice sounded distant. I assumed it was a bad line.

'Are you in Ganja?'

'No, I'm at the flat,' he gasped. 'And I haven't eaten for days. I won't eat unless you come to see me.'

Oh no, I thought, this was his new plan, to drag me down, just as I was getting started in my new job. My first instinct was to hang up, but I knew I couldn't. Suleyman never did anything by halves. There was nowhere to escape to; if he wanted to track me down, he would. As it was nearly lunchtime, I thought maybe I could manage the situation.

'I'll buy some food and be there in half an hour.'

I dashed out, annoyed by my inability to say no and Suleyman's narcissistic selfishness. The traffic was horrendous. It took forty minutes to reach his block, so I called Emiliya and said I would be popping into a school on my way back from lunch, to give myself more time.

It was painfully familiar going up in the lift to Suleyman's flat, as I remembered my captivity all too vividly. I felt like I was walking into a war zone without a gun. The door was on the latch. I gingerly crept in and headed towards the groans in the living room. The curtains were all shut, the flat full of shadows. I imagined myself in a horror movie, descending broken steps into a cellar, all my senses shouting *Don't go in there!* but I continued, my fine body-hairs prickling with dread.

I did not see Suleyman straight away because he was slumped on the floor, his back against the sofa. I went to open the curtains.

'No, don't,' he moaned, 'I can't bear you to see me like this.'

However, when my eyes had got used to the semi-darkness, I could see well enough. There was a syringe on the floor and a jar containing a dark-red liquid, which, even from a distance, smelt like blood. The crook of Suleyman's arm looked bruised. Why was he drawing his blood out? He looked a mess, so much thinner and deeply unhappy.

'I brought you some food,' I said, putting out some *pirozhki* on a large plate.

'I won't eat without you,' he said hoarsely.

I sat on the sofa, trying to ignore the syringe and the blood. It was hard for me to stay. I had seen my mother's slit wrists when I was only six years old. I didn't know what to say or do.

'Work,' he croaked, 'they need supervision… produce needs to be ordered. Please help.'

I made him sip some water, as my head whirled. How could I do three jobs at once? I was due to give my first lecture at the university today, but the state he was in made my mind up. 'Give me the number. I'll make the order. You can settle with them when you feel better. I'll pop to the office and check on them when I've got time,' I said.

As I got up to leave, he grabbed my leg. 'Don't leave me. I don't know if I can survive this pain.'

'I have to go to work,' I said slowly, speaking to him as if he were a toddler.

'Promise you'll come back tomorrow. I swear to God, I won't eat unless you are here.'

I knew this was emotional blackmail, but I felt unable to ignore his manipulative demands when he looked so ill. Now I would have to continue to lie to my new colleagues.

I returned to the office and, after talking vaguely about the school I had just "visited", I prepared another stack of applications, made more school enquiries, surreptitiously ordered the sanatoriums' supplies, then made a mad dash to my old office to check on things there, before arriving to give my first lecture at Western University, with five minutes to spare.

Although I was well prepared for this first lecture on international law, I was so exhausted that my hands and voice shook. I tried to feign confidence, but eventually gave up on making a good first impression on my ten masters' students, and talked about the history of international law, reading some passages from my notes, hoping that I didn't drone on like my boring lecturers at Baku State University.

The next day was a carbon copy of the previous one, except that Suleyman looked frailer and needier.

'If I die, it'll be on your conscience. You can't leave me like this,' he said, after we had eaten and I had assured him I was monitoring his office, until he 'recovered'.

As the days passed, I felt my levels of tiredness and misery rising. It was virtually impossible to juggle so many activities. I used various pretexts to disappear for long stretches of time from my new job. I thought it was only a matter of time before I was found out. I had to call schools from my mobile in taxis, recording the conversations in a notepad balanced on my knees and still submit regular reports to Jeremy. I hated lying, but Suleyman seemed to be declining and I was truly worried about him.

As we entered the second week of Suleyman's self-harming, his depression worsened. The flat stank because he had not showered in days. I sat there feeling disgusted, forcing myself to share the food I had brought, amidst the bloodstains and the stench.

'I would really like you to shower,' I broached the subject.

'Why bother? I don't want to,' he said bleakly.

'Would you do it for me?' I asked hesitatingly.

He turned his pale, gaunt face to me, his large nose protruding more than it had before, reminiscent of Baba when he was fighting cancer. That had been heartbreaking. To see a once powerful man diminish into a helpless skeleton. Could that happen to Suleyman?

'I would do anything for you,' Suleyman whispered.

'Let's start with a shower,' I said brightly and supported him to walk to the bathroom. I hated going into that room where I had taken so many miserable baths during my captivity, but I gritted my teeth, helped Suleyman undress and seated him on a plastic stool under the water. I left him there, on the pretext of calling work and shot into the living room to find his mobile. I found it on the filthy floor. I searched through his address book and, keeping an ear out for Suleyman, I dialled his older brother's number.

'Elmar?' I spoke urgently. 'This is about Suleyman. He is in a critical condition. You have to take care of him. It's your responsibility. Come today, leave now, he's really bad.'

I hung up the phone and placed it back exactly where I'd found it. Suleyman was dressing, judging by the sounds from the bathroom. By the time he finally emerged, I had tidied up the room. I insisted he went to bed, then returned to work armed with another lie.

# 16.

# PROPOSAL

My plan must have worked because, after that day, I did not have any more phone calls from Suleyman, but I kept checking in on the procurement team staff for a few more days. Once they demonstrated that they could handle his absence, I stopped going there and could finally concentrate on my new job. Jeremy and I were both pleased when applications started coming in, some of which looked quite strong. My teaching at university also went well, and I had good feedback from the dean and the students. Life was turning a corner.

One October morning, Farida surprised me with a visit. She was dropping something off for Nigar, who was in the next-door office, but wanted to chat with me too. Once Emiliya and Mehdi had gone for a tea break, she said, 'It probably won't come as a surprise to you, but Polad is very attracted to you. He wonders if you would like to meet for a chat, so you can get to know each other better, before things perhaps progress to the next stage.'

I was lost for words for a moment. Was this the start of a fairy tale or a potential nightmare? I tried to sound nonchalant. 'Sure, give him my number, there's a park near my flat. Maybe we could go for a walk on Sunday morning, around 10am?'

'I'm sure he would love that.' She beamed.

I tormented myself for the rest of the week. On the one hand, I wanted to look perfect for my date: I bought a pair of jeans, which I had to zip up lying down on my bed, and planned to team them with a lilac top. On the other hand, I kept worrying about what might transpire after this first date.

If it got to the point where he proposed and I said yes, then the next step traditionally was for his family to come and speak to my family. I couldn't send them to Nana. She still thought I was working in the States somewhere. Nor could I send them to Mama, whose whereabouts I still didn't know. My uncles lived far away in Moscow and hadn't seen me for years. Worst of all, there was the lie I had told to Farida about Suleyman being my uncle. Denying his existence now would be very suspicious.

It seemed an insurmountable challenge, fraught with multiple pitfalls capable of exposing my sordid past, but I stubbornly refused to back down. A very young and naïve part of me still believed in miracles. Amina would have thought of something. If Polad did fall in love with me, wouldn't he take me for who I was? That was unlikely. I dare not tell the truth, especially since I was working with Nigar.

On Sunday morning, I got up early to dress and put on my make-up. My heart was racing because this was the first proper date I'd ever had. When there was a knock at my flat door, I was surprised. It wasn't even 9:30am and Farida had asked Polad to meet me outside the block. Perhaps he was as excited as I was? After a quick glance in the mirror, I flung the door open, then shrank back in horror. Suleyman was standing there.

'You look fancy,' he said, raising his eyebrows. 'Where are you going?'

Flustered by the lack of time before Polad was due, I couldn't come up with a lie and knew that getting angry with Suleyman for turning up unannounced might cause a scene, so I just blurted out, 'I have a date.'

'What? Who with?' he demanded.

'Don't do this, Suleyman,' I implored. 'We always said that our arrangement was temporary and that one day we would move on. Well, today is that day for me.'

'Well, I just came to say thank you for looking after me and saving my life,' Suleyman replied, as he walked jauntily into the flat. He had no intention of leaving any time soon, by the way he lolled on the sofa.

'I have to go now,' I said firmly, although I was now feeling twice as nervous as before. Suleyman's mood went from nonchalant to distressed in a split second.

'Please, don't go. It'll kill me,' he howled, collapsing on the floor. Then he did something I hadn't seen him do in five years, he started to weep uncontrollably. Did I pity him, or was I repulsed by him? At that moment, I couldn't tell. Then my survival instinct saved me.

'We'll talk when I get back. Right now, I have to go,' I said.

He started sobbing louder as I closed and locked the door, then dashed to the lift. On the way down, I took several deep breaths and flattened my hair. Polad sat in a flashy car, with music booming out, his dark sunglasses concealing his eyes. He smiled and pointed to the seat next to him. Deciding it was safer to drive off somewhere with Polad than have Suleyman follow me downstairs, I got in.

We were quiet in the car. Polad pretended to listen to his music, while I tried to hide my preoccupation with Suleyman and my future fears. The fact that I was sitting in Polad's car by myself meant an implicit yes, in traditional terms, and the meeting meant to iron out the details of the next step.

He stopped near a small park with a broken fountain and some young olive trees. He opened the door for me, and we started walking side by side. I found his nearness electrifying. With fleeting sideways glances, I admired his tall, athletic body, as he spoke, until his eyes met mine and I looked away, as was expected. Although I had been with many men before, this situation was far more emotionally intimate than I had ever experienced.

'Tell me something about yourself,' he said, as we settled on a sheltered bench.

'Where do I start?' I said, buying myself a few seconds. This was by far my least favourite subject. I told him about my academic accomplishments and work, but he interrupted me.

'I know all that stuff. Tell me about yourself. Have you ever loved before?'

'No!' I knew my answer was too quick, but I wanted to reassure him, and my mind was battling images of my past. 'And you?' I asked.

He shook his head but didn't say anything. Was he telling the truth? If I could lie so easily, what was to stop him doing the same?

After a couple more conversations that petered out, Polad moved on to the main reason for meeting up. He said he wanted his family to visit mine the very next week, so needed my mother's phone number to give his mum.

I said the first thing that came into my head. 'You give me your mum's number, so my family can phone her first. They have to travel from Ganja, so it might be best for them to contact your mum when they are in town.'

We walked a bit further and then headed back to the car. His mum's number felt like it was burning a hole in my pocket. How was I going to handle this situation? Even if I could fool them somehow now, how could I sustain those lies into the future? I knew it was madness. I should stop it now, by saying I hadn't gelled with Polad or something similar. Bow out gracefully and possibly save my friendship with Farida and Nigar. However, my desire to have a normal family life was so strong, I couldn't give up on that dream.

★★★

Suleyman was still in my flat when I returned. My heart sank. He lay fully clothed on my bed, his eyes red with tears.

'How did it go?' he asked, not hiding the bitterness in his voice.

'It's not what you think,' I said, defensively. 'It's serious. He wants to send his family to see mine, next week.'

'That's the funniest thing I've heard in ages,' chuckled Suleyman. 'What family?' His gloating spiked my mood.

'Well, thanks to you hiding me away, I don't have one, do I?' I was infuriated with his attitude because I blamed him entirely for this situation.

'Let's not forget why I did that,' he replied sagely.

'Here we go again. You will never let me forget, will you?' I snapped.

'Let me help you,' he said, sitting up. 'Please, I told you I would do anything for you.' He reached out to hug my hips.

'How can you help?' I said, trying to wriggle out of his grasp.

'Let me represent your family. For the past few years, we have been like family. I kept you away from trouble. I supported your studies, your work and your growth. This is the next natural step.'

As he spoke, his hands started to wander all over my body. Was this the price for his help? To have sex with him? He read my mind, as usual. 'I'm so weak, I can't perform any more,' he said, mournfully. I stiffened, hoping he wasn't going to break down again. I hadn't got his brother's number. 'I just want to feel your body next to mine,' he said sadly, 'one last time. Then I'll do anything you need me to.'

I had been right, but what other choice did I have? Reluctantly, I let him undress me with trembling hands. His feelings seemed genuine and, whether it was because he needed me, or because I knew this was the last time, I let him caress my body, though it all felt so wrong. I had just given my word to Polad, and was now in the cloying embrace of my nemesis.

Suleyman appeared to be weak and impotent to start with, but he soon became aroused and climaxed over me. All I felt was guilt oozing through me, any vestiges of self-respect left in tatters for betraying Polad so soon after our meeting. As Suleyman lay panting next to me, I rationalised to myself that one more encounter with him did not make me any more spoilt goods than I already was. This was the last time. I hadn't yet had a chance to discover if I would fall in love with Polad, but I definitely felt a spark growing between us and I was willing to do anything to regain my respectability and see if I could lead an honest life with him.

I gave Suleyman the precious number as we sat drinking tea afterwards.

'Can I really trust you?' I asked. I still wasn't sure.

'Can you really afford not to?' he replied.

★★★

I could not sleep the night before their meeting, so I was jittery and short-tempered at work, jumping each time the phone rang. Suleyman was meant to meet with Polad's family that afternoon, so I wouldn't know the outcome until after work.

When I left the building after six, Suleyman was standing outside. 'What are you doing here?' I hissed, suddenly alarmed. 'How did you find me? What's wrong?'

He was so well dressed; a crisp, expensive shirt, a brand-new suit, a smart tie, a fresh haircut and even some cufflinks I'd never seen before. He looked like he was about to marry someone himself.

'Relax, everything is all right.' He smiled broadly. 'I think the meeting went well. All is in order, except for one little problem.'

'What?' My heart plummeted.

'Someone has stolen my phone.'

'What do you mean? Who could have stolen your phone?' Had he left it in his car?

'I foolishly took a bus. Someone picked my pocket. I could not call you, so I went home to fetch my car and come here. I didn't want you worrying. Now I need to go and report the theft to the police.'

It all seemed unlikely to me. Suleyman on a bus and someone getting close enough to steal from him? I hadn't seen him on a bus once in all the five years I'd known him.

'Don't believe me? Come to the police station, then.'

'I don't want to. I don't have the time,' I said truthfully.

'I just arranged your future,' he yelled, 'but you don't want to support me in such a small way? Come with me now!'

Anxious to avoid attracting my colleagues' attention and, against my better judgement, I climbed wearily into his car and he drove to the police station. I sat minding the car, while he went to collect the form he needed to submit. I still doubted him. Why was he bothering to report it? Hundreds of phones were taken every week, and I don't think the police ever found any of them. He could just buy himself a new one. What was this really about?

As I stared out of the car, I suddenly recognised the area. I was in the backyard of Farida's multistorey building. This couldn't be a coincidence. My anxiety ramped up. I considered getting out of the car and hailing a taxi, but then I noticed the keys dangling from the ignition. Someone might steal his car and it would be my fault. I did not notice Suleyman had returned until he opened the boot and jolted me out of my thoughts.

'Stay there,' he said firmly. I think he could see I was worried. 'I've got something for you.'

My unease doubled. What was he up to? I couldn't antagonise him because he might call Polad's mother and tell her the truth. He came to my open door with an exquisite pair of high-heeled, golden, patent leather shoes.

'Aren't these perfect?' he said, kneeling in front of me. For a second, it looked like a scene from *Cinderella* as he fitted the shoes on my feet. 'They suit you and will go so well with that magenta-gold suit I bought you recently.'

I could not argue with his taste, the shoes were lovely and they would match that outfit, but I was embarrassed by the looks of passers-by.

'Please get up now,' I said, 'I need to go.'

'There's nothing more I can do here, so I'll take you home.'

I had held a faint hope that he would say goodbye in the courtyard, but he followed me upstairs and started to undress the moment we got into the flat.

'No!' I exclaimed. 'You promised last time was… the last time!'

'That was before I discovered you could wake the dead,' he replied, loosening his tie. 'Everything is fine, don't worry. Think of this as a celebration shared by good friends. You really are amazing, you know. Now come here, let's not fight on such an auspicious day!'

I was on his hook again. My body was rigid with hatred: hatred of him, hatred of my stupidity, hatred of being a woman. I ground my teeth with resentment of his enjoyment, as he ground into me, oblivious.

I couldn't speak to him and, after cleaning myself up in the bathroom, I sat in the kitchen cloud-watching. Their vastness seemed to put everything in perspective. Ours was such a little drama compared to them.

Suleyman came to find me eventually and tried to coax me back into the bedroom, swearing on the lives of his children that he wouldn't touch me again but would support my marriage.

'You won't come back, ever again?' I asked drily.

'I am a man of honour. Of course not,' he said earnestly.

I still slept fitfully, in the living room. The next morning, when I went to the wardrobe, he was still in bed. I felt him watching me make my selections.

'Aren't you going to wear your new shoes today? They look wonderful,' he said, getting dressed himself. 'You will let me take you to work, won't you?'

'No, Suleyman, I won't. Remember, we agreed last night, it's over. Everything is over.'

'You are right, of course,' he said, with a mock bow of submission. 'Everything is, indeed, over, today. But humour me one last time and wear that gorgeous outfit with your new shoes to work.' He clasped his hands as if in prayer and gazed at me puppy eyed.

I agreed just to shut him up, though the shoes were not very practical to walk in. I banged the door resoundingly on the way out and caught a taxi to work, still on edge. I was relieved to find the office was empty, so I didn't have to chat and could start on the newly submitted application forms straight away.

I sighed inwardly when my office door flew open. It was Nigar. I was puzzled because she worked in the main office, a converted flat next door. Nigar hardly ever came to mine, which was in an adjacent, but not directly connected, former shop. I gave her my best welcoming smile, but she stormed furiously towards my desk and shouted, 'I want you to pack up your stuff and fuck off right now.'

'What? Why?' I said. 'Nigar, please calm down and tell me what's happened.'

She was beside herself with anger. Her eyes were full of hate, her sensual mouth twisted and her slim frame rigid.

'Don't bother playing the innocent good girl with me! He told us everything! Do you hear me? Everything! Have you got any idea what you have done to my brother, to our whole family? My mother hardly slept last night.'

I was dumbfounded, shocked by my own utter stupidity and the sadistic brutality of Suleyman's revenge. She came around the table and, for a moment, I thought she wanted to hit me, but instead she stared down at my feet.

'And you are wearing those shoes! That was the last piece of evidence he gave us. He showed them to us and said you'd wear them today, if we still had any doubts about what he had told us. I never ever want to see you again! Do you hear me?'

I knew she meant it, but I tried to salvage something from the situation. 'I'm so sorry, Nigar. You don't understand, he's a monster. I... I... accept there's no chance of a wedding now, but...'

'You are joking!' Nigar cut in. 'You're a fool!' She started to laugh hysterically, walking away from me.

'I can't leave this job,' I said, louder than I meant to. 'I have nowhere else to go!'

Nigar stopped laughing. She glared at me as she approached and leant over my desk. 'Do I look like I care?' she said, menacingly. 'If you don't leave nicely, believe me, I'll make your life a living hell. One way or another, you... will... leave!'

Before she left the room, she turned round and said, 'He's an ugly person, that Suleyman, inside and out. But he loves you, doesn't he? He loves you very much. I'll give him that.'

When she banged the door shut behind her, I collapsed, sobbing. The shards of my shattered dream cutting deep into my heart, I blamed only myself for this awful mess.

# 17.

# SET UP

Nigar kept her promise. After that morning, life at work became a living hell, a soulless wasteland. She spoke to all of my colleagues, apart from my boss, and convinced them to ostracise me. I didn't know if she had disclosed the facts of my past or used some other leverage, but not many people would talk to me socially, not even to answer my morning 'hellos'. When someone made tea for the office, I was left out. When there was a meeting for people to share their concerns or ideas, I was ignored.

Each new social stab weakened my resolve to stay. I knew that finding a new job would be difficult but maybe it was best to leave. Suleyman had orchestrated this situation so well: ruining my marriage prospects and my career opportunities in a single stroke. He obviously thought I would have to return to work for him, but I couldn't face that, so I increased my efforts recruiting schoolteachers for the two programmes, until the application numbers had risen to eighty-four and fifty-six respectively. When I went to share the good news with Jeremy, he said he needed a quiet word.

'Gulya,' he said, clasping his long fingers together. 'I've

heard some rumours in the office relating to yourself.'

*Here we go*, I thought, miserably. Nigar must have convinced him to fire me. I tried to think of a way to explain the situation as a misunderstanding, but he continued. 'I personally don't care about your past. I don't know what went on with you and Nigar, but I have been crystal clear with her: that I value your contribution to our team. As long as you work well, you're staying. Don't let me down, Gulya.'

'Thank you, Jeremy,' was all I managed to say. I kept myself together as I gathered my paperwork up and left his office. Only then did I rush to the toilet and let tears of shame and gratitude run down my face.

\*\*\*

Jeremy's faith in me professionally kept me going towards the month's deadline. I amplified my efforts, while suppressing my grief over being ignored. This was made easier now Emiliya and Mehdi spent the majority of their time in the main office and, instead of going through to Jeremy's office to report on my progress, he visited me once a day, standing in the doorway and smiling, while I updated him on the rising numbers.

It was one day, while I was reporting to Jeremy, that I suddenly saw Suleyman standing across the other side of the wide corridor behind him. Not wanting Jeremy to turn round, I carried on talking, but knew I was gabbling. Suleyman was gesticulating that he would cut Jeremy's ponytail off or hit him on the head. Unaware, Jeremy started talking about a complaint against me.

'Gulya, I've had an angry email from the head of both programmes in DC,' he said, not noticing how pale I had become as I quietly wished Suleyman dead. He was still making rude gestures while I struggled to concentrate on Jeremy's words.

'Why is she so cross?' I said, surprised since I had been making such good progress.

'You haven't answered a single email from her in the past month.'

'I haven't received an email from her for days,' I said, praying that when this conversation ended, Suleyman would let Jeremy return safely to his office. So, I opened my computer and said, 'Please come and take a look.'

While Jeremy perused my inbox, I walked to the door and shut out Suleyman's ugly face. I didn't want to call the police unless I absolutely had to.

'It gets quite draughty in here,' I said brightly. 'You can see there's not a single email from Washington in my inbox,' I said, returning to my desk.

'Hmmm, I can see that. Nevertheless, she has set up a meeting in two days at 5pm Baku time, it's morning in DC then. You'll need to come to my office to speak to her.'

Jeremy probably wondered why I opened my office door so cautiously for him to leave, but he didn't ask. I watched him walk away, ready to call the police if anything happened. I relocked the door and stood against it, feeling very vulnerable. There was nothing to stop Suleyman attacking me here, given that my colleagues had practically moved to the main office now. I told myself to stop worrying. He wouldn't risk someone hearing me.

To distract myself, I started trawling through the

deleted items folder and the spam box to see if I could find any stray emails from the DC office, but couldn't find any. When Emiliya came to collect her bag, I asked her.

'Emiliya, I know you've been corresponding with the DC office since the start of the programme. Have you received any emails in the past month?'

Emiliya hesitated before replying. I could see a mix of emotions crossing her face. She seemed to have joined the general boycott, having hardly spoken to me for weeks. Then I saw her face relax. 'Listen,' she said, 'I personally have nothing against you, Gulya. Shit happens. My family refused to speak to me for months after I told them that I was in love with a Russian man. Your life is your business; but I hope you understand, it was made clear that I had to be either with you or against you. There was no middle ground. I'm finishing here soon, remember. I'm the part-timer and I really need a good reference for my next job.'

This was the longest conversation I'd had at work in weeks, except with Jeremy. It felt good hearing someone acknowledge the situation. Being ignored had nearly driven me mad.

'I understand,' I said. 'I would have done the same, probably.' She looked relieved. 'So, have you had any emails from Washington?'

'None,' she said, heading out the door.

After lunch, Emiliya came back to work at her computer opposite me. Although she was not as chatty as she used to be before Nigar denounced me, she appeared friendly. The radio purred in the background while I entered details on the database, until someone knocked on the door, causing me to flinch. The tall man that entered was not Suleyman. I sighed with relief.

'Excuse me.' He was confident but polite. 'I am here to find out the results of the secondary school competition. My nephew applied,' he explained. He was in his early thirties, wearing a sharp grey suit. He was not classically handsome but had a ready smile and the sort of charisma that commands immediate attention.

'Mehdi manages that programme. He is out of the office for a short while,' I informed him.

'No problem,' he said. 'If you don't mind, I'll wait for him.'

He made himself comfortable at Mehdi's desk, sitting back in the armchair, as if he owned the place. As Christina Aguilera sang 'What a Girl Wants' on the radio, Emiliya and I exchanged puzzled looks. Then, he got up and without asking switched the radio channel. 'This is my brother's radio channel,' he said, grinning, 'I highly recommend it.'

What an attention-seeker, I thought, and tried to concentrate on the music – because he certainly had mine. I recognised Mariah Carey singing "Thank God I Found You", which sent a familiar tingle down my spine. *No, not again*, I told myself, sternly. I tried to focus my wandering mind on the database figures, which now seemed to be dancing in front of me.

The next song was by fellow Azerbaijani Aygün Kazimova. I remembered watching her perform live one New Year's Eve when I was still working with Amina. Aygün had had difficulty keeping her music on her stand because it kept collapsing. She had eventually kicked the stand away, thrown the music to one side and improvised confidently. Suddenly, I realised Mehdi's visitor was speaking to me.

'My name is Rasul,' he said, 'and you are…?'

'Gulya and this is Emiliya,' I said.

Emiliya smiled and raised her eyebrows at me. She kept stealing looks at Rasul, then looking at me. I tried to block them both out by disappearing into my database. I didn't need to get involved in any gossip.

'Is it always this quiet in your office? It's all go at mine!' he exclaimed, stretching his arms out.

'Where do you work?' asked Emiliya, while I continued to feign indifference.

'KGB,' he said, clearly pleased to see our reactions.

We sat in stiff silence until he got up and approached my desk.

'Would you do me a huge favour, Gulya, and pass my phone number to Mehdi? Or better yet, perhaps you could call me yourself when you find out if my nephew passed. Here's his name. I pray that it's good news for him. My sister will be the proudest mother alive.'

I looked at his phone number. I would not forget it: 0552225555. I noticed his long fingers and his graceful gestures. I could feel my face blush, so I kept my head down, cursing my pale skin.

'Call me with any news,' he said, kindly pretending not to notice. 'I'll be waiting. Goodbye both.'

'He's so into you!' Emiliya gabbled as soon as the door closed, just like her old self. It was good to have a friend in the office again.

'Come on!' I laughed, raising my hands and my eyes.

Then, worry kicked in. Would she tell Nigar, giving her more ammunition to throw at me?

As if reading my mind, Emiliya shrugged. 'Don't worry, Gulya, tomorrow is my last day. I won't say anything. Call him now, make some excuse to start talking to him. That's what I'd do.'

Buoyed up by her enthusiasm, I dialled Rasul's number. Thankfully, the signal didn't connect. I passed his number to Mehdi when he returned and decided it was best to forget about our visitor.

★★★

I was sad that Emiliya left the next day. I was pretty sure she had been spying on me at one point, but we parted on good terms and I felt lonelier without her. My timekeeping was the current instrument of torture at work. If I was more than a minute late to work, or after lunch, someone would alert Jeremy and I would find him waiting in my office. It felt awful being under constant surveillance. Nigar was obviously intent on fulfilling her prophecy. It was only a matter of time before I slipped up in some small way and she would pounce.

There was something terribly wrong with the correspondence with Washington. I was nervous as the day of the meeting arrived and I would have to explain myself to the programme manager. Before heading to the meeting, I searched through all my emails again, but there was nothing there. Perhaps there was some old correspondence in Emiliya's mailbox, I thought, so I opened her computer, and rummaged around. There was nothing in the inbox, outbox or even in the deleted items.

I was about to close her computer down, when I noticed an unfamiliar folder called SysUS. Curious, I clicked on it and gasped. The folder contained numerous unread emails whose subject lines became more and more terse. They had all been automatically directed to this folder, which Emiliya had probably deliberately ignored. Now that she had finished her contract, no one could hold her liable. She had received a glowing reference letter from Jeremy.

I rushed to his office, alarmed at the implications. He came and looked at the evidence, shaking his head, his kind eyes sad and disappointed.

'We'll fix this,' he said. 'I'll have a word with everyone concerned. Don't worry, it will be fine.'

I wondered whether this was what Emiliya had meant about taking sides. It was very clever of someone, but I would never know if that clever person was her.

\*\*\*

Although the situation at work stabilised after Jeremy cleared the air with the DC office, Suleyman was still coming to my work. He continued to mime threats to hurt Jeremy, there were silent phone calls and he hung around outside. One day, I decided I could not tolerate the stress of the situation any more and went to confront him. I instantly regretted speaking to him because his response was so predictable. 'I want you to come to my flat tonight, to talk, otherwise, I'll have to see about your boss. He spends too much time in your office. Unless you want to be blamed for his injuries and get fired, you'll have to come.'

Once again, I believed I had no choice, but when I

arrived that evening, I quickly realised Suleyman was drunk. There were kebabs and an open bottle of vodka on the table.

'Have some,' he said, pushing an overflowing glass towards me.

'No, I'm not here to socialise. What do you want from me now?'

He chewed silently on a kebab, then downed another vodka. I had never seen him this drunk.

'We are over, Suleyman.' I said steadily. 'How can you think otherwise, after you betrayed me? This performance has got to stop.'

'It'll stop when I say so,' he retorted. 'How dare you talk about betrayal after dumping me like this?' His words tasted as bitter to me as the vodka he was drinking.

I could see it had been a mistake to come here: he wasn't going to listen to reason.

I turned and walked swiftly out of the flat, breathing a sigh of relief when I pressed the button to call the lift. But before it could arrive, I heard the flat door click open. Suleyman emerged and began to stagger towards me. I darted to the stairs, in case he tried to follow me into the lift. Despite his drunken state, he managed to catch up with me on the ground floor. I turned, shouting, 'Leave me alone!' just in time to see him reaching for my head, but too late for me to dodge. I screamed in horror as he dragged me towards him by my hair then bashed my head against the concrete wall.

'You are mine, Gulush! Do you hear me?' he roared.

With my ears ringing, I scrabbled to push back from the wall. I was shocked to my core. Suleyman had been verbally and sexually abusive, but he had never beaten me. I whimpered in fear, trying to wriggle free, but he held my hair firmly, pressing my face against the wall with increasing pressure. A searing pain pulsed through my nose. Blood started to trickle down my lips and chin.

He was trying to destroy the only two things I liked about myself: my brain and my nose. A sudden rage shot through me, a drive to survive fired my muscles and I found the strength to fight. I kicked back at his shins, catching him off guard. Using the wall as leverage, I pushed him away with my whole body. He lost his balance, but managed to grab my left hand and twisted it. I yelped in pain as one of the diamond rings he had bought me dug into my middle finger, piercing the skin.

Then the street door clanged open as a man carrying his shopping walked into the lobby. Suleyman moved away from me. I stood motionless, bleeding, overwhelmed with shame, my eyes begging for help, but although I was sure he saw me, the man carried on, walking past us towards the lift, as if we weren't there!

Panting and dizzy, I found myself unable to move as Suleyman hissed, 'See, no one wants to help a whore like you. It's just you and me now, and you'll do as you're told!'

He started to press my face against the wall again. I was sure he was intent on damaging me for life. Give him what he wants, my survival instinct told me.

'OK, OK,' I cried.

'OK what?' he said, his breath hot and acrid on my neck.

'I'll do what you want,' I said.

'Louder!' he said, releasing me to gloat at my defeat.

'I'll do what you want!' I shouted.

'That's better. Now, come here and kiss me, properly.'

Swallowing down my blood and pride, I tottered towards him. I shut my eyes as his mouth pressed down on my painful, blood-caked lips for a lingering kiss, like that of an onscreen romance. It seemed an eternity before he pulled away, smacking his lips as if relishing the taste of gore.

'Good,' he said, with a vampiric smile of red-stained teeth. 'Go home and clean yourself up. You look disgraceful. I expect you back here tomorrow evening. Wear those golden shoes,' he said, disappearing up into the shadows of the stairwell, so light on his feet now that they made no sound.

A gentle rain had begun to fall as I retrieved my fallen bag to limp home. I welcomed its healing chill, which soothed my skin and kept most people indoors. Of the few who, like me, had no choice but to walk in the night, most were wrapped in hooded jackets or hidden under umbrellas.

At home in my little flat, I ran myself a deep bath. The perfumed salts stung my wounds, before they soothed me, as I sobbed. My nose didn't stop bleeding for ages and bruises blossomed all over me, especially on my face. I could feel the skin raw and raised on the back of my head as I washed my hair in the cooling water. I was so tired and disorientated that a bit of me was tempted to just sink under the water and stay there. I resisted that impulse. I wasn't going to let Suleyman push me there.

After my bath, as I applied ice to my face to ease the swelling, I thought of going to the police, but quickly decided that was pointless. It was always a woman's fault here, especially if Suleyman, on paper a respectable businessman, disclosed my past to them. Neither could I go unannounced back to my family, looking like this. Nana was too old to know the truth, I thought, and Mama was caught up in her own struggles. Once again, I felt I had no one to turn to, until an absurd idea entered my head. 'He's so into you,' the ghost of Emiliya's voice said. I picked up my phone and dialled the number simple attraction had etched into my memory: 0552225555. This time, despite the hour, he answered straight away.

'Rasul *muellim*, this is Gulya,' I said shakily. 'You gave me your number when you were making enquiries about your nephew at ACCELS. You said I could call you.'

'Of course, I remember you. Sadly, Mehdi told me that my nephew didn't pass. I was starting to lose hope that I'd ever hear from you. How can I help?'

'It's a long story, one for the daylight. Have you got time to meet me tomorrow?' I asked. What was I doing? *You have had enough*, came the answer.

★★★

The next day, I called in sick. I met Rasul in a café, which seemed especially discreet and dimly lit. Rasul lit a cigarette and, after a brief hesitation, offered me one too. I hadn't smoked for years, but in the circumstances, I accepted with relief. I needed to take the edge off my pain and my nerves. Though my face had told much of the story for me, while we sipped coffee and smoked cigarette after cigarette, I told him everything I was prepared to share.

I had learnt the hard way that lies would only fester and destroy. Besides, working for the KGB, he could find out anything he wanted to. It was still a huge risk to share my vulnerability with him, but I knew there was no other way forward. His face seemed warm and empathetic as I ended with the events of the previous night.

'I have told you all of this because I truly have no one else to ask. Can you help me? Perhaps if you spoke to him, as a KGB officer, he might leave me alone.'

Rasul sat back considering, then he smiled and said, 'Yes, of course. It'd be easy to do that for you. Believe me, I know how to speak to bullies. He won't bother you again.'

I was so grateful I forgot protocol for a moment and reached to hug him. He felt warm and muscular, despite my aching left arm.

★★★

A few days later, Rasul called me and said that the matter was resolved. Although I asked him several times, he never disclosed the tactics that had rendered such excellent results. I never did see Suleyman again after that, though my fear of being stalked and attacked by him never did completely disappear. Sometimes, when I walked around Baku, I thought I saw his face amongst the passers-by, but he was never there.

Rasul insisted on calling me regularly to check how I was. We both saw our friendship as platonic because Rasul was married with his wife expecting their second child. Although I found his presence supremely comforting, I accepted the facts. Our café meetings felt innocent enough, being an open environment, but whether it was because of my loneliness at work, or because of gratitude, I gradually felt my feelings towards him changing. His company felt like a breath of fresh air.

One evening, he took me to a café with an intimate atmosphere: the lights were low, the cosy seats were pushed close to each other, there was relaxing background music and no other customers. I was trying to celebrate my recent twenty-seventh birthday and had dressed in my favourite beige trouser suit, which always made me feel more attractive. Rasul's proximity made me tingle that evening; the scent of his cologne, his hand casually brushing against mine, his voice, it all felt so tantalising. As we chatted, I was suddenly moved to kiss him. His reaction was unexpected. He covered his face and seemed to be shaking.

'I'm so sorry,' I said, instantly regretting my impulse, 'that was wrong of me.'

'No, no, it's not that,' he replied, tearfully. 'It's just that… it means a lot to me.'

'I'm so sorry,' I said, standing up. 'I have no intention of tearing you from your family, Rasul. Thank you again for what you did. I'd better leave. It's for the best.'

He reached gently to hold my hand. 'I care about my family, of course I do, but I'm not in love with my wife, nor she with me. I never have been. I have seen other women. I would walk into a room, see a woman, decide I would have her and then pursue her until I had. When I saw you, it was different. I thought "she will be mine". It was not just a physical feeling. It was deeper.'

He rose, held me and kissed me, just like that. It was both unexpected and exciting. Was this yet another man

341

taking advantage of my vulnerability? It felt so good, for once, I didn't care.

That was the start. I had my own flat, so we didn't have to sneak around to find places to be together. The physicality of this relationship never felt transactional to me. Being with Rasul always felt reassuring. I loved every hour I spent with him, even though, no matter what was going on, he always went home to sleep.

★★★

The final figures for my two projects at ACCELS were one hundred and fifty-six applications for English language teachers and one hundred and thirty-one applications for civic education, respectively.

'For the first year of a programme, this is an exceptional result,' Jeremy said.

I organised a panel of independent judges to read and select the long list and then the finalists of the competitions. Everything was done anonymously. Even I didn't know who the winners were.

For the awards graduation, I hired a local museum, near Fountain Square. It was an unusual choice, compared to the anonymous hotel reception rooms favoured by my colleagues, but I had stumbled across the museum a few weeks before and thought it was an amazing space and managed to charm the director into letting me hire the largest exhibition hall for our graduation ceremony.

The guests – teachers, school directors, representatives of the Ministry of Education and US Agency for International Development – really enjoyed looking at the historic artefacts. I greeted every one of them personally to make them feel welcome. Jeremy was impressed by the standard of catering, the turnout, the publicity and feedback. It was a proud moment for the whole team. Jeremy ended up using my speech, as he had not expected he would be asked to make one, while I spoke spontaneously, from my heart.

18.

# COMPLETION

A few weeks later, the delegation of eight teachers travelled to the USA for a life-changing six-week training experience. I had bought their tickets, arranged their visas and organised their transport. The first programme was a resounding success.

The second programme participants, who were due to travel to the USA a few weeks later, now became my focus. They all needed to improve their English before leaving.

Jeremy told me he'd been speaking to the director of the The American Bar Association – The Central European and Eurasian Law Initiative (ABA-CEELI).

'Do you know John? He's such a lovely man.' I didn't, but I knew that the ABA-CEELI was the organisation that ran the Jessup Moot Court Competition, which I had previously entered. 'He and his wife have volunteered to help our participants with their English. Here's his number,' said Jeremy.

I called John and arranged a series of meetings at their offices, so the programme participants could spend time with him and his wife, learning about life in America and improving their English comprehension.

I was impressed by the stunning location of their

offices, opposite the Boulevard and the Caspian Sea and right next to the iconic Maiden Tower, the symbol of Baku, at the edge of the Old City. The building was airy and bright, featuring a large law library, amongst other things. The training took place at the far end of the complex. I took care of every detail of these meetings, from the itinerary to the food and notebooks. I sat with the participants at their table, looking out at the Caspian Sea, revisiting my dreams of living in the USA. From what I'd heard, my fantasies of sweeping streets and washing dishes in Miami were just that, fantasies.

On the last day, while participants busied themselves with a delicious lunch, John asked to see me in his office. *What's wrong?* I wondered as I followed him.

'I've been watching you throughout this training series, and I think your performance is exceptional.'

'That's so kind of you to say,' I said, relaxing.

'I want to offer you a job here, as a staff attorney.'

This was incredible: a legal position in an American organisation, working on the Rule of Law project and legal reforms. Not only my perfect job, but a one-way ticket out of the silent treatment and other torments I'd had to endure in my current job. John took my silence for a hesitation.

'Of course, you may not want to leave your current job,' he said.

'No, it's not that at all. I'd love to work here. Yes, please!' I said happily. I returned to the training session beaming.

As we were packing up, I couldn't help overhearing John speaking to an employee outside the doorway. 'We have two prosecutors visiting from Miami. They are supposed to be training students for a mock trial but they need someone to interpret for them over the weekend. Can you think of anyone?'

As I emerged from the room, he was still there, and I found myself going up to him and saying, 'If you still need an interpreter, I'm free this weekend, if that would help. I think it would be a useful experience for me.'

I had no real idea how much experience it would offer me. The weekend was dynamic as there was a packed schedule. The time flew by. I felt like I had already started my new job. Simultaneous translation turned out to take up a lot of energy, but I was joyfully exhausted.

On Sunday night, feeling satisfied about my work with the American prosecutors and the Azerbaijani students, I lay on the sofa watching a programme about an Azerbajani women's rights protection organisation. They were talking about domestic violence. I wondered how they might classify what happened with Suleyman. Was him locking me up domestic violence? I had known about abuse from when I was a child. I had seen Mama and my aunt beaten, Nana had told countless stories about Baba's aggression and I'd heard her chat with neighbours about their experiences. How could one organisation hope to eliminate all that evil? I felt physically sick as these thoughts triggered a flashback to Suleyman's deliberate attempt to break my nose and destroy my brain. I shivered, paralysed by the memory of it all, fighting to shake off this oppressive cloak. I dragged myself into the kitchen for some hot tea, adding a large slice of lemon.

As I returned to the room, I thought I heard a voice so familiar that I nearly dropped my mug. How could it be? I stared at the TV screen in utter bewilderment. There, larger than life, was… Mama! She was the representative of the women's rights organisation and was slowly dictating the number for the hotline. I rushed about like a headless chicken looking for a pen and finally managed to write the number on my arm, just before the programme finished. Then I sat staring at it wondering what to do next. It had been so long.

It was days before I mustered the courage to call her. I hadn't tried to get in touch with her for years. What pain and suffering had I caused? What if she did not want to speak to me any more? I carried that number around everywhere with me, but always found a reason not to phone it.

It was coming up to Mama's birthday on the 23rd of August 2002 when I finally punched in the number. 'Mama, it's me, Gulush. Happy Birthday!' was all I could say.

She instantly started to cry, just like she did when she rang me to say I'd got into university ten years ago. She didn't cry as long this time.

'When can I see you? I was so scared that I'd lost you,' she said.

'Well, I'm back, Mama. I'm sorry. I tried to find you, but I didn't know your address.' This was partly true, I hadn't had her address; but then again, I hadn't tried hard enough to find her.

'Write it down now. We're in the Old City, near the second city gate after the Maiden Tower.' I knew exactly where it was. I had been near there when flat hunting with Suleyman. 'You can come today? Nana is here for my birthday.' Suddenly there was much excitement in the background conversation.

★★★

It was so strange reconnecting with Mama after so many years. She had told me on the phone that she had managed to pull through the hard times and had bought a one-bedroom flat in the Old City, dilapidated but close to the city centre and all its amenities. She had thought I was too busy in America to have time to contact her, but she had never stopped praying that I would.

I paused outside the flat door before knocking, unsure what to expect, but I needn't have worried. Everyone was pleased to see me. The surprise on my siblings' faces was priceless as they bounded towards me. My heart ached to see how much they had grown. I hugged them briefly then rushed into Nana's arms. We squeezed each other tightly, our tears mingling. Then Mama came and put her arms around both of us. She still looked beautiful but worn out from working to defend women going through the same experiences that all three of us had endured. No one asked any questions about where I had been. It seemed they had all been fed the illusion of my blossoming diplomatic career by Nana; though I thought Mama sensed something in me closer to the truth. We embraced as if I had never left.

'When are you coming back again?' Nana asked as she and I lay snuggled up together on mattresses in Mama's living room that night. I breathed in her familiar scent. It reminded me of the days in Ganja when we had had too many visitors for weddings or funerals; Nana would lay mattresses next to each other on the floor and we would sleep all together in the same room to accommodate the guests.

'Soon, Nana, very soon,' I said, stroking her greying hair and soft face, though I wasn't sure what I was going to do next.

It took me a long time to fall asleep that night, as I suddenly realised I did not want to go back to my flat. I was tired of being alone and I never felt safe there because I still feared Suleyman might return. I had stayed away from Ganja, all this time because I feared the tradition of arranged marriages there, but what if I could bring Nana to live with me in Baku? I had enough savings now to buy a larger flat, with the various gifts and salaries I had amassed, and I could sell my jewellery if necessary. This idea was so appealing, I found myself sleeplessly planning every detail.

Mama swept into action when I mentioned it over breakfast. 'Put your shoes on and follow me,' she said.

'Why? What's the hurry?'

'There's a flat two doors away that's up for sale,' she beamed. 'Let's go see it. Maybe it's the solution.'

Leaving Nana supervising breakfast, we entered a courtyard property, a duplicate of the one I had rejected before. Neighbours peered from their windows, following our every move, but now I saw them as the friendly, concerned faces of people who wouldn't walk past a girl in trouble. On the top floor, an old Russian lady opened a world-worn wooden door to show us the eighty-one square metres of her flat. There were two bedrooms, a living room, separate kitchen, a long corridor and an outdoor toilet. It currently looked too dingy and dark for my liking, but it had not been renovated in a long time; its location was perfect at the very heart of Baku's Old City, right around the corner from Mama's, so Nana would have company and help from my siblings and Mama when I was at work. Both Western University and the ABA-CEELI were a five-minute walk from this place.

The woman wanted eighteen thousand dollars and would not budge on the price. I only had fifteen thousand, which I could get straight away. However, when we told Nana about the flat, she said that she had three thousand dollars saved for my dowry and would be happy to contribute that. She had somehow realised that I had different priorities for my life now. I knew the decision was impulsive, but I wanted my family back together and, if that was the price, that was the price.

We three went together the second time and I paid a deposit and agreed a date for the legal formalities to be the very next week. Then Mama took Nana to Ganja to fetch her secret hoard while I stayed with my siblings. Everything happened so quickly. I went from being utterly alone in the world to buying a property for Nana and I close to Mama and my siblings. As before, the legal process took minutes and, on the 30th of August 2002, I became the owner of my second flat, only a week after reuniting with my family.

I still kept most of my past hidden from them. I had to keep track of my lies, listening first and carefully censoring my replies. On the last weekend of a scorching August, Nana and I went to Ganja where she paid a neighbour to bring some of our old furniture to our new flat in Baku. Shadows of distant memories coursed through my mind as if from another lifetime. We drove through the painfully familiar streets and entered our old home, now an empty shell of its former hustle and bustle of life when there were

350

fifteen of us living there. This was a new chapter in our lives, which would hopefully bring happier times than the one that began with my single ticket to Baku.

# EPILOGUE

The 2<sup>nd</sup> of September 2002 was my first day working at ABA-CEELI, exactly ten years since I stepped foot in the Prosecutor's Office. I now had a new home, my dear Nana cooked up a feast every evening to greet me after work and Mama and my siblings stayed over any weekend I was "away", for I had kept my old flat secret from them, as a place to meet with Rasul and as a financial investment for the future.

Jeremy had offered me a pay rise and promised that I could have an annual trip to the US for professional development, but I had said a firm no to that, explaining that since I had trained in the law, I needed to follow that path. I did not mention the attraction of new colleagues who would treat me with respect: that had not been Jeremy's fault.

John, my new boss, found my teaching experience a great asset and assigned me to a legal education reform project where I would be collaborating with local universities to help make their teaching more interactive: less like the tedium I had experienced at Baku State University.

I was heading to my new desk that first day when John called me to his office.

'Do you have a boyfriend?' he asked me.

It was a strange question to ask on my first day. I felt myself starting to worry. Had my past followed me again? My relationship with Rasul was now a full-blown affair. Had John heard about that?

'No, I'm single,' I lied hopefully, smiling. 'Why do you ask?'

'It's just I want to send you on a work trip and I wanted to make sure that there won't be any objections from a significant other. The prosecutors from Miami were so impressed by your work style that they have insisted you join their team on a visit. Can you bring your international passport to work today?'

'Yes, of course.' My eyes widened with surprise.

'They are taking a delegation of high-ranking Azerbaijani judges, prosecutors and lawyers to visit the federal and state penitentiary system in Miami. You will be a part of that delegation. You'll need to get ready to leave next week.'

'I'm going to Miami?' I said breathlessly.

'Yes,' John said, smiling at my reaction. 'Indeed, you are.'

I walked in a happy daze to my desk and sat down. Someone turned up the news on the radio next door. What was happening? The presenter was talking about the construction of the Baku-Tbilisi-Ceyhan oil pipeline that was due to start on the 18th of September, sanctioned by the presidents of Azerbaijan, Georgia and Turkey. It would be finished in late 2004 and cost nearly three billion dollars. The first tanker of Azerbaijani oil would hit world markets at the beginning of 2005.

I sat in front of the balcony door, staring at the Caspian Sea for a long time. Such news sounded as seismic as the changes in my life. I, a former clerk in a Prosecutor's Office in humble Ganja, would be travelling with the judge of the grave crimes court, a senior representative of the State Prosecution Office and other well-known law professionals.

I remembered those desperate nights in Suleyman's flat, when my biggest dream was of going to Miami, to sweep the streets and wash dishes in exchange for my freedom and safety. Now all my hard work was finally paying off, I was going on my own terms and I had earned it fair and square. With calm determination, I got up and went home to fetch my passport and tell Nana and my family the news, this time the truth: I was going to America.

# ACKNOWLEDGEMENTS

This book could not have existed without my partner Alex's invaluable support. He should be awarded a sainthood for his incredible capacity to stay and hold the parts of me that used to feel full of distress and shame. The writing of this book began way before I put pen to paper, so to speak, in September 2020, when I first met Alex, and all my history started to unravel.

To start with, we had to navigate some difficult flashbacks and my deep rejection of parts of myself that didn't fit in with my idea of who I should be in this world. Alex has been able to love me back into wholeness, where I was finally able to accept my past with an honesty, humility and softness I wasn't able to master on my own.

I wrote much of this book in France, where Alex and I walked and talked about the scenes from this book for hours on end. He helped me to identify my blind spots and see the full picture.

'No fudging,' he used to say softly, helping me commit to the truth over and over again.

Writing down this part of my history was not an easy process. I remember thinking, 'Why am I doing this to myself? It was hard enough to live through this hell the first time around.' The answer, which emerged in the context of so many healing sessions with some amazing practitioners over the course of the last decade, was always the same: I want to set myself free. If you've ever held space for me, please know that I feel an immense gratitude to you for helping me to get a step closer to birthing this book.

In my life, there have been two beautiful souls – Colin Harrison and Fanny Behrens – whose depth of practice and devotion to truth became transformative substance for my life. With infinite patience and consummate skill, they walk alongside me for the long journey of growing up and awakening.

I'm also immensely thankful to Edward Mannix, my Compassion Key teacher, for helping me heal some gnarly wounds and embrace my gifts as a healer and teacher, as well as Joel Young, my Non-Personal Awareness teacher, who helped me to not take things personally and taught me how to be a skilled practitioner.

I want to acknowledge my editor Ali Stubbs and my publisher Jen Parker at Fuzzy Flamingo for their invaluable support in bringing this book to fruition.

Given the context of this book, what are the chances that I would be blessed with two beautiful children? Caspian and Jasmin, you are an absolute miracle in my life.

# ABOUT THE AUTHOR

Born in the seventies during the Soviet rule of Azerbaijan, Gulara was raised in the semi-poverty of rural Ganja by her very strict and traditional grandparents in a large multigenerational household. Being extremely bright and competitive by nature, she excelled at school, becoming an accomplished violinist and gaining a place to study law at Baku State University. After achieving her master's degree in international law, Gulara became a university lecturer, while also working on educational reforms for the American Bar Association in Baku. With the support of first the British Council and then the University of Birmingham, she was awarded a master's degree and a doctorate in European law. She went on to lecture at the University of Birmingham for fourteen years. During this time, she travelled extensively in Europe and the United States promoting the rights of minority communities.

A mother of two young children, she now lives in rural

Devon within the beautiful Dartmoor National Park with her partner Alex. From this tranquil setting, she devotes herself to her family, her writing and her work helping women and men free themselves from the shackles of abuse and trauma. She's a certified Compassion Key, Non-Personal Awareness, Family Constellations and Identity-oriented Psychotrauma Therapy practitioner, Soul Motion Dance Teacher, Spiritual Acceleration facilitator and Reiki Master. Using this unique blend of healing methods, she supports her clients in transforming their lives.

Azerbaijan remains close to her heart and each year she spends time with her extended family in Baku where her mother runs a refuge for women and children experiencing violence and exploitation.

If you read this book and the content has resonated with you, you may wish to access Gulara's home study course "Reclaim Your Feminine Power", which she is gifting to her readers. The course will help you to heal any ancestral, parental and personal experiences of sexual trauma using her intergenerational trauma healing framework:

https://gulara-vincent.mykajabi.com/fragile-freedom